THE
LOS ANGELES
REVIEW

THE
LOS ANGELES
REVIEW

VOLUME 8

FALL 2010

THIS ISSUE DEDICATED TO JUAN FELIPE HERRERA

Editor	Kate Gale
Managing Editor	Kelly Davio
Contributing Editor	Mark Doty
Prose Editor	Nancy Boutin
Fiction Editor	Stefanie Freele
Nonfiction Editor	Ann Beman
Poetry Editor	Laurie Junkins
Translations Editor	Tanya Chernov
Book Review Editor	Joe Ponepinto
Production & Layout	Elizabeth Davis
Design Assistance	Peter Davio
Marketing	William Goldstein

The Los Angeles Review is a publication of Red Hen Press

Advisory Board

Janet Fitch	Lawson Fusao Inada	Li-Young Lee
Carolyn L. Forché	Robert Peters	Amy Tan
Judy Grahn	X. J. Kennedy	Helena Maria Viramontes
Michael S. Harper	Galway Kinnell	Karen Tei Yamashita
Garrett Hongo	Yusef Komunyakaa	Ray A. Young Bear

THE LOS ANGELES REVIEW (ISSN 1543-3536) is published by Red Hen Press.
Copyright © 2010 by Red Hen Press

The *Los Angeles Review* is published twice yearly. The editors welcome electronic submissions of fiction, nonfiction, poetry, book reviews, profiles, and interviews. Please go to www.redhen.org/losangelesreview for guidelines and reading periods. All rights revert to author on publication.

Subscription rates for individuals US $40.00 per year. Libraries and institutions $44.00 per year. Subscriptions outside the US add $5.00 per year for surface mail or $10.00 per year for air mail. Classroom and bookstore discounts available. Remittance to be made by money order or by a check drawn on a US bank.

Acknowledgments: The work and ideas published in the *Los Angeles Review* belong to the individuals to whom such works and ideas are attributed and do not necessarily represent or express the opinions of Red Hen Press or the any of its advisors or other individuals associated with the publication of this journal. Certain works herein have been previously published and are reprinted by permission of the author and/or publisher.

Congratulations to Christina Rosalie Sbarro, winner of the Ruskin Art Club Poetry Award. Her submission, "If You Fall It Is Your Fault," can be found on page 209.

Juan Felipe Herrera's poem "They Whipped Their Horses—Mud Drawings" reprinted by permission of the author.

Juan Felipe Herrera's "Mud Drawing #3—The Kalashnikov" reprinted by permission of the artist.

Visit us online at www.losangelesreview.org

ISBN 978-1-59709-500-6

The Annenberg Foundation, the City of Los Angeles Department of Cultural Affairs, the Los Angeles County Arts Commission, and the National Endowment for the Arts partially support Red Hen Press.

Contents

Fiction

<u>POETRY</u>

To Our Readers

Clouds shaped like plaster crumble over Los Angeles.
If Vatican City were inside L.A., Angelenos would scrape
the paint off Michelangelo's ceiling and sell it
on Craigslist, assuring themselves the studios could hire
enough Michaels and Angelos to construct replica chapels
on the backs of their lots, which stretch for as far as six days.

Steve Westbrook, "The Space between Fingers"

The Los Angeles Review with its lively group of editors has become a West Coast presence. The last issue had a picture of the bridge going into Pasadena: the suicide bridge. Somehow that felt fitting as we moved to Pasadena on January 15th. As if running a non profit isn't crazy enough, let's move to a new city where we know very few people, and let's take on a permanent commitment to paying for space and utilities. We could have stayed children, but we opted for adulthood with its challenges and agonies. With great power comes great responsibility, as Spiderman likes to point out, and this is a city where we don't have conversations with Jesus, but with Spiderman or Superman. We're all about creating a real city, or one that looks real. Story telling is all about the intellect meeting the imagination.

The sadness of American stories comes through here, the meth, the neglect, the abuse. There are families that don't quite come together, but hang like a sail coming apart, and can't catch any wind. There are ants slaughtered in the kitchen by the loving couple, like the founding of America itself, a long story of genocide and slavery while the white people claimed "in God we trust," and sang of purple mountains' majesty.

It all feels like the tainted stories of the end of the world and the big bang at the beginning. The very end could be an explosion of light, a collision of the Milky Way with the Andromeda Galaxy. There are trapdoors and tunnels in these stories and poems that lead to other stories, the ones that have to be unearthed, but even those stories, once they are pulled out into the huge Western expanse and bright air, might not be the real story.

We collect work for this review not because it is true or insightful, but because it is the kind of language and dream on paper that makes you wake up at night and wish that you could be another person, live another life, maybe not a better life, but certainly a wilder one.

If we could, maybe we would love, but in these stories, we've mostly forgotten how.

Rusty Barnes in "An Explanation of Love," ends his story with this:

> And then there's now.
> Someone said to me once that God is in the details. Look at the red smear on Maryse's face where she hit the sideboard when she fell, the pale blue vein skirting her temple, the fluttering pulse at her throat, the needle in her arm. If God is here or there or anywhere at all, his bastard son too, they both can come down right now and explain this love. I have all the time in the world.

The interviews with Juan Felipe Herrera and T. C. Boyle give us writers deeply involved in Southern California's immigrant culture, and indeed most of the work in this magazine feels like it bubbles from the melting pot of West Coast multiplicity of voices. We feel the dreams out of reach, we feel the sunlight beating.

JUAN FELIPE HERRERA

They Whipped Their Horses – Mud Drawings

They whipped their horses down the mountain as if they had erupted from the heart of Africa. As if Africa itself had sent them to us. But, we were Africa. So we stood there.

Facing me. Janjaweed. Standing. His killing was done. When I looked up I knew then that the spidering was just beginning even though my village was burned to the ground. Everyone had been cut down by the Kalashnikov. Kill what next? I asked. Even if the barrel is empty the killer still loves to hear it spin. Feel it click on target.

Abdullah kept repeating things. He stopped speaking like he used to. After a while his words resembled the Antonov. The bullets. The shrieks. Those things flaming out of the cracks of the sky, the earth, the night and the day. After a while he just mumbled and stuttered. How could the singer of the village not sing again? Lose all his melodies.

The horses never ceased from galloping. Every bullet that shot out from them made them kick faster made them fly made them into something that broke apart across the desert.

On the mud walls of the cave where we hide, I have drawn many things that have happened to me and my village. I have drawn the shapes of the voices, the explosions, the attacks and burnings, faces and scattered blood. Rotten flies and charred ants, the broken jaws of the Kalash. All the dreams and the screams – they echo in the cave. Even the Janjaweed's crazy televison talk. How he rides with his men in search for us. When he is lost and mad he sits near the cave without knowing it. He directs a little television game with his guards. Then he laughs waving the Kalash in the air. There are only three of us left. Abdullah who spits out words here and there like bullets. Zeyi who builds tiny schools with the wings of dead beetles and sticks. And me. I am the son of Muhammad and Nasra, grandson of Um. Wait. My mother ahead, guiding us. She carries a hungry child on her back. This is how she carried me. It is a mirage. It is a wing of ash sent to me from the ancestors who live at the foot of the mountains. Follow her steps to Senegal, perhaps from there I will reach you. Wish I could find the words to tell you tell the story of my village in Darfur. I leave these drawings on the wall.

YUSA ZHUANG

Preservation

*Miss Wong Sin Yah: On June 13th, 1967 she was arrested with more than 300 patriots
for demonstration in support of the struggle waged by detainees against persecution.*
                                        —*from* Socialism That Works . . . The Singapore Way

My mother is on the lawn. She is sweeping, clearing the dead leaves.
It is noon; the shower has fallen. I am just having

the first meal of the day. I spent the night reading
over and over her prison poems

written on scraps of tissue, meaning to decipher the life behind
the small and fading words . . .

In prison, my mother slipped memories into the pages of her *Kamus Umum*
to hide them.

Forty years
and over half a life before her, she pressed the musky tome
into my hands. Careful, she said. Otherwise

your father will throw everything away.

CHARLES HARPER WEBB

Genesis

A shriek yanks me out of the tax-bog
where I'm groping for deductions to save me.
Five feet away, Erik stands, a finger jammed
into my office wall, as if saving
a Dutch city from the sea. I lunge to pull

the finger free from the slammed door
that's trapped it, then gather him in
the way Mom used to gather me.
"It'll be okay," I soothe, and check to see
if the bone's broken, the nail crushed.

The hand looks better than it feels, judged
by his howls. Those times I dragged him
out from underneath his play-pen pad,
or saved him from some chair
that he'd turned into a barred cell,

the fact of freedom stopped his cries.
This time, the pain hangs on as tightly
as he clings. Soon enough,
he'll shove away—hide his injuries,
and hold his wails inside. He'll learn

about shared DNA, but barely care
as his life's barge slips from this time
when his flesh feels linked to mine.
Even now, as the hammer-blows
in his finger subside, he wiggles free.

Decades from today, mugged by the IRS,
flung into adult muck darker
than the tarriest night, will he dream
of a flowered Eden, a God whose touch
could change pain's glare to healing light?

STEVE WESTBROOK

The Space Between Fingers

Clouds shaped like plaster crumble over Los Angeles.
If Vatican City were inside L.A., Angelenos would scrape
the paint off Michelangelo's ceiling and sell it
on Craigslist, assuring themselves the studios could hire
enough Michaels and Angelos to construct replica chapels
on the backs of their lots, which stretch for as far as six days.

It would be so much easier if everyone believed in the nonsense
of God, a lover shaped like your father or granddad
who somehow does not gross you out with his constant
come-ons or spittle, but always protects you, or sometimes
on a whim, rubs a cheese grater over your skin
and squashes the heart of your son like an insect.

Such is the comfort of He who says love
when the subtitles read asphyxiation, or
the whole film is dubbed with Randy Newman lyrics.
Michelangelo said his feet danced by themselves.
He also said his belly hung like an empty sack
and his brain had fallen backwards.

When I was a child actor, I wanted Dad
to stick his head through a cutout circle
in a painted wood plank, the kind you find
at the carnival, where a bearded lady chases
an Easter Bunny, who is hopping after St. Francis,
and there are holes everywhere in the wood and signs hanging

from holes labeled Princess or Dragon or Fuckup, and Dad
can choose any one and pose without shame or commitment,
and I can take pictures or throw a giant wet sponge
or grenade at his face. God, how I miss connecting
with family, hands almost never quite touching, and then
the director yells cut, or an earthquake nearly levels the city.

STEVE WESTBROOK

Men Who Don't Believe Much in Language Find it Difficult to Express Their Belief

1.
When I was young, I scratched seven flakes from my scalp
and molded them into a man. He lived like dust on the carpet,
said he was my dad, then kicked me out of the house.

2.
I've seen footage of the Taliban destroying Buddhas in Bamyan:
vast sandstone robes exploding in showers of smoke.
I've seen California missionaries whitewash cave paintings
on YouTube: by proclamation of some order, fathers
reenacting fathers step off their mules, make the sign of the cross,
and graffiti Graffiti Rock with a mixture of holy water and Whiteout.

3.
Granddaddy painted self-portraits as animals eating animal carcasses:
he was a lion eating a gazelle and also a gazelle in a lion's mouth.
He was not a talented artist.

4.
If you cup a friend's testicles and hold them like a seashell
close to your ear, you can hear the Y chromosomes cursing
each other: conquistadors trapped in a long house.

5.
It took me until adolescence to move into a better creation myth,
the one told by who was it—Mohammed, Joseph Smith, maybe
Bob Hicok? Here, scripture says there is great pleasure
in putting your penis in the hose of a vacuum cleaner
and pressing the on switch.

6.
There is also great risk.

Mrs. Finch

Strangers at our front door posed a threat. They might find out what we were really like when no one was watching, and what we were like was *unlike* everyone else in 1960s La Crescenta. They were white, Protestant, athletic, optimistic, politically conservative; we were hysterical, chaotic, hypochondriacal, pessimistic, leftist-leaning Jews. And to make matters worse, my father was running an insurance agency out of our house. He believed that all anyone had to do was complain to some authority and we would be put out of business.

So when the doorbell rang that morning, I let out one horror movie scream to alert my family to the potentially lethal incursion. Fighting the urge to run, I froze instead, while my 14-year-old brother Paul parted the curtain and tentatively peeked out the window.

"It's only Mrs. Finch," Paul yelled, loud enough for her to hear. He made no move to open the door.

In the bedroom, my mother held out a leg of my father's pants which he stepped into like a small child. "We're coming," she screamed back to Paul. He still made no move to open the door. I scrunched in next to Paul and peered out the window. Mrs. Finch was standing on our front porch, her dull brown hair tied up in a bandana, three tightly wound pincurls peeking out in front, a small concession to vanity. She was carrying pamphlets and had a determined look on her face. "Uh-oh," I said.

Ella Finch and her family lived across the street in a house set back, down a long, unpaved gravel driveway. Her front yard bore no lawn, only colored stone, forbidding cacti, and more gravel. Mrs. Finch spent a lot of time outdoors, "gardening," though nothing green or obviously alive emerged from her hands. Still, her ministrations were an object of regular interest as Paul and I frequently watched her through binoculars as she tended to her cacti, or hauled gravel from one side of the yard to the other.

A prominent member of the local church that most vocally dominated community life in La Crescenta, Mrs. Finch divided her fellow gentiles into two groups. There were those who might say they believed in Jesus—the Catholics, Episcopalians, and members of more liberal Protestant sects—and those who, like herself, had an already-punched ticket to Heaven by virtue of having been born again. If Mrs. Finch regarded even the other Christians around her as not

Christian enough, converting a family of Jews constituted her personal extra-credit assignment from God. And we were the only Jews she had cast eyes on in her life except for those depicted in her garishly illustrated King James Bible.

My father had his own slightly skewed Freudian interpretation of Mrs. Finch's behavior. "Ella Finch," he'd proclaim, "has sublimated her sexuality with religion." Or more crudely, "That woman just needs a good *shtup*." The cure was not to be delivered anytime soon. Her husband drank Budweiser for breakfast, spoke with a snarl, stalked around in paratrooper boots, and refused to be baptized. They slept in separate bedrooms, each in a single bed. A picture of Jesus hung over hers.

My father arrived from the bedroom, and I stood beside him as he opened the front door, the still-locked screen all that separated us from our neighbor. Mrs. Finch was dressed in her usual attire—denim pedal pushers, white peds, and navy blue slip-on Keds. She had an angular body, bony and gawky, revealing no breasts or hips, and her face was deeply lined from hours spent in the sun.

"I don't need to come in," she said, "I just thought I'd bring you over some of the new circulars from our Church." She clutched a fistful of brightly colored cartoon-illustrated materials. "You know, God hasn't given up on you yet." Though Mrs. Finch had stopped smoking when she became born-again, she spoke with the voice of a smoker, gravelly with a flattened Midwestern accent that reminded me of John Wayne. I tried to disappear behind my father's rotund body, but Mrs. Finch put her face up close to the screen and lured me out.

"Deb-bie," she said, exaggerating the two syllables of my name, "Did you know that Jesus came to save you, the Jews (she elongated the vowel sound so what I heard was Juuuuuuuuuuuuuuuuuuus), your people, and YOU betrayed him." I tucked my head down into my chest. My family had done it again.

My father opened the door a crack as she handed me a glossy two-pager titled "The Good News about God." In full-color, storybook-style drawings, Jesus tended a flock of sheep. Light radiating from his hand, Jesus touched the head of a small blonde child. Jesus was dressed in full Biblical garb, but the boy who smiled beatifically from under his touch looked like a character from *Fun with Dick and Jane*. He had a contemporary haircut, and wore a short sleeved sport shirt. He could have been one of my classmates. He did not look Jewish.

On the back of the flyer was the same picture that hung over Ella's bed: Jesus, a handsome young man in profile, hair and beard the color of an Irish setter, eyes also reddish brown and turned heavenward.

"You were the chosen ones, the *Jews*," Mrs. Finch said, looking down at me with a cross between pity and disdain. "And when you refused to recognize Jesus as the son of God, you made God's daddy very, very sad." A wave of shame swept over me.

I remembered a time when I was four. My friend Janie and I were swinging on the swings in her backyard. It was dusk on a Fall day, the air growing cold, and about time for us to go in. Janie slowed down her swing, and began to trace circles in the dirt with her foot. As if unaware of my presence, she broke into *Jesus Loves Me*. Janie had five brothers and sisters and an always overwhelmed mother. She sang the song to herself as a balm, her eyes glazed over as she swung rhythmically from side to side. The song, a source of comfort to her, felt like a stake through my heart. Jesus didn't love me, he didn't even know me. *Jesus* was a word we didn't say, a god we didn't believe in. If I said the name *Jesus* to my ultra-Orthodox Jewish grandmother, she'd slap me across the face for blasphemy. Our own God's name was supposed to be unsayable. It had never before occurred to me that Janie was Christian, and now there was a breach between us that could not be repaired.

Mrs. Finch was still talking. "Jesus is standing and waiting at the threshold of your heart," she said, "all you have to do is invite him in." I shut my eyes and imagined my heart, a rough-hewn sort of Valentine, ruddy and beating. Its door was that of a cuckoo clock I'd seen, through which two carved wooden children revolved on the hour. The red-haired god stood before the door's threshold, his feet just off the ground, a nimbus glowing around his head. Just as Mrs. Finch described, his hand beckoned. "And once you let Jesus into your heart, you'll have a personal relationship with God; you'll never have to feel alone again."

This was tempting; I was a very lonely child. I shut my eyes tighter and waited. If what Mrs. Finch said was really true, then I should be able to *feel* the truth of it; I should be able to test if something was true by the way it felt inside. I let Jesus stand at that door in my mind, and waited for some kind of sign. If there were no sign, then I'd have to conclude that it was all just the product of my own imagination. The same imagination that was always getting me into trouble, convincing me I had botulism or tetanus, or that wearing the wrong socks on the wrong day would produce some dire outcome. I was, as my mother never ceased to tell me, "a highly impressionable child." Susceptible to believing way too much *mishegos*.

But what would constitute a sign? A shift in the wind, a light in the sky, a warm suffusing sensation in the center of my chest, a bird alighting at my feet? The other day, a sparrow had flown into our living room and become trapped, frantically banging against the panes of the big picture window. When a bird flew into your house it meant someone was going to die, a friend's mother had warned. "Nonsense," my mother said, "that poor bird just got distracted by its reflection in the window, it doesn't mean anything." With a broom, she gently coaxed the bird back to freedom.

"Heaven is a beautiful, beautiful place, Debbie. More glorious than any place you can even imagine." Mrs. Finch had moved her argument up a notch and was laying out the ultimate payoffs. "And Hell is more horrible," she cautioned, gritting her teeth.

I'd seen the flames of hell in cartoons, yet the prospects of eternal damnation felt distant and abstract compared with the pain of the mental limbo in which I now resided: Jesus might be real, might be waiting for me, but I couldn't get to him because I couldn't differentiate what was real from my own imagination. And I had to be sure because the consequences of what Mrs. Finch proposed were more monumental than she seemed to realize. How could I tell my grandmother that I had taken Jesus into my heart? If she would slap me across the face for saying his name, what physical damage would she inflict on me for converting? How could I continue to live as a Christian in my family? Would I hang up Jesus's picture beside the *Shabbos* candles? Put a cross next to the Mezuzah? And what about the Jewish injunction against graven images? That picture of Jesus was as graven as they came.

And even if I did this, would I cease to be a Jew? The difference between me and the other children in La Crescenta seemed ineradicable, not a product of what I believed but woven into my core. No matter what I did—in my eyes, in Mrs. Finch's eyes, in God's eyes—I would never be the little blonde child in the circular. I heard my father's warning: "Converts, hah! The Nazis didn't care who had converted; once a Jew always a Jew. Even if you had only a tiny percentage of Jewish blood, you were a Jew to them all the same." My mind went to a regularly played-out fantasy: the stranger at the door transformed into the gang of Nazi soldiers coming to take us away to the Camps.

The door to my heart closed, and Jesus, now a mere cardboard figure, was whisked away like a stage prop.

"Ella! Ella!" my father's tone sounded conciliatory as he tried to interrupt what had turned into a shrill tirade about our culpability in the crucifixion. Mrs. Finch was no longer gently upbraiding us for our understandable mistake of failing to recognize Jesus as our savior; she was railing against us as savage murderers. My father smiled his most ingratiating smile; his paranoia made him congenial. What if Mrs. Finch decided she didn't want those Jews running a business out of their house and called in those faceless authorities we lived in fear of? He had to be nice to Mrs. Finch. But how nice? Nice enough to take the blame for killing God? Nice enough to convert? Or would diversion work as well?

"Ella, the Romans killed Jesus. We Jews wouldn't kill one of our own. . . . Why don't you come in for a piece of coffeecake?"

My father opened the screen door and let Mrs. Finch into our house. From the kitchen doorway, my mother glared. She never liked to let Mrs. Finch gain full egress. Wide-eyed, Mrs. Finch took in the art prints in our living room: Degas's dejected *Absinthe Drinker* on one wall, Renoir's *Gabrielle with a Rose* (and a nearly exposed nipple) on the other; both in ornate Baroque frames. Then there were the Socialist magazines, the Yiddish newspapers, the fine layer of dust on the artificial roses in the vase at the center of the dining room table. Although all the houses in our tract were similar, the contents of ours looked nothing like Mrs. Finch's.

"Ev," my father said to my mother, who was still hiding in the kitchen. "Can you bring out some coffee and pastry?" Seeing there was no getting Mrs. Finch out of our house, my mother made instant coffee and brought out the babka. On weekends, we drove thirty miles into the Fairfax district and bought it at Canter's.

"I've never had coffeecake like this before," Mrs. Finch said, letting the cinnamon streusel melt in her mouth. "It's delicious." I was still musing about what would happen if one day I actually did feel the Christian god's presence enter my heart. Would I be able to keep it a secret or would the transformation show on my face?

"Isn't it tasty?" my father said, as if expecting the pastry to perform its own subliminal conversion, as if Mrs. Finch's sudden affection for the cake might convince her to let us Jews off the hook so we could continue to bake it in peace. My mother stared into her coffee cup. "Can I pray for your family to see their way to God?" Mrs. Finch said, her eyes filling with righteous tears. I put a piece of babka into my mouth. Its sweet familiarity entered my heart. I didn't need a sign: This, *this* I knew was good.

"Why don't we pray together?" my father said. "We both pray to the same God as our Father." My mother cast my father a contemptuous look and went back into the kitchen. Mrs. Finch sanctimoniously took my father's hand into hers, shut her eyes, and began to intone earnestly, "God, let these wayward Jews, your people, come to know your son, Jesus Christ, the savior of us all."

"And let all of us," said my father, "Christian and Jew—all your children— continue to dwell together as neighbors in harmony. Amen." He pronounced the last word with a short "A" the way Jews said it.

"Amen," Mrs. Finch said, elongating the "A," gentile-style, and jockeying for the last word.

Cinnamon, along with many other ubiquitous substances, sometimes made my father wheeze. He began to clear his throat, and then to cough. As phlegm accumulated in his respiratory passages, his cough grew wetter, and began to sound as if it might bring the coffeecake back up at any moment. It got Mrs. Finch to her feet. "Well, I'll leave these circulars with you, then," she said, fleeing our house and letting the screen door slam behind her. My mother came back into the dining room.

"What do these *goyim* want from our poor lives?" she said, sweeping the pamphlets off the table and into a wastebasket. I held onto the flyer Mrs. Finch had handed me for a moment longer, taking one final longing look at Jesus's visage, and then added it to the trash.

As crazy as my Jewish family was, I suspected that Mrs. Finch was even crazier.

J.M. Huscher

Divided and Conqured

In 1991 the Soviets retreated from Eastern Europe, taking with them the rigid, state-enforced atheism, opening the door wide for Bible-believing missionaries like my parents. My brother, sister, and I packed our suitcases alongside them, and the five of us moved to Budapest in August of that year. In an effort to gain credibility, and thereby a means of sharing the good news about Jesus with the locals, my parents enrolled me in a public elementary school. I faithfully attended classes despite not being able even to say *I don't speak Hungarian*. Teachers would put their hands in the small of my back. They'd push me around the school as if I was broken machinery, or awkward furniture.

By November, the novelty that made this seem more like vacation than real life had worn off. I didn't get along with my classmates. Judit still slapped my ears whenever I forgot she was behind me. Ignác still stuttered when he tried to read and still punched kids daring to call him a gypsy. I had reached a sort of truce with most of the others. They taught me swear words, which I pretended not to know when my father asked me about my school day. They drew crude portraits of our teachers, showing them to me during breaks, making sure to point out that such and such a teacher was pooping. They repeated the word for this over and over until I finally said it after them. During class, they asked me to pass their notes, which I did. I passed them, and I never got caught. I showed them how to wrap the notes around the ink tube of a disassembled pen and to stand and carry the pen across the room right in front of the teacher. This was the sort of idea that would have raised any one of them to legend status. It elevated me to somewhere near normal. An awkward truce developed between the Hungarians and me. We didn't like each other, but we didn't clench fists in our pockets as we passed in the halls either.

It was Ignác who first insisted that all the boys should decide whom we were in love with—that we should divide and conquer our female sixth grade counterparts with unprecedented efficiency. Ignác was the only one of us who had kissed a girl, and one of two who had smuggled pornography into the boys locker room before school. Because of his experience with women, we trusted Ignác's opinion on the matter.

And so in the locker room before gym class, the boys stood in their white underwear and white tank top shirts, reading down the list of girls, each one calculating the rankings in his head. Ferenc, second or third in the hierarchy of boys, chose Andrea, who was much too smart for him, but similarly ranked among the girls in our tally of desirability. Hajnalka, whom we all suspected to be part-Russian, figured high on the list because her parents owned something. I forget what. Peti claimed her the way a man plants a flag on an island. "*Enyém*," he said. Mine.

At one point, Peti and Ferenc counted through the girls on their fingers, trying to establish a specific order of desirability. This exercise devolved further with "*Nem lehet*. No way is she prettier," and "*Hogy ö? Na ne már*. I can't believe you would choose her." Ignác, the tallest and strongest of us, chose Betti Kralik, with whom he did not stand a chance in hell. He used the word *szerelmes*, love, when he picked her. "I will be in love with Betti," he said. That was how I knew. I too was supposed to be in love.

Betti Kralik had brown hair, straight as nails, without the slightest hint of a curl, not even where it met her forehead and ran straight backwards toward her ponytail. The best student in class, she wrote and wrote in her notebooks as the teachers lectured on, and while she wrote three times as much as anyone, she also knew that much more. Whenever Betti bent over her desk to write, pen poised, she would twist her head slightly to the left. With her right hand, she then would whisk her ponytail over her right shoulder. Quick and instinctive, the movement held poetry—hair flipping up through her fingers as she tilted her head. She was beautiful without trying. I couldn't fault Ignác for choosing her.

Our gym teacher yelled at us twice before we left the locker room; we had wasted two whole minutes of class. A squat woman, Ildi Néni always stood with her legs wide, making her even shorter. She wore her spiky black hair short, too. The only gym teacher I ever had that never actually performed any exercises, she watched us as we ran circles around the basketball court for ten minutes at the beginning of every gym class. Standing mid-court, spinning slowly to capture our every move, she yelled at us as we trotted past.

Ignác positioned himself five steps behind Betti, her ponytail bouncing up and down with perfect rhythm against her back. As her right foot hit the ground, the ponytail fell against her right shoulder. Left foot, left shoulder, hypnotic swirl of hair.

But Ignác wasn't watching Betti's hair. He watched Ildi Néni, and every time the gym teacher turned her back, he thrust his hips, stuck out his tongue, and made his eyes wild. He pumped his hands into fists and acted as if he was pulling something on top of himself, presumably Betti. I knew what it meant. The boys made those same gestures and that same face when they passed the pornography around in the locker room. I started to feel anger toward Ignác, but not enough anger to do anything.

Betti, Ignác, and I formed a train half a lap ahead of the rest of the group. The three of us ran harder and harder: Betti because she could, Ignác because the rest of the boys snickered and laughed, and I could feel my ears getting hotter and my heart pounding faster. Ildi Néni yelled at the rest of the boys. Then several things happened at once.

Two of the boys were laughing so that they had completely stopped running. Ildi Néni took a step toward them to give them a piece of her mind, which was something she was very good at. As soon as she took that step, Ignác, with the eyes of the whole class on him now, raised an open right palm straight up in the air. He swung it around in two giant circles like the lonely blade of a windmill. Leaning forward and sprinting past the unsuspecting Betti, he swooped his hand down with amazing speed, swatting her backside with a smack so loud, I winced. Betti's run faltered to a stop. Ildi Néni turned to see Ignác trotting forward as if nothing had happened.

My school days were normally so full of confusion and misunderstanding, but not today. Without even thinking, I leaned forward, exhaling a heavy gust. Lifting my feet as fast as I could, I leaned in and turned the tight corner, Ignác in my sights. Like sprinters I had seen on TV, I made my fists into two straight lines. I breathed through clenched teeth. He was five feet away. Now two. I could have reached forward and punched him in the square of his back. But I didn't. Running behind him, my anger building, I leaned forward again, trying to pass him on the outside.

"Yankee," I heard him say.

In my head I called Ignác *cigany*, gypsy.

He lengthened his stride and started to pull away. He was so much taller than I, but I couldn't let him win. I had to match him. Even when he made his hands into straight lines like mine and lifted his knees higher, it didn't matter. I was gaining on him. We raced for almost a full lap before I finally passed him and began to pull away, lapping the slower students at the back of the pack. I felt their strange looks, but didn't care. I passed Anita, who wasn't even trying. I passed Peti, cursing me under his breath.

From behind me, I sensed Ignác. He spoke only loud enough for me to hear: "Stop running, *kurva geci*."

I kept running.

My heart beat in my fingertips. In the backs of my eyeballs. In my lungs and my throat. In my legs, pushing me faster. In the anger pulsing at my temples. I didn't like what love meant to the other boys. They treated me like that, too. Like I didn't have a choice in what would happen in my life. Betti shouldn't have been the punchline to the joke. I shouldn't have been one either.

A fiery pain crept into my right hip, but anger spurred me on, triggering a daydream. A future version of myself had time-travelled back to see me at this very moment. And in this moment, I did something better—ran faster—than anyone else. I convinced myself I was standing up for Betti, even though I wasn't sure that's what was happening. My legs felt like bags of sand. Heavy and tired, I kept up the sprint.

I advanced around the corner to where Betti should have been, but she wasn't. She had left the gym in tears, and hadn't seen any of what happened. I imagined that she had heard Ignác call me a *kurva geci* and had figured that I was out here running my legs off for her. I imagined it even though I knew it wasn't true. Ildi Néni stood near the two boys who had quit running. She eyeballed me with an expression between pride and surprise. I could feel her gaze in the side of my head, but I refused to look back. She blew her whistle, and we slowed our strides. As our feet stuttered to a stop, our rubber shoe soles slapped the gym floor, echoing off the tall walls like a toppling drum set. We gulped air, putting our hands over our heads as we knew we were supposed to after a long run. My lungs were dry, but I felt like I was drowning.

I didn't know if I was in love with Betti or Andrea or Hajnalka or even Anita just then. I wasn't what the other boys were, and if they were calling that *szerelmes*, love, then I was pretty sure I didn't need to be in it. I only knew for certain that I felt big. Bigger than an airplane. Bigger than my school. I could have smashed a village under my feet. It wouldn't have mattered in what language they begged for mercy. But I didn't feel like destroying anything. I felt the way a mountain does as the clouds crash around his head, the rivers flow from his kneecaps, a climber stands on his shoulders, and wildfires burn at his feet. The only way I will ever be in love, I thought, is if it feels like this.

KATHLEEN GUNTON

This Brough of Bells

Every morning at 5:30 you are baptized in the truth of what it means to be a nun.

—Let us bless the Lord.

You don't even think about which sister is on call. You only know it is not you today, which means an extra fifteen minutes of sleep.

—Thanks be to God.

You answer as the pewter bell wakes you from sleep. The bell moves on to the next curtained cell. After twenty-two years you know the cold floor, and the cold water in the pitcher and basin next to your single, wrought-iron bed. You dress in the habit, all by touch, no mirror needed.

Wool serge pleats confirm front and back and cape and veil.

You make your way down three flights of stairs, addressing St. Joseph The Worker at the first landing. St. Theresa offers you her bouquet of roses on the way down if you can just keep a holy silence today. The roses aren't real, but the Rule of Silence is understood.

You enter the chapel. The dome of your world. You sing it into silver, chanting Psalms.

At breakfast God signs his name to the bell that marks a new day. The mother of God asks you in her silent blue morning way to give up your will when the Superior assigns duties.

—Sister, there are altar linens for the wash. And parish records need to be completed today.

—You answer yes to everything and bow with acceptance even though a walk outside in the garden would have been nice.

Over the years it seems you are always one bell short of obedience.

Just last week you took the long route to the Post Office so that you might watch mothers with their children playing.

The need for mothering is very strong you thought as you smiled at the child who was asking

—what means *nun*, mommy?

You remember. Was it ten years ago now? Antonio, that handsome fix-it man. He was anointed God-sent by the whole Order, as he traveled from convent to convent, repairing and patching. Such a generous man.

—Please show Antonio to the ladder in the storage room, sister.

You were coming up the stairs when your hand missed the rail and he caught you, saved you from a fall, saved you from the dust of the cellar.

—Sister, forgive me for saying it, but you are very beautiful.

You shook off the compliment then, but still today you can hear his deep voice. Yes, you can find that voice tucked away like an extra cup of chocolate in winter. You drink it slowly. Before darkness falls you had hoped to be a bell to others. It did not happen today.

God is wearing you down, maybe like the polished black oxfords you wear that look good but are killing your feet lately.

—Why, Sister, they look brand new, when you asked for another pair of shoes.

During your holy hour you think about leaving, quitting. It wouldn't be easy. A.W.O.L. In formation when someone left, they always called it *At War Over Love*—God being Love, of course.

There would be lots of forms, maybe you'd need to say things . . . things that you know are better left unsaid. Besides, if you stay just two more years, your likeness will appear in the diocesan newspaper.

—25 Years of Service it will read.

Perhaps you will get mail from people who have known you; your brothers and sisters will call to congratulate you. They'll promise to write more often.

You will sign your vows again. You will continue to work for God.

ORMAN DAY

A House Aquiver

Early in the night from our unlit porch,
three firm knocks on the door of our rented house
startle Dad in his easy chair, resting his arthritic feet,
lazing in sleeveless t-shirt, pajama bottoms.
Dad straightens up, shushes us with a finger,
Mom steps into the glow of our black and white TV,
a variety show that makes my sisters giggle,
darkens the room with a twist of a dial,
whispers, "It must be the church."

No time to neaten *Life* magazines, Nancy Drew books,
pick up Mom's yardage cut into dress patterns.
Doreen drapes a towel over the parakeet's cage,
Candy, Laurel, and I sit motionless on the floor
beside a plastic bowl of green clustered grapes.

Though we pray in the pews at First Methodist,
we're not going to welcome members
of the stewardship committee come in their ties
to ask Mom and Dad for their yearly pledge.
I hope one isn't the accountant father of a cute girl
who lives in a hillside home with a pool,
all the chocolate chip ice cream I can eat.

I'm a teenager, a leader in the youth fellowship,
I know what my parents would be embarrassed to say:
Dad has bills for remedies that don't work.
Mom has run up our account at Penney's,
where she sells bolts of cotton in the basement,
I'm a growing boy, never enough meat at supper,
my sisters have cavities, their shoes wear out,
we bought our car used, it needs an exhaust pipe.

I have my own offering envelopes,
each bearing a date, looming in a pitiless box.
Often I forget to bring the envelope to Sunday school,
spill my coins anonymously into the circling basket.
By August, I'm oppressed by the debt owed my pledge.

If we let them in our door, clear a place on the couch,
the men will tell us it's tough raising four kids,
but don't forget the poor widow, her gift of two mites.
My parents wouldn't be expected to pledge 10 percent,
part of our tithe might slide into a Christmas kettle,
purchase a pencil from the blind man on Brand Boulevard.
If Dad says he prefers to give as he can without envelopes,
they'd say God and the budget demand a commitment.

Just a little something.

The laymen must sense that ours is a house aquiver
with palpitations, the heavy sighs of held breath.
They don't adjust their eyes at a chink in our curtains,
only tap twice more before leaving us alone
on the scariest night of the year.

I think of their act of charity every time I'm phoned
by a hireling of the firefighters or the state troopers.
I tell them I'm pension-less, on Social Security, a poet,
but they keep knocking and knocking
until I finally ask, "Do you really want my last cent?"

DAVID WAGONER

Saved

Have you been saved? The teenage girl wants to know
    through a crack in my door
        which is about as open as I feel
this morning in my secular robe
    and sandals. Her straight hair
        is cut a little too short of her jaw-line
for her good face, and it's been baptized
    an unhappy yellow. She holds in one hand
        (thinly disguised by leaflets)
a diet-pop can and rattles it at me,
    smiling. She doesn't wait for an answer
        (which is the right move on her part
for both our sakes), then hands me a flier
    through the gap between us. Our God, I see,
        is just around the corner
at the repossessed and yesterday-empty
    but fundamentally sound church, which shall remain
        nameless as it was in the beginning.
We're having a pizza prayer meeting on Friday,
    she says, *with faith games. Come on by.*
        It could change your life. Before I can think
to tell her why I won't be there in the flesh,
    she leaves us both unchanged by our faith games,
        with our same lives and our fates better than death.

DAVID WAGONER

What to Do about the Monster in the Back Yard

We can see it through the window, lying there
still breathing yellow smoke. How many want to
give it something to eat? How many want
to poison it? How many want to go
out the front door right now and never come back?
Does anyone know what we can use against
this bony-headed, spike-tailed, cockle-kneed,
snaggle-coated clump that's already broken
the hot tub and the incinerator door?
How many want to kill it with kindness?

MARK JAY BREWIN JR.

Jersey Devil

Struggling to survive with twelve children, [Mother Leeds] became distraught when she
realized that yet another addition to her overburdened family was on the way. Cursing
her hopelessness, she cried out in disgust, "I am tired of children! Let it be a devil!"
                 —*James F. McCloy & Robert Miller, Jr.,* The Jersey Devil

Whenever the ruddy dusk swallows the sandwash, the barrens,
children fed on devil stories tramp the woods' footpaths.
They shoulder branches whittled to spears and prowl
the rock shore, wade into bog shoals and back—legs stained
from the creek ore and muck. From rickety forts,
they map and raid the scrubland. They palm knives,
scour the tree line and timber shanties, ramble home
toting their marsh-blackened boots. The children peak
through curtain gaps during summer downpours,
play lookout from the covered porch—this is how they keep
the family mutt from slaughter. They wrestle the stream-
snagged lure with the thought: *it's him.* The wild thing
that snakes along the forked river as the brave

plunge from the dock ledge into rusty water.
The shadow that buries its hoof trail under pine needles
skirting abandoned deer stands. The savage who loses
its wing-scrape and forked tail in the wind-churned oak boughs.
And when night paws at the window, the light-empty bedroom
fakes the creature's black-jack lair, dreams flash
the mud-padded fur coarse as bark, wild fangs like a jaw of briars.
Mothers and fathers wake at the sound of their own
sharp gasps, bawl and whine the Jersey Devil hunts for them.
The children light house lamps at the same black hour,
sweet-talk and shoo away the wicked. They stare beyond
the glass-pane and drapes, the yard fence like a band of teeth,
and wonder if they are already tucked in the beast's belly.

MARK JAY BREWIN JR.

From These Split Ends

— for Jessica Keough

After I proposed marriage, we decided
to start cutting each other's hair.

First time, I was drunk on vodka tonics
and used poultry shears, but she trusted me

enough to score off a few inches.
We did it standing in the apartment's

old cast iron tub, naked, my hands trembling.
Her curls made it difficult. The blades

didn't trim right, and I strained to snip each lock.
While inspecting the workmanship,

I dropped the shears, nicked her ankle.
I forget exactly how she reacted, but it was calm—

something of a soft glance down.
As I palmed the clutch of her strands,

worried over the neat horizon of her cut,
her manner suggested to me, *there is time to get better.*

Split ends in the wastebasket. Her right arm
over her breasts. I brushed off a lone hair

perched on the crook of her arm
and offered my hand to ferry her out of the bath.

TARA MAE SCHULTZ

To Love a Lamb

The sheep bleat outside the window
while the ram dances in the kitchen.
Rejected by its mother, it slept
on a pile of blankets in our room,
drank from a bottle in my hands.
Tomas says it has fallen in love with me;
it runs into his knees whenever he gets too close.
The children that are not mine, but his,
worry it will butt them. They lock it
inside the spare bedroom on their weekends.
I stroke the wood of the door, wanting
to hear a baby bawling. Instead I listen, lonely,
while it bleats on the other side.

Tomas tells a story of a ram
that knocked its owner over in the fields
and when he tried to stand,
knocked him down again.
His son found him come daylight,
nearly dead, bleeding from the ears.

When Tomas comes home, grimy
with sweat and dust from the lumberyard,
I peel his shirt off him like an onion's skin,
smell his musk mingle with the beef in the oven.
Is another woman running her hands
along his back to feel the strength
of his muscles, hardened by labor?
We should take the ram to Ben's.
I shudder, mutely agree.
Dressing later, I discover his dirt
has darkened my torso.
I push the ram outside that night

and cry next to Tomas in bed, listening
as it bleats and runs itself into the back gate.

In the kitchen the next morning,
I hold one of the new hen's eggs,
palming the warmth from the hen's hock.
Tomas and another farmhand
rope the ram to take it to Ben's—
Ben with his dull calf eyes,
his filthy, bloody apron.
The ram will not last feel the love
of my motherly touch.

My hands cut celery, prune weeds, wait.
Tomas returns with the ram
wrapped in tissue in a small, cardboard box:
four pink chops, each shaped
like half of a heart, leathery and heavy.
I feel their weight, miss the feel
of the ram's snout at my breasts.

For dinner, we eat them seasoned with rosemary.
His children laugh with their mouths full,
remark how wonderful the ram tastes,
tell their father that he won "the battle."
Upstairs, I put a robe over my nightgown,
walk out to the pasture where the sheep
rip the grass out by the roots,
and sleep in small groups. Some
patrol the paddock for predators.
I smell their wool,
see a ewe lick the ear of a lamb.

Tomas finds me later crying.
What's wrong? He asks.
I follow him into the kitchen,
drag out the cardboard box
from the trash, and stare
at the blood smeared on its insides.

BOB PERKINS

The Archimedes Palimpsest

1.

They killed the lamb
for dinner and for profit.
Flayed it, split and stretched its hide,
sold the parchment to men
who rewrote Archimedes there.

Someone scrawled an Aristotle critique
over the parchment.
Later, medieval Christian tastes
cut, folded, scrubbed it clean
(almost clean) and twisted
the sheep's skin for a prayer book.

Just last century,
some Frenchman faked illuminations
to increase its market price.

Now, sheepskins upholster sports cars
and the digital palimpsest
is on the net, a Google book.
Oh, lamb.

2.

Above Tom's Place, off 395,
I sit beside Rock Creek
and watch the flow.
 Holy, hypnotic, the motion distracts
from displays of standing waves and eddies,
leaf and sky reflections
flashing on the stream's stretched surface.

If I look at them
I cannot focus on the creek bed's rocks
or shadows, and whichever avatar I choose,
the clear water itself slips by unseen,
almost absent
unless some trout swims there.

3.

First I sought your pink,
your so-white skin beside my brown,
your unpainted lips, eyes, breasts, hips—
tried to know you in sex.

The fluid years drift by, draw tighter.
The mass of your kindness leaves its mark.
So do our quarrels and congruences.

Sometimes I see flickers deep within,
sometimes I hear our humdrum babble,
sometimes your body grips me once again,
sometimes I am distant.

Lives are too large for telling.
I say, "Ink. Fish. Love. Skin,"
one word at a time.
I should shout all my words at once
like a creek,
like a bleating beast.

DARLIN' NEAL

Blue

My grandmother chopped the first snake I ever saw in half with a hoe. I wasn't afraid. Neither was she. Then I learned, anyway, it was only a king snake stealing the eggs. When I found out she died, I was sitting on a porch. I'd just left her bedside, made it down the road before the tornado tore over the hospice. A TV inside the house made the porch glow in flashing neon. Above was a blue moon. I couldn't get over how she died on that blue moon and how spooked her children were that the life had left her body and headed out with that tornado beneath that moon. How much sense it made to everyone. My dress felt cold against my skin. My mother-in-law was in the house behind me, where I'd asked her to stay and leave me for a little while and let me just be sad. She kept telling me not to. She was so confusing. Her husband brought me a stiff drink and we laughed about being watched through the window in that neon glow. That last night of my grandmother's life, all the snakes hid in the woods. I watched the moon wishing to have time back and in awe that it was hanging up there, blue.

AARON ALFORD

This Is Radio, Kid

I fear my grandmother sounds foolish; she mispronounces words she shouldn't. She's a smart old lady, a pistol. She looks great in yellow, curves still intact—such a catch. Yet more and more of her words come out wrong. Instead of retiring a sentence with *et cetera, et cetera*, she says *excedra, excedra*, which sounds like a pain medication, something you take for stiff joints.

Out on the town, Grandma orders tai chi lattes and buys cookware from Williams-Samoa. At home, she saves receipts in a vanilla folder and sends me emails from her Yoohoo account.

And when her knees do, on occasion, get stoved up, she takes a couple Isbuprefen.

Once, on the way to Wal-Marks, she asked about my radio.

"Who is this you're listening to?"

"Foo Fighters," I tell her, turning it down. "Just a band that's out now."

"Oh, yes. *Food* Fighters," Grandma says. "I've heard of them."

My mother says to leave it alone, let her think she knows something. "All her friends are old and can't hear what she's saying anyway."

But this isn't exactly new for me: when I was a boy Grandma sliced reddishes and squarsh from Papa's vengetable garden; she warshed and wrenched clothes, folding them away in her chester drawers, and several Christmases in a row she supported my Ninjun Turtle addiction.

Some of that's regular Grandma stuff, some of it's Southern—I'm fine with all of it, as long as it's just me and her.

Now she spends her summers in Washington State, where there's too many Indian turkey-yaki restaurants, far away from the Texas summers Papa could no longer weather. They found a retirement community outside of Olympia, where they're a hit. People there love the way they talk. They serve iced tea on their porch, which holds up to twenty octogenarians, depending on space for wheelchairs and walkers, excedra. None of their neighbors, who hail from all over, are from the South; we're talking people who keep their clothes in bureaus or dressers, who've never warshed a load of whites in their lives, and whose excuse for moving slow, using a cane, is never because they're stoved up with arther-itis.

"Let her talk like she wants," Mom says. "Why does it bother you so much?"

Because it's embarrassing, how the retired couples from in-state giggle when Grandma can't pronounce their hometowns, the small settlements scattered around Puget Sound named by ancient people. Nisqually. Skokomish. Yakima. Puyallup. Out Grandma's lips, they become someplace else.

Because Grandma called to say Papa left the door of his Toyotie wide open all night, battery run dead by sunup, and soon the rest of his mind will go.

Because among the retirees is a pack of widowers who jockey for soon-to-be widows like my grandma, and I assume that, sociable as she is, she'll eventually need to take another partner, a gentleman friend. One widower, who's outlived two lovers since his wife, is looking for his third. He scoots past Grandma's porch and prays please God every day for Papa to keel over. And I know he's not listening lovingly to Grandma's sweet drawl, her gold rings clinking against her tea glass. At the potlatch fashion show she was the spriteliest model on the catwalk, swinging her hips, dressed up like Mae West—they still call her that some nights on the porch, and when she jokingly replies, "Come up and see me sometime" (a line she never flubs), it's all the old coot can do to keep his walker off her porch steps, aching to pull one over on the gal who probably can't even say *Skookumchuck*.

Right now, Papa still on the porch, I want Grandma to speak clearly to her audience. I want her to tell her new friends how she sang on the radio in Houston when she was young. How she warmed up with tricky tongue twisters. *Unique New York, Unique New York.*

She should imitate the director who drilled her before broadcasts: *Why so much makeup, kid? This is radio, not the pictures. You wanna sound pretty, then smile while you sing.*

Chin up, doll. Loud and clear on that last note.

Et cetera, et cetera.

EMMA RAMEY

Looking Up Only Strains One's Neck

My abdomen is swollen—
a sad state of affairs—
and of course I am dying.

I must be, no matter the doctor's words.
Always assume the worst.
Those are the words of a survivor.

Or else. If I am to be positive,
(says my mother, says the love of my life)
it is the beginning of time,

right there in my gut.
The universe expanding
out of nothing, out of worry.

I should sing it a lullaby,
serenade through womb,
the beginning of all things.

And how fast it is expanding—
my reproductive organs, gone,
my intestines, my stomach, gone and gone—

until I cannot breathe and the vision
becomes just flashing lights,
a star here and there, a sun,

a ring of planets,
and what song to sing—
a hum, a howl, gone and gone.

AUBREY HIRSCH

Multiple Sclerosis FAQ

Q: What is Multiple Sclerosis?
A: Multiple Sclerosis is a disease of the central nervous system. The disease erodes the protective myelin sheath around nerves in the brain and spinal cord. This causes a range of degenerative symptoms, always unique to the individual.

Q: Who gets Multiple Sclerosis?
A: Your father.

Q: How can I catch Multiple Sclerosis?
A: Multiple Sclerosis is not contagious. You cannot catch Multiple Sclerosis. As your father becomes sicker, however, you will probably experience many of the same symptoms he does. Specifically, you can expect to face nausea, confusion, dizziness, loss of appetite, and depression.

Q: What are the symptoms of Multiple Sclerosis?
A: Initial symptoms include tremor, slurred speech, numbness and weakness. Later, the patient my experience loss of vision, fits of anger, the inability to make breakfast in bed for your mother, difficulty swallowing, diminished capacity to talk earnestly and meaningfully about what is happening, trouble helping you with your math homework, optic neuritis, emotional distance, loss of ability to play chess, unemployment and/or divorce.

Q: What causes Multiple Sclerosis?
A: Medicine has yet to come up with a definitive answer. Heredity may play a small role (*very small*, the doctors assure you). Some research suggests that environmental factors might be associated with certain cases of MS. You cannot dismiss the possibility, however, that God is making your father sick because you are a bad child.

Q: What can I expect after the diagnosis?
A: It depends. At your house, everything is the same at first. Your mother reads everything she can get her hands on, but your father doesn't want to discuss it. The more your mother reads about weakness, fatigue, and loss of muscle control,

the more time your father spends exhibiting his energy and strength. He bounds up flights of stairs with a basket of clean laundry pinned against each hip. He walks you and your sister around on his shoulders, ducking the light fixtures and ceiling fans. He flips pancakes high in the air, throws softballs, turns jump ropes, runs in front of kites and behind two-wheelers. Once, and only once, he roller-blades the length of your driveway and partway down the street. For years his rollerblades sit in the garage, shiny and black, monstrous next to your miniature multi-colored versions.

Q: Does Multiple Sclerosis always progress the same way?
A: No. The course of each patient's disease is unique. In the months after the rollerblading, your father gets quieter, slower. He falls through a glass door and you drive him to the hospital where he receives eleven stitches. He stops being able to change light bulbs. He can no longer shop for groceries. He stops being able to make your mother happy. After the divorce, he loses his eyesight for a while, then gets it back. Once, your boyfriend has to carry him from the couch to the bedroom because he is too weak to stand. You teach him to play euchre on a Thursday. By Saturday he is good at it and you are glad to have something you can do together. By Sunday, he has forgotten completely how to play and your sister—who wasn't there when he was winning, really winning!—gets upset at you for trying to teach him such a complicated game.

Q: How is Multiple Sclerosis treated?
A: While there is no cure for Multiple Sclerosis, some treatments have been prov-en to slow the progress of the disease. First, you give your father weekly shots with a big needle. Then, you switch to daily shots with a small needle. Your father says he likes this better, but it is difficult to know for sure. When the daily treatment becomes ineffective, drive him to the hospital once a month for intravenous infu-sions. You will sort of miss injecting him. It was the one thing you could do to help. Now you don't feel involved at all.

Q: Is there hope for a cure?
A: There used to be among the members of your family. You would go door-to-door in the cold gathering pledge money for the annual MS Walk and spend no small amount of time internet searching "MS treatment research." But as your father gets sicker, the cure seems farther and farther away. Now when you watch him use his hands to gingerly place his feet on the footrests of the wheelchair, you know that it is too late. A cure wouldn't help him anymore.

Q: What supports are in place for patients with Multiple Sclerosis?
A: At first, your father doesn't need a lot of help. *This isn't so bad*, you think. You can deal with this. When he does need something, your mother is there. Then, slowly, more things fall to you: changing the filters in the furnace, vacuuming the stairs, adding up the plus and minus columns in the checkbook. When you get your driver's license, you log hundreds of miles between the pharmacy and home, the MS center and home. When your mother leaves, you learn to make coffee. He asks for the remote, the TV guide, more potato chips, if you can look for the phone, if you can fold his laundry, if you can skip your "thing" to take him to the doctor. He never asks to talk. You act like everything is fine. *The party?* you say, *It's okay if I miss it.* Your father always says thank you, but never with too much sincerity. That would mean you were giving something up. That would mean you were sacrificing. That would mean something, everything, was not fine.

Jill Maio

Tallying

Rosalie seems different. Tits for one thing, but Pete shouldn't be noticing those. A couple days into his return there's a snow day, and by the time he gets up, she's already trudged little canals down the driveway, down the road and back, left wet, wooly-smelling things on the heater, and set up a full-fledged science lab on the kitchen counter. "How'm I supposed to make breakfast?" he says, blinking. He pushes her jars and vials toward the sink. She pushes them back, glares up with her grasshopper eyes. "Quit it." He still feels like Goliath around her.

Shivering Goliath. The window above the sink is open, letting in a thousand icy needles per second. He tells Rosalie to close it, but she ignores him, and he doesn't feel like hearing himself say anything else. He goes to his room, pulls on a thick pair of tube socks and zips a sweatshirt over his tee. Puts the hood up. When he comes back he finds some leftover macaroni and cheese; he leans against the fridge eating it in cold clumps from the Tupperware and watching his sister, who, with yellow dish gloves loose on her hands, is squirting some harsh-smelling chemicals into a bottle. She adds tap water and shakes the bottle while the tits move side to side under her shirt. She turned 15 in October—just before he got the boot—must be happy they finally sprouted.

When he asks what she's doing, she tells him it's none of his business.

"Are you mad at me?"

"I'm concentrating." She turns to the sink, still shaking the bottle. Her hair is tied in a ponytail, long and straight down her back. Pete got their father's curls, but keeps them shorn.

He leaves a little mac and cheese in the corner of the Tupperware so he can stick it back in the fridge instead of washing it. When he's about to return to his room, Rosalie unrolls the top of a paper lunch bag and dumps out a whole mound of Sudafed packs. He stops. "What do you have those for?"

"A project. Never mind."

He looks again at the glittering cluster of vials down the counter. "Isn't that how they make meth?"

Her quick little fingers are spitting all the capsules from their blister packs. She twists them open, sends powder snowfalling into the stainless-and-glass smoothie blender. "Hope so," she says.

Ro's only a year younger than he is, but half his size. Small and delicate like an insect. Their parents used to say that Pete used up all the flesh when he was born and just left scraps for the second kid. But he did leave her the brains, as their mother still likes to remind them both, and those brains are supposed to take her sailing into the ivy-league and then on to med school.

He looks at the little doctor again. "Crystal meth?" When she tells him she tried some at a party, his head starts clouding over. "You? A party?"

"Me," she says, peering into the blender. "A party. Then I heard what the guy paid for it and told him I could do him cheaper."

"Do him cheaper? Is that how you drug dealers talk?"

"I haven't actually dealt anything yet. But yeah, that's how we talk." She looks up, sticks her tongue out.

He watches her break open the last of the Sudafeds. Her nails are bitten past the crescents. Rosalie is supposed to be reading late at night in her bed, or building little things with the tools their father left behind. She isn't supposed to go to parties, take drugs, get in trouble. That's his job. She pours denatured alcohol out of a can, presses a button, and the blender whirs angrily.

"You have a recipe?"

Her shoulders hunch up for a second, fall back down.

"You're not going to blow up the kitchen, are you?"

"Would you have a problem with that?"

Clearing off a section of counter next to the stove, he hoists himself up. "I guess not, so long as I can save the ice cream in time." He saturates a paper towel with some of her denatured alcohol and presses it to the long scrape up his fore-arm. Stings—must be good.

"How'd you get that?" Ro asks.

"Broken window. Car we found."

The car was abandoned on the sketchy back road into the city, and if he and his friends hadn't broken in, someone else probably would have. Nothing worth-while inside, anyway. He takes the paper towel off and the air bites down. What is denatured? He can't begin to guess, nor does he understand how the lye and engine fluid and all the rest of Ro's stuff is going to turn the Sudafed into meth. He believes she can do it, though. You can ask Ro a ridiculous question—how a seed grows into a carrot, how a plane stays in the air, why it snows—and her eyes will dart around for a few seconds and then she'll tell you. As if the world has written all its answers out on thin air, and his sister is one of the few who can read them. Maybe it's the grasshopper eyes.

Starting to feel dizzy, he inspects one of the little jars glaring like jewels on the countertop. The liquid, cloudy and heavy at the bottom, has cleared to a bright sliver of ultra-clarity on the very top. When he picks up the jar the liquid jumps, swallowing the sliver back into the murk. He puts it down behind the others.

"Where'd you get all this stuff? Where'd you even get the money?"

"Around. I was stashing the supplies in your room while you were away."

"You were in my room?"

"Took a shit in your closet, too."

He looks at her, not sure she's kidding until he sees the little upwards tug at the corner of her lip. "Fuck you, Ro," he says in appreciation.

Pete is a vandal, a thief, and a bad influence. He crosses the yard and his feet break the icy crust on top. The snowstorm is just about over; everything is clean, sharp, and quiet. The last flakes come drifting down from some softer place. He turns his face up to catch some, sees a bright flicker of lights through the trees, and his heart speeds up. Snowplow, that's all.

Opening the kitchen door, he's overcome by the chemical stench. Rosalie, with the rubber gloves on again, is bent to eye-level with the countertop, drawing the clear stuff out of a jar with her eyedropper. Without looking up, she says, "Want to help me get some fans going?"

He salutes and brings them in from the garage.

She turns a knob on the stove, startling awake the ring of blue tongues; when she settles them down, she puts on the mixture and looks nervous for the first time all day. He offers to try the stuff when it's done, so if there's something really wrong Rosalie can call for the ambulance. "Come on," he says, "would you trust me to take care of things if you got all fucked-up?"

She agrees, draws up a stool and tends the pan while he wanders in and out, calling his friends to see if anything's up for tonight, playing a few rounds of Doom.

When he comes back, the stove is off, and Rosalie is slumped there, staring into an empty Pyrex dish. The air is bitter cold and the fans are still at maximum whir. He asks what happened.

"No crystals," she says bitterly. "I was probably too chicken with the HCl."

Ro hates to get things wrong. It must feel weird if you're not used to it. He points to the little bit of liquid left and asks, "Would it work like this? Could you sell it as teensy little shots?"

She frowns while he sops up some of the liquid with a scrap of paper towel, balls it, and swallows it with a gulp of water. It's the most horrible, unnatural thing he's ever tasted. After chugging some fruit punch from the bottle, he manages a grin. Ro looks back seriously. Holds the look unblinking.

"Shit," he says, "I'm not just going to let you stare at me," but she follows him into the living room and perches across from him. He flips on the TV. While a trio of furry monsters debate how many pies are on a table, he tries to determine whether or not he feels normal. It's hard; normal ceases to exist the moment you start thinking about it. Eyes blinking, check. Heart beating, check. Turbulence in stomach, check. He has no idea how the body works, 18 million feet of intestine and good bacteria and bad bacteria and some mush in his skull in charge of everything. Except for when some fried drain cleaner steps in to man the controls for a while.

Looking worried, Ro says, "You okay?"

"Nothing's happening. You want to try again?"

"Another batch?" She shakes her head. "Don't have time. Unless you think Mom might want to help when she gets home." She laughs and so does he. Mom, ha.

Pete wakes up seeing police lights, bright and insistent, hurting his head as they pulse all that sharp blue in. But when he finally raises his lids he sees he hadn't woken up the first time; it's morning in his room, with bright white sun, and his eyeballs feel like they were soaked in lye and baked. And there's pounding outside his skull as well as inside. The door opens halfway, pushing against some dirty laundry.

"Pete, you'll miss the bus."

"Too much snow," he mumbles.

"The roads are fine."

His mother's voice is clicks and beeps. He opens his eyes again and sees her in the doorway, fastening the clasp on her watch, wearing a skirt and jacket that say she's ready to do her lawyering. One foot back out in the hall. "You getting up?" she says. She doesn't want to come in any farther. Fine with him.

"I didn't hear Rosalie in the shower yet," he says.

"She's sick—staying home."

"Me, too. I don't feel good."

"Oh, come on."

He turns over, drives his face into the pillow.

"Damnit, Pete, please just go."

He waits to hear the frustrated clop clop clop of her heels back down the hall. Pete is a vandal, thief and bad influence, a lacker of motivation, a faker of sickness, and he drifts back into sleep listening to his mother's shovel scrape snow in the driveway.

Rosalie says her head hurts too, but she makes them hot buttery toast with cinnamon sugar, and it's so good they go through half a loaf of bread. They eat on the couch, curled up in velvety throw blankets, and watch a few game shows before getting down to business. More TV voices float into the kitchen whenever he and Ro aren't saying anything, which is most of the time, and it's nice that way.

The chemical smells start swirling again. Pete takes his seat on the counter, resting his head against the cereal cupboard. Its warm yellowy wood has been shellacked so many times that his hair sticks. He wonders how his mother, who's been on a mad, two-year tear of home renovation, has allowed the cupboards to stay this long. Rosalie nudges his leg to get in the dishwasher for the measuring spoons. He watches her measure out lye in the smallest one, drop it in the bottle and start shaking. She'd have made a good doctor. Might still, of course, but then again, she might become a good drug dealer. Shake shake shake, side to side to side to side. Little weasel. That's what their dad used to call her. He can't remember if there had been a name for him.

"Hey, Pete?"

"Yeah?"

"Stop looking at my tits."

A rosy flush starts at his ears. "Maybe you should try a bra."

She grins, shakes the bottle harder.

While Rosalie camps in front of the stove, Pete watches a soap opera in the other room. A woman with turquoise eyes has come back to town after being thought dead, but she doesn't remember anyone or anything—even breaking up her sister's marriage, even poisoning the head of the big corporation. "I'm called Jane now," she keeps telling people.

"Ro?" he hollers. "How does amnesia work?"

"Not like that," her voice comes back.

A few minutes later, he hears a whoop. Rosalie's gotten crystals, and he runs into the kitchen to watch the liquid bubble off around them. "So beautiful!" she says, sounding for a moment just like a six-year-old. The crystals are pinkish—Ro says it's from the red dye in the pills she used this time—and Pete jokes that Barbie would be proud. He's kind of proud, actually. The little weasel can do anything.

After it dries, they each snort a tiny bit off the cutting board—just enough to get their hearts pounding, to get their teeth tugging them out of the house to the sunlit snow and the fresh, fresh air. They run down the street packing and hurling snowballs. Ro's aim sucks, but she throws hard, calling, "Die, stop sign, die!" before exploding the ball on a nearby tree.

They cut into the big field between their house and the neighbor's, and survey the gleaming expanse. Not even animal tracks. Snow everywhere, hard and clean: a foreign brightness snuffing out what's beneath. With a yell, Pete throws himself into it and rolls, feels the ground harder than it looks, feels the snow bite into his exposed wrists, ears, neck. He lies utterly still for a minute, seeing how long he can take the cold, pretending to be frozen solid. When Ro steps close he reaches like a zombie waking in the grave, and yanks her down by the leg. She squeals, laughing as she hits the ground.

He thinks they must have played like this sometimes when they were little, but he doesn't really remember. He looks at her face, wet with snow, cheeks bright and Barbie pink. He needs to tell her something. "Don't keep snorting it, Ro, the meth kids all look like shit. Go back to your books, okay?"

"I'm not going to snort it; I need it to make money." She sits up, swats the snow off her clothes. "So did you and mom make up?" she asks.

"I guess."

"What was it like living at Dad's?"

"Not good."

She nods.

"What was it like here?"

"Same as usual," she says, but then she works her jaw forward and back. "Your room felt like the room of someone who died." She looks at him. Great big eyes a little scared.

It suddenly occurs to him to ask Ro why she needs money, but she doesn't hear him or just doesn't answer; she's gotten to her feet and started off around the edge of the field. Her footprints are shadowy blue. The sky is going dark so softly, so early, and everything feels paper, paper thin.

What if you could give yourself amnesia? he wonders. Give it to yourself like a gift. No longer a vandal, thief, bad influence, lacker of motivation or faker of sickness. No longer a stainer of sheets, a taker of seconds, a leaver-up of the toilet seat, a C and D-getter, a teaser of fat kids, a forcer of sex. If you could suck yourself clean out with a giant soul vacuum and start over.

Placing one foot carefully in front of the other, Rosalie moves around the field, closer and closer in; unspooling under her feet a giant spiral. A car swims slowly toward them and past, policing sharklike in the snow ocean. Taillights red red, and the brakelight on top, cinnamon red-hot red. It gets smaller, turns down their driveway. Ro isn't looking; she's intent on the tighter and tighter turns of her feet, and the curved blue line that is just now reaching the very center.

The car enters the garage and goes dark. When Pete sees the door roll down behind it, he remembers that they left the stuff out. All of it, spread across the countertops and stove. She will see it in twenty seconds, maybe thirty, depending if she has bags to set down before she turns on the light. His poor mother. Clopping around hallways all day trying to keep her company out of trouble, then coming home to the empty packs of Sudafed, the whirring fans, the bottles and jars, the pink crystals. She's not an idiot; she watches the news. But he'll say it's his, it's all his, and that will be the last straw and probably better for everyone.

"Hey, Ro," he says, not loud enough for her to hear. He imagines her footprint spiral seen from a plane, a spaceship, a floating heaven. Hey, up above! Hey, look! We're down here on this cold, white page. With too-thin eyelids and mush in our skulls and god knows what coiled up in our hearts.

From the center of the field, Rosalie starts running her spiral back out to the edges, ruining her careful line, racing, stomping, kicking up snow, treading as hard as she can.

STACE BUDZKO

Health & Beauty

You have to understand I haven't seen Wes in ten years, maybe more. I'm home visiting family.

But back then when we were working at Jonesy's Filling Station his girl died in a car crash, leaving him with their twin daughters, Jasmine and Poppy.

See there was this Sears truck and that metal sidewinder was rolling down Route 77 when it lost break pressure on the berm by the new wind farm. For hours the road was emergency lights and barricades, queen sleepers and loveseats. Traffic had to be rerouted. The wrecks were taken to Georgie's lot across town.

When Sergeant Hilton came by the shop to give Wes the news, he brought him outside to the picnic table where we kept the used oil. All you came away with was how Hilton thumbed the inside edge of his police cap the entire time. And what a sad sack of a job he had.

After, Wes went about his business. Nobody said a word.

For the rest of the day I took my cues from Wes—feeding him wrenches, throwing him the lamp. As he carefully fine-tuned the rebuilt in Auden Hammel's pickup, you could hear the pumps ticking away—click, bell, click—it was the worst song ever.

Now here in the IGA, Wes stands in Health & Beauty. His cart is filled with a large bag of Friskies and an assortment of frozen South Beach dinners. There's a case of Bud, too.

—Well if it isn't Jonesy's best gas attendant, he says.

—Nice to see you, Wes.

We shake.

What I notice first is where Wes missed shaving. Next, that familiar gas smell. I'm reminded how he'd clean his hands with an orange before his girl picked him up at close.

—So what do you know about these? Wes holds a package of pads. With Wings, it reads.

Quickly, I do the math. Jasmine and Poppy are at that age. As we stand in the aisle, I hope the power fails. Or a shoplifter is apprehended at gunpoint. Anything to forget the fact none of us said anything worth a damn to Wes that day. I feel small and weak, and certain.

—You should be fine, I say.
 He tips his chin, winks.
—Thanks, Pump, he says. I could always count on you.
 Liars both, we go our separate ways.

MEGAN GREEN

Bloom

then one day it happens that the carpet beneath
her knees is the same institutional blue as yours
or the street out the window behind her becomes
your childhood street, the street with the bushes
that smelled like semen when they bloomed,
the street with the one dog that every kid shared,
the one who answered to Roy and Max and Precious,
who got scratched behind the ears or kicked in the ribs
depending on the day, the kid, what happens is that
the girl stops suddenly, she empties herself, she
becomes blessedly singular and hollow and she
rises with the grace of someone freshly knighted
and she turns the corner of your street, she walks
past the bushes, past the dog, past your father
with his briefcase and his eyes full of smoke,
she opens the door to a house you haven't seen
since you were 12 years old, but you are there,
somehow, and she knows it, she wants you to follow her,
so you enter the sinister sweetness of the night,
white petals soft as milk everywhere, and her back
comes in and out of focus like memory and then
you're at a midnight diner and she's ordering pancakes,
a huge stack of them, a mountain of them, and you
can see her swallow them, I mean you can see them
as they're going down, her throat is transparent
as a drinking straw, but she doesn't seem to mind
you watching each bite clink down her throat like
wishes in a well and her make-up is thick as paste
but her hands are made of mist and she sees you
noticing them and she plays a song on the jukebox,
don't be cruel to a heart that's true, and she asks you
to dance so you take her in your arms and she looks at you

like you're an idea that just occurred to her and she starts
to laugh and laugh and laugh and suddenly you feel sick
with the scent of everything blooming at once
and you say, *maybe I should take you home, it's late,*
where do you live, and she's still laughing but you
can't hear it over the dog barking in the distance
and then she looks at you and she says *you know where*

MEGAN GREEN

Ants

They enter through the power outlet in the kitchen,
a slow red current through the cracks between the tiles.

At first we do not mind. They want sweet so we give them spice,
concoct a chili powder paste, dip in a finger, draw a crude

circle around their entrance like some ancient ritual, a warning.
Then we find them in the cupboards, raping the honey jar,

the corn syrup. We brainstorm deaths: boiling water, dish soap.
Finally we scatter traps black as bombs, a tiny domestic ambush.

We begin to despise them. Their ambition, their frailty.
I trap one in the glass lid of a saucepan, watch it frantically

pace and circle. It's silly, a melodrama, a soap opera,
a high school Hamlet hamming it up for the crowd,

but then I don't want to watch anymore, his desperation won't stop,
he is still making these delirious laps, drunk with a wild

and innocent fear, a child running from a burning building.
I remember a video I watched once, two sickly ants

making a bridge of their bodies for the others to traverse,
how still they were, how resigned, the others simply happy

to have a gap filled. My husband says they don't feel pain.
He presses them out with an index finger, like a lover's gesture,

while I sponge them from the counter like strawberry seeds,
something incidental, already dead. I don't like to see their legs twitch.

I like the white expanse of clean counters, spice jars sweet
as sleeping babies in their rack. The trapped ant is still circling,

wild and violent, a flying spark, something broken. I release him.
Because he loves his life and I love mine. Because I have never

made a bridge of myself. I might kill him in an hour but now
I lift the lid, watch him crawl toward the honey, like a guest,

like I have all the sweetness in the world to spare.

MICHAEL HEMERY

Like It Mattered

"The trees are aware of us," Stacie said, walking through the park.

I entertained my wife's statement for a moment. She said trees are conscious of movement, the squirrel skipping its tail on a branch, the wind from our strides brushing tips of bark. She said they sense vibrations from our words. As we move through their space, they're whispering. They know about us, even before we arrive.

The late-March afternoon was still brisk, my breath visible as I stirred in thought.

After less than a mile, I asked what she thought about the baby nursery's color. I said maybe a muted green or a duo-tone with a bold border to separate.

Stacie hushed me. She said not today. She said she didn't want to talk about bumper pads or cribs anymore. She asked if we could walk like the trees knew we were there. Like it mattered.

After a minute I mentioned the high chair with the highest safety rating in the *Consumer Guide* book.

Stacie shushed me.

I said we needed to add a bouncer to our registry.

She held her finger to her lips.

I said, "No baby talk at all?"

She shook her head.

I asked, "If they are aware, then don't you think they'd like to know? Wouldn't they be interested in the baby? In our lives?"

Stacie didn't answer, but continued to walk, her shoes displacing mud on the rain-soaked trail. Quiet utterances.

LARS NORDSTRÖM

Cape Shoalwater, Washingtonkusten

Jag kör åt sidan och går ner till stranden
för att inspektera hur havsströmmar och flygsand
håller på att bygga om udden—
en arbetsplats utan början eller slut.

När jag återvänder ser jag en minnestavla
på andra sidan vägen, en flyttad begravningsplats:
"därför att erosion hotade de ursprungliga gravplatserna."
Ett tjugotal namn, några finländare,
en svensk, en okänd "Man found on beach"
en vinterdag 1898.

En lönnlucka öppnar sig—
till golvet i farmors kök
där jag sitter och räknar en skatt
av ett- och tvåöringar under ett samtal
om farfars bror, sjömannen som
inte fanns på några fotografier, som
försvann i en storm eller ett krig

Stilla havet dånar, sanden driver över asfalten,
jag minns knappt farfar längre, huset är rivet,
mynten indragna, mamma och pappa utsuddade,
jag själv en främling som sätter sig i bilen
och spårlöst kör bort i ett främmande land.

LARS NORDSTRÖM

Cape Shoalwater

I park and walk down to the beach to inspect
how ocean currents and shifting sands
are reconstructing the spit—
a job site without beginning or end.

Returning, I notice a memorial plaque
across the road, a relocated cemetery
"because erosion threatened the original gravesite."
Some twenty names, a few Finns, a Swede,
an unknown "Man found on beach"
a winter's day in 1898.

> A hidden trapdoor suddenly opens onto
> grandmother's kitchen floor where I sit
> counting a treasure of old copper coins
> during a conversation about
> grandfather's brother, the sailor who
> was not in any of the family photographs,
> who had disappeared in a storm or war.

The Pacific roars, sand drifts across the asphalt.
I barely remember grandfather, his house torn down,
the coins no longer in circulation, mother and father erased,
I myself a stranger who gets into his car
and drives off in an alien country leaving no tracks.

LARS NORDSTRÖM

Barfota i snön

Du kommer ut ur bastun
insvept i ett moln av ånga,
glider ner i det kalla, svarta karet:
Tempelklockor tonar bort i universum.
Medan du står där och lyssnar
på tiden som porlar i stupröret,
på vinden som nosar över snön,
passar mörkret på att göra en
snabb avgjutning av din kropp.
Huden börjar vakna och ännu
en gång har livets centrum
hittat dig därför att du stått
alldeles stilla.

Lars Nordström

Barefoot in the snow

You come out of the sauna
wrapped in a cloud of steam,
glide down into the cold, black tub:
Temple bells fade away into the universe.
While you stand there listening
to time gurgling in the downspout,
to the wind sniffing across the snow,
the darkness takes the opportunity
to make a quick mold of your body.
Your skin begins to wake up and
yet again the center of life
has found you because you have stood
absolutely still.

MATTHEW LABO

Colfax Street Lullaby

Sunlight cuts through my vertical blinds, waking me. Tired, I stand before the bathroom mirror, nothing more than a stack of bones sheathed in skin. At this moment I resort to self-deception. Artful and well-practiced at the craft, I once again appear whole.

Dressed in yesterday's clothes, with no shower and no shave, I make the call. He picks up, thank God. I say, "meet me somewhere," and he obliges me, giving me a location in town.

In my car, which has become a roving dumpster on wheels, I feel slightly anxious. There's a ten-minute drive ahead of me and I go fast, too fast, with a glove box full of unpaid traffic tickets. The court dates written on them have come and gone. I fear a traffic stop beyond all else at this point, but I arrive early, as I always do, and park against a fence between two other cars and shut the engine off. I wait. Looking up at the trees, I notice that fall has arrived. It means nothing to me.

The money is clutched in my hand as if it might disappear. I grip it so tightly, the possibility that it will disintegrate becomes real. So I relax, putting it between my knees, still balled up. I pick it up, straighten it and count it again, not because I believe that it isn't all there, but because it will help me pass time. Then, for a brief period, I focus my vision on the entrance to the parking lot as cars drive by. No one pulls in. Things aren't happening fast enough. Five, ten, twenty minutes go by, and he is late. I pick up the phone and dial his number, which happens to be the only number on my cell phone's call history going back months. It rings and rings before going to voicemail. I shut the device. Then, a car approaches, and for a moment, just a moment, I think it's him. It isn't. I try the number again and get more of the same. I don't panic, but panic is right behind me, and it lets me know that it has my back.

Five more minutes pass, and I think: *he isn't coming because he doesn't have anything to sell me and won't admit it.* Another minute or two elapses and no one shows. Now I panic. My nose is running and my stomach's in knots. Sweat forms on my brow and my hand runs through my hair then slides tightly down the back of my head and neck with a great deal of tension. The thought of going even one more hour is something which, at this point, I am not willing to contemplate. I drive onto the highway.

I head towards Colfax Street in the badlands where a few messed up things have happened to me in less than a year, like nearly being Shanghaied by a street urchin, locked up on an ordinance violation, and robbed. Strangely enough though, I feel exonerated for deciding to go there simply because I feel that I have no choice. My symptoms with each passing minute begin to worsen, their effects pulsing through me like impending malaria. They sap me of wellness and of strength and security, and the feeling, the knowing, that they will be upon me in short order is overwhelming, so I stop the thoughts.

I pull into the shit-hole. An old black man sits in the sun on a rusty folding chair, looking at me. He knows why I'm there. He gives me an admonishing look. Continuing on, I scan the area for young men in the baggy garb they wear like uniforms. But none are about, so I park and get out, hoping to make contact with someone yet unseen whom I will not know and whose true intentions will be a mystery to me. They will ask me to hand them my money. They will probably say, "I'll be right back," and my inner voice will tell me not to trust them, but it will also tell me that my other choice sucks too. Suddenly, a voice issues from behind a building.

"Yo man, over here," a young Latino boy calls to me. He wears a black hooded sweatshirt and a gold necklace. I go to him.

Cupped in his hand is the artificial happiness I need right now more than anything, or at least I believe that I do, and he puts it in my palm before I even give him my money, which I do seconds later. All of it. *I'm going to be all right*, I think. Furthermore, he makes me take down his cell phone number and asks for mine, but doesn't give his name. I become momentarily at ease, and at the same time, anxious to leave this place. Relief courses through me like fuel through a gas line as I walk back towards my car. Seconds later, I see something: a black-and-white sedan. The driver, a large man in blue comes to a stop behind me. He flashes lights, gets out, and yells, "Drop what's in your hand. Drop it right now and get down on the ground."

I scream something incomprehensible, instantly powerless over any and all circumstances, as I see the Latino boy tackled by another cop, his money flying in the wind.

A hand grabs my wrist. But instead of a callous hand, it is a surprisingly soft one, a woman's hand. For a few seconds I'm cloudy-headed, though I hear the nurse say, "Matt, it's okay, you're talking in your sleep. Bad dream, honey?"

She's like an angelic apparition, all in white at the foot of my hospital bed. I open my eyes and look up at her. I'm sweating, and relieved instantly. "No," I tell her and then pause. "It was my life."

SUSAN L. MILLER

"*the* might have been"

(after a letter from Robert Lowell to Elizabeth Bishop)

I like to imagine them, young then,
walking together: the tall dark hornrimmed
pelican, and the stout, graying sandpiper,

their pants cuffed at the ankles, their feet wet
in the spume. The beach was veined

with a line of crushed mussels. In the air,
a sharp smell, and translucent crabs
washed up in the shallows. They would have met

in transit—he between wives, she
between continents. Maybe that day

he felt slightly subdued, bending
to her, solicitous, not bothering
to be clever. It was an afternoon like others

friends have shared: each of them silent
not in caution, or anger, not to withhold

love from one another, but in observance
of what they would not say. I know
it happened. And who knows how she felt—

the moment it became clear through
a gesture, his hand in the small of her back,

a look, that his friendship stood
at the water's edge and wished for immersion.
There he loomed in all his broken majesty,

sad and loved before her hard-won balance.
I've stood there. I like to think she weighed it

in her mind, present, unasked for, and
declined, and that she knew her reserve
would secure their friendship until they died.

I like to think she regarded the horizon,
and for that moment it didn't appear to shake.

Осип Мандельштам

Silentium

Она еще не родилась,
Она и музыка и слово,
И потому всего живого
Ненарушаемая связь.

Спокойно дышат моря груди,
Но, как безумный, светел день.
И пены бледная сирень
В черно-лазуревом сосуде

Да обретут мои уста
Первоначальную немоту,
Как кристаллическую ноту,
Что от рождения чиста!

Останься пеной, Афродита,
И, слово, в музыку вернись,
И, сердце, сердца устыдись,
С первосновой жизни слито!

1910, 1935

Osip Mandelstam

Silentium

It is not born yet,
It is music and word,
Of all that thrives, therefore,
It is the unbreakable thread.

The calm sea's bosom exhales,
But day is insanely bright.
It is foamy lilac-white,
In its black-azure vessel.

And found again in my mouth
Its dumb primeval state
Like a pure crystal note,
Immaculate in its birth.

Stay, Aphrodite, as foam,
While words, to music revert,
And heart, from heart, with guilt
To primordial life returns.

1910, 1935
Translated by Don Mager

COREY GINSBERG

Closed Doors

Vic returns to the family room carrying a trash bag full of boxes in his lanky, outstretched arm. He sets it next to the couch where I'm sitting.

"We've been saving these for you," he says as he brushes the skin of dust off the faded poinsettia wrapping paper. I would never guess he's almost ninety from the effortless way he lowers himself onto the couch.

"You didn't have to get me anything." I look at my mom in the love seat across from me, then at Dorothy, hunched over in the easy chair. Her spine is bent into a comma, the weight of the past eighty-four years grinding her down. My throat suddenly hurts and I can feel blood rush to my cheeks.

In the first box is a porcelain doll with frosted gray eyes, staring out through a plastic case. I hold it up and smile the kind of smile that glosses over every-thing that can't be said. Like how their oldest son, Milo, my biological father, left my mother the week before I was born to have an affair with his client, how he robbed us while my mom was at work, how he began sending me letters when I was seventeen claiming that "Spirit" told him the time was right to reach out, how I called him a "fucking bastard" and a "sad man" in my last letter to him seven years ago, during my sophomore year in college.

"Wow," I say as I hold up the pale doll. "How beautiful. Thank you so much." The smile expands on my face and stiffens into a rigid "U."

I look across the living room at my Uncle Mark, the man I just met, who is in town from Utah visiting his parents for the holidays. Mark had pulled me aside earlier and apologized on behalf of his brother. "It wasn't until I had kids of my own that I realized just how awful what Milo did to you and your mother was," he said, his brown eyes and long forehead catching the low kitchen light. "I know it doesn't mean much now, but I'm so sorry." Even though he's trying not to be obvious, I can tell Mark's taking me in, noting each of my features like I'm a famous painting he's trying to burn into his brain to tell his brothers and kids about later. What will he report?

"Go ahead and open the others," Dorothy screams. She moves her thinning, red curls away from her ear and adjusts her hearing aid with the hand that's not gripping the arm of the seat.

It's been almost twenty years since I've been to Vic and Dorothy's. My mother and I stayed in contact with them until I was nine; we did the compulsory visits twice a year that usually ended with a promise of more meetings, of keeping in touch throughout the holidays, of them coming to see me compete in swim meets at the natatorium down the road, and them not showing up. Three days ago my mom ran into Vic at Trader Joe's—a store she's only gone to a handful of times since it's so far from our Pittsburgh suburb.

As I sit on the scratchy brown couch and try not to fidget, I tell myself there's no such thing as coincidence, that my mom and Vic were meant to be next to one another at the checkout line at that exact moment—him a half hour from home buying a panettone, my mom killing time before a centerpiece-making class, shopping for multi-vitamins and white roses. I tell myself this isn't about what Milo did, and it's not about me. I run my fingers through the doll's blond wavy hair, and they get caught in a knot.

I open the second box and pull out a tiny pink sweatshirt. For a second I'm not sure what to do or say; I can't tell whether it's a children's size or if it's sup-posed to be for the doll. Dorothy grins at me as I hold it up, so I pretend it's the most beautiful thing I've ever seen. "It's perfect," I say, staring at the flimsy cotton rather than her face.

"It looks small." She inches closer and squints from the tip of her seat to get a better look.

"Nah, I think it will fit." I hold the shirt at an angle toward my face so she can't see the tag that says "7/8." I try not to think about this bag sitting in their closet for twenty years, gathering dust, waiting for the indefinite date when they'd see their granddaughter again.

In the next box is a pair of Lee blue jeans—the straight legs not much longer than my forearm. I don't know if my legs were ever thin enough to fit in pants this small, this straight.

As I bunch up the last bits of wrapping paper that have floated onto the car-pet, I wonder who this person is they've constructed, this granddaughter they've pieced together from the few bits they have—a hand-sketched Christmas card from 1988, a ceramic snake made in my second grade art class, and a photograph of me with my younger brother and sister, back when I still had bangs and made pillow forts.

My photo is on the corner of their coffee table, next to pictures of cousins I've never met, an uncle I don't know, and a father Mark tells me quit his job as a stock broker and is now working as a marriage counselor. I try not to act curi-ous when Milo's name is mentioned, try to look uninterested, as if this man who impregnated my mother is nothing more than a sperm donor with a burnt orange mustache. I try not to have any reaction at all—to construct a face that's as blank as the one I rehearsed in front of the mirror before we left.

There are moments during the two-hour visit when I can't bear the thought of it ending, when I try to think of avenues of discussion we haven't tapped, topics we can talk about that don't mention Milo or my dad Mike and how he's been the father to me Milo never wanted to be. It should be easy, considering there are nearly two decades of events to catch up on. But it's not. I pour more sugar into my coffee and pretend it tastes good. I take another cookie out of the tin and everyone glances at me as I bite into it. I laugh too loudly at comments that aren't that funny and chew the scraps of chocolate with deliberate bites till all that's left is a bitter film in my mouth.

Then there are moments when I wish we hadn't come, that my mom had gone to a different supermarket, that I hadn't agreed to open this door that's been closed for so long. Being back in their house is like standing on the median of a highway, watching cars speed past in both directions, unsure of which way to step.

My mother finally speaks up. "Well, we have to be going. We've still got some Christmas wrapping to do," she lies.

Mark stands and embraces me, a firm bear hug that engulfs my broad shoulders. As we walk toward the door, he gives me his cell phone number. "If you ever have any questions, you know, about Milo or anything, you can call me," he offers. I thank him and nod, and wonder if he knows I'll never call.

At the front door, Vic wraps his arms around me, eyes brimming with tears. I look at the carpet. "You have no idea how much this meant to us, to Dorothy," he whispers before letting go.

Vic helps Dorothy to stand, and leads her to me. A frigid burst of air rushes in through the storm door.

"Honey, thank you for coming to see us," Dorothy says. Her chin quivers.

"Sure. Thank you, gra—" I start, then catch myself mid-sentence. I almost say "grandma" but can't make the word roll off my tongue. It's stuck somewhere inside the banks of my brain, rolling between synapse and sound factory. I know how much it would mean to Dorothy to hear me say it; she watches my face, waiting— but I can't do it. Calling her "grandma" would imply a pretend past, an impossible future of weekly calls, birthday cards, subsequent visits. And it would mean acknowledging Milo as my father.

When I hug her, Dorothy feels jagged in my arms, her shoulders brittle like chicken bones. As I stand halfway out the door, I'm flooded with the thought that she will die soon. There will be a funeral, and the family will fly in from the west coast. Milo will be there, and so will his girlfriend and her children— the ones I'm told by Mark call him "The Buddha" because of his philosophical inclinations. As my hands swim beneath the soft folds of Dorothy's sweatshirt, I take in the warmth of her body for one long second and try to commit this feeling to memory, knowing that when the door closes behind me, I may never see it open again.

AMY LEACH

Love

LOVE-IN-IDLENESS

In the year 3,000,002,010 the Andromeda Galaxy is going to collide with our Milky Way. At first this sounds miserable, like a collision of two birdflocks. But galaxy members fly farly, not tip to tip. In a galactic collision the stars do not actually collide—as with crisscrossing marching bands, only the interstices collide. (Oh, to be like a galaxy, to mingle without wrecking. But then we would have to be composed of so much more sky.) The spaces between stars are wide enough that thousands of galaxies have to converge before the stars will crash.

But, unlike the gaps between clarinetists, a galaxy's gaps are sometimes inflammable. Our encounter with Andromeda will be a predicament after all if the meshing gaps explode. It will feel like being threshed by fire, and it will disturb the Earth's biosphere—the rummaging turtles and yawning bunnies and cherry-composing trees. Afterwards the Earth will plod round its normal route but gaunt, irrelevant, having lost its beautiful flocculence, its beautiful freight.

But what with all those rich, though knocked-apart, ingredients, some rematerializing should eventually happen. And which of the Earth's biospherical items might return first? Not the ones that were tinkered into existence, for there will be no tinkerers in the beginning. Ingeniously small, ingeniously fluffy dogs, for example, can be expected to take many centuries to come back, as can the hanging gardens of Babylon. Derivatives not only take a long time to derive, but also, once derived, they usually require husbandry. Even if a little fluffy dog did appear without being invented, there wouldn't be anyone to shampoo it and rub its tiny teeth with gauze and trim the silky hairs from between its toe pads. It is hard to walk on silky feet, the little dog would slide, and who knows into what— a tarpit? Similarly, the hanging gardens would soon be a hanging matted mess without any husbands.

In the contest between the cultivated pansy and the pansy's scruffy foreflower, the wild viola, for which will soonest reappear on the blasted planet, the viola, also known as love-in-idleness, will surely win. Even with their faces so fat and cheeks so bright, pansies have the more nervous constitution, the constitution more like bubbles. They are subject to pansy sickness and unless regularly tufted do rot and snap at the heel. Pansies, therefore, will need the world to be prepared with responsible tufters before they come back. But violas, though dismissed in our windowbox age for being too indiscriminate-growing, too easy, for having lax standards—they even grow in the serpentinite barrens of Blaxland—the bumpkin habits of the violas will give them an advantage on a world that's lost its windowboxes. Love-in-idleness may even anticipate the thrips and the bees and the pluvia moths, for although these exploited hexapods are prerequisites for windowbox-flowers, love-in-idleness is a self-seeder.

So when the belated magpies are reassembled, and the belated stoats, and voles, and cotton-bolls, there will be no reason for them to be threnodious and back-looking—they shall be high-hearted from the start, for green will already be at large. Love-in-idleness, that frivolous, haphazard, twiddly weed, that untutored flower, that plant heretofore regarded as Not Serious, will already have threaded the Earth with revelry; for as it grew uncritically before the collision, so will it grow afterward.

What would spring forth on an irrelevant Earth but a plant that had been happy on irrelevant earth anyway—hedge bottoms and snowy boulder fields and sloe-shrub patches? What might venture onto a thripless planet but a flower that had preferred steeps and flats, norths and souths, dry badlands and soggy sumps, springs and summers and winters and falls, a flower that had taken root wherever it found a sliver of dirt, even slurry-soil in a slit in soft green rock, as if it just wanted to grow, grow, no matter where? Other flowers are pinpoint flowers; love-in-idleness is miscellaneous. It is not orderly like ice but mazy, veering, like melted water.

And so, when the Earth begins to undishevel after the Andromeda undoing, love-in-idleness will be the first to return; along with moonlight. For love is as idle as moonlight, and has as many prerequisites.

LOVE-IN-A-MIST

Love-in-a-mist frequently gets planted next to spectacle flowers. Love-in-a-mist has spectacles too—flowers blue like jungle butterflies—but it blurs them under fronds. Extracted from their mist of frond-wisps, *Nigella damascena* flowers resemble triple-twining paper stars. However, a *blurred blue* flower looks like any other blue blur: love-in-a-mist's flowers could be blurred racquetballs, or blurred poison-dart frogs, or little unventilated heretics huddling in the foliage.

Being reticent, then, generally green-looking, love-in-a-mist is a perfect Nearby Plant for ostentationists. If you are an orange slipper flower or a fuchsia knapweed or a ruffly silk-white peony, then you will want love-in-a-mist as your Nearby Plant. You can be a jewel and it can be your setting; and in return for its assisting your allure, you can exhort it every morning: "The greatest need in the world today is the need for modest flowers, meek flowers, flowers who will abnegate regard and let green leaves overlie them."

Because it shrouds its prettiness, love-in-a-mist allows people to regroup while they are between-peony. When we look at ruffly peonies all we can think about are ruffly peonies; the same with pininanas. If not for an interpolated margin plant like love-in-a-mist, our thoughts would be inane like sneezes: "Peony! Peony! Pininana! Peony!" Peonies ruffle their petals excitingly; love grows in a mist and lets us meditate on peonies.

Why did love become love-in-a-mist, why did it efface its posture? Was it truly in deference to the flaunty flowers? Is love-in-a-mist not rather a commemoration of Friedrich Barbarossa, drowned in the Saleph River, his drowned-blue face surrounded by the weedy-green tresses of the siren who dragged him under? Or is the blooming behavior of love-in-a-mist simply a result of its experience, same as the experience of many loves grown diffident, blooming but hunching under screens? Not all loves and not all flowers are granite-petaled. Love-in-a-mist's flowers may have decided to avoid the open as swimmers decide to avoid the snakepond.

Once we shipped love-in-a-mist to space to observe the effects of cosmic conditions upon it. *Terrestrial* conditions, it seems, had caused love-in-a-mist's blue flowers to retreat beneath a feathery green cloud of foliage, for on Earth exposed flowers get sun-grieved, rain-frayed, frost-brittled. But space is kind; space greets papery blooms of love not with petal-twisting kicks of wind but pacifically.

When it returned to the Earth from the universe, our love-in-a-mist plant was unaltered. But maybe if it had stayed up for more than a week, love-in-a-mist would have mutated into love-out-of-the-mist, its stellated sapphires rising from their green diffidence and regaining Aplomb and Posture. Then again, given centuries in the tranquillity of the cosmos, love-in-a-mist in space might only ever become love-in-a-mist-in-space, having suffered too many smarts on Earth to ever lose its huddle, to ever dispel its mist.

LOVE-LIES-BLEEDING

Flowers are commonly known for having pink sprees or yellow sprees and then sticking the following week out, before they revert to stems, sere, unvisited except by munching deer. Ackee flowers, for instance, spend all their glow at once and thence proceed to fruit duty and seedhead service. But the Tassel Flower is ruby-red as a bud, rubier-red as an adult, and rubier-rubier-red from then on.

When planning a tasteful garden, as when planning a tasteful robe, one places the tassels on the edges. Thus the crimson Tassel Flower can be seen growing on the borders of bundleflower gardens and gardens filled with toadflax and grindelia and green-winged meadow orchids and agastache and holy ghost and iceland moss.

The Tassel Flower, also known as Love-lies-bleeding, is assigned to garden borders not only because it is tasselly but also because it can be trusted to stay where it is planted, to not redeploy itself. Love-lies-bleeding accepts the purposes of Horticulture. In contrast, if you decide to border your garden with fairies or bluebirds, they will escape their appointment as only the rootless can. There are in truth two ways to escape: the bluebird way and the dandelion way. Bluebirds defect, like bubbles and luck. Dandelions, on the other hand, escape like secrets: sprawlingly. Plant a dandelion border around your garden and soon your garden will be a dandelion fair.

Love-lies-bleeding escapes in neither fashion. It stays in the parish where it's put, using its energy not to strew about and hold a tassel exposition in your garden; nor to decamp; but to bleed. Now most bleeders who devote their energy to bleeding end up paler than when they started bleeding. Fringillines and phalaropes, if pierced, fleetly expend their several teaspoons and then are bankrupt like broomstraw. Small fringilline birds are so soon sapped that within minutes of being punctured they can only dream of the days when they had blood: fringillines-lie-dreaming.

There are some things you can do forever. Given a deep enough shaft, you can fall forever. You can forget forever, and disintegrate forever, and you can laugh for a very long time. But you cannot bleed for long—not you, not citruses, not twites or treepies, not orangequits or plushcaps or jewel-babblers, nor any creature whose vessels flutter with warm, swirling, cell-bearing plasma. Either your leak will mend or you will become void.

Only love can bleed forever; only love has endless blood. Only love's slender drooping tassels can bleed yet grow stronger, bleed yet grow brighter; redder, redder, never spent, never phantasmal-gray. Maybe, if it only gets kicked, then love is love-lies-dented, and in a few days it replumps. But when it suffers a terrible wound, love seems able neither to heal—to grow substitute tissue over its damage—nor to run dry. The other name for love-lies-bleeding is *Amaranthus*, and *Amaranthus* means eternal and unfading, and even after the *Amaranthus* plant fails and drops to the Earth, its flowers are brilliantest bleedingest sheddingest red.

LOVE-BIND

Love-bind is an Earth-hog. A rampant plant, it stampedes ten meters per season, sprinkling 100,000 seeds per year. It binds the forest, wraps and winds it in itself. Forest, are you there? All we see are forms—linden forms, lentisco forms—all engulfed in uncontrollable green love. After years, O trees, of slow-layering labor, of soft blond sapwood maturing into dark sturdy heartwood—you were overcome in one season! Once distinct, once fingertipped with intricate twigs and buds, you are now merely the prop for scrambling love.

Dear people, track your offwandering donkeys with care, lest you get blitzed by rushing love in the green-mad forest and become another of its shapes; for love-bind overtakes all but the rapidest donkey trackers. Moss and mushroom communities are defenseless against love-bind, being stay-put.

Could we marshal all our myrmidons and send them in, with spikes and pikes and poison, to argle-bargle with the love-bind, even they might become shapes, myrmidon-shapes, blanketed in greenleaf. Burly armored warriors are no safer from being waylaid by love-bind than the slight nymph Dryope was from being transformed into a trembly poplar, no safer than small bland beach animals are from being overswept by seawaves. *Clematis vitalba* never goes feeble-brown; it ever reaches, ever enwraps, like the effusion from some fanatical knitter's speed-needles.

How different the practical plants, like drupelets and teff! For them we have to till, for them we have to hoe, pulling weeds out, pushing pods in, beseeching the sky; then *if* the sky is benevolent our nurslings *might* shuffle thinly out of their seeds. If you have time, you can do a simple experiment in comparative botany: sit down in your yard and chronicle the order in which different plants travel to you. After maybe a decade radishes will creep from the east, with radish ministers. Radishes are like aristocrats, they require an entourage. Then three years later, you may notice some cucumbers at your feet, escorted by weeders and slug-shooers and attendants holding humidistats. But earlier, much much earlier, weedy love-bind will have sped to you, surrounded you, leafed you, and kept going. Weedy rambling love arrives within weeks, without squadrons of nurserymen, in an onslaught, its own sponsor.

And if the wind could blow so far, perhaps the moon too would be draped in love-bind, since palest things on Earth, most moonlike things—drudges, and graves of drudges—themselves become swathed once in love-bind's vicinity. Then along with the other shapes you see drudge-shaped love and grave-shaped love. The stars, even, might get dragged into love's all-draping project, the sharp pointy sparkles of Acrux and Spica buffered with leaf-weave—Dryope-stars—if only the seed-bearing winds weren't altogether impounded on the Earth, or if the stars weren't so extra-atmospheric.

Love-bind turns everything into a dubitable green figure. Once-unambiguous mangadous, once-dapper pineapple-gadrooned credenzas, once-natty hat-stands—all rendered approximate by overrushing love. The love-trammeled are no longer spruce, no longer chiseled, no longer emphatic. Considering a mystical green ectomorph, one might wonder: "Tetzel the tavernboy? Beanstan the barrelstaver? Wictred the twit? Maybe a butternut seedling?" Overgreening love converts the Nest to a Was-a-nest, the Wiliwili to a Was-a-wiliwili, Upholsterers to Were-upholsterers. Everything becomes erstwhile; and in this way love-bind is like time and obliteration.

Yet perhaps the erstwhiles are not so desperate to get free. What looks like a tedious costume from without may feel different from within. Perhaps love-bind not only wraps but procures, even translates. Perhaps its underpinnings are not thinking, "Quit me, Love, I'm no girder," but "Green me Love, green me on, quit me not, twine me with your fresh pressing weight. Once a success, now a success-weed, I look just like the booby-weeds over there, the idiot-weeds and the wretch-weeds. Still I wish to never be rid of this leveling leafage, for once my heart was pasty, but now my heart is green, growing-green."

There are many ways to be transfixed, and no season is safe. If it is winter you may be transfixed by ice; if it is springtime, by firefinch music or phoebes singing or the squeaky compositions of foxkits. And if it is summer, you may be transfixed, like Dryope, leaf by leaf, by clambery vine-winding love-bind. For love, onslaught-love, beleafs all things.

DAVID LaBOUNTY

considering apples and other things

you're worried
about this

the ease
of your
thoughts
as you
consider
adultery

how your
face is
studious
and blank
while you
think about it

the way
your face
is the same
as your
wife's face
when you
see her
at the grocery
store selecting
apples, feeling
them in her
hand while
checking
them for
bruises

picking
only the
brightest
apples to
come home
and live
in the fruit
bowl in
the middle
of the kitchen
table, apples

shiny enough
to absorb
that natural
warmth, to
reflect that
chronic light and

you wonder
about God
in all His
merciful
savagery

how it
is that
some
apples
are good
enough to
be eaten

while other
apples are
so casually
thrown away

RUSTY BARNES

An Explanation of Love

They say get into the ambulance, go with your wife, and I do. Everyone ignores that she's not my wife anymore. Maryse's into the habit of listing me, forgetful maybe, because the police call me first, before they call her last husband. The EMT is busy making sure the bag of fluid empties correctly into Maryse's arm. I'll be damned if I'm not in the place I swore I'd never be again, holding her hand through another fit.

The driver is young, the ambulance is bulling every curve like a scared dog, lifting me off the ground with every bump. He considers this an emergency, and the EMT is back with me so she can't tell him different. Maryse is pale on the gurney, her arms strapped down. I think about it for a moment and move my hand into hers. She won't remember it, but it feels right.

• • •

The first time I held her hair out of the toilet while she puked, the feeling I had was pride; this is the way it ought to be, a man, me, helping his wife, her, through occasional difficult times. Except that it became every weekend and sometimes during the week if I didn't watch her: the vodka disappearing, the boxes of white wine on the weekends, the four-drinks-an-hour pace she set when we went out.

• • •

"She'll be fine, sir." The EMT, Rosie, pats me on the arm, a firm professional move. I approve of it, though it doesn't help.

"She was fine when I met her, but not many days since," I say. The van slows slightly to take the curve at Jones's corner, and I lean back against the shelf.

"I understand, sir." Rosie lowers her eyes, takes a quick look at Maryse's face and scribbles something into her notepad. Maryse's head lolls to the side, mouth open, and I get a quick glimpse of what she might have been like as a child, sleeping in a bed somewhere in that nebulous haze of remembrance, a worn-bare teddy tucked into her arm.

• • •

Three years ago—a bare three years—I asked her for a divorce when she came home from work sloppy-drunk and dropped on the floor in front of me, giggling in fits, her skirt askew. She passed out and woke in the bed where I put her and tried to climb on the couch with me. She fell again and broke her wrist. This was the first hospital trip. I loved her then.

• • •

And then there's now.

Someone said to me once that God is in the details. Look at the red smear on Maryse's face where she hit the sideboard when she fell, the pale blue vein skirting her temple, the fluttering pulse at her throat, the needle in her arm. If God is here or there or anywhere at all, his bastard son too, they both can come down right now and explain this love. I have all the time in the world.

COLIN POPE

Goodwill

for Jennifer Wrisley, 1980-2010

This was right after you killed yourself.

We pulled you from the house as a mortician
pulling organs from a body. We boxed you all up.
Then a van came to clean the house
and another to take all of you away

though nothing and nobody
was willing to let go yet. There were little cries
like organs being pulled from a body.

This was right after you killed yourself.
You told us not to embalm you. They put your ashes
in a box and we took you home.
A different home. On a plane. There were forms.

About a month later, a woman at the store
took you from a hanger
in front of my eyes. She stretched you out a little
to see if you'd fit. She put you back.
The hangers were everywhere as I looked,
squeaking back and forth. Everyone

was there for you.

Brandon Courtney

Cupped Hands: The First Boat

To fill your mouth with coffee, a tablespoon of sugar, *& not* swallow; to practice drinking water from another's cupped hands, lithe fingers like wicks caked in wax—the color of Mississippi pearls pulled from a bed of loam.

We learned early on how to close the throat of the river with rough-cut stones gathered from pastures, learned to measure distance in the space between lightning flash & thunder clap—to pray on the rosary of rain.

Delirious & fever stricken, you imagined your skin as the milky backwash of bones forming oars, rowing your body through the tunnel of light at the end of your life; the spiral, the whirl—the pattern and the patterns within patterns.

We looked away from your face only briefly, looked again: the eyes cannot bear to be emptied like a bowl, opened like a book, filled like a boat—closed for sleep.

Above, the stars were folding themselves into shapes we could hold in our hands: impossibly white candles, usable fruit from trees, ribbons to bookmark our dead in the earth.

Here, the wasp enters the apple, calls it heart—here, a mouth, here cistern, the place where heaven collects under the tongue, & how the sound of it all forces the hand to invent new instruments.

& to think her wedding ring, which she lost in the field of foxtail barley pulling bed sheets from a bowing laundry line before the storm, ensured a proper burial. Inside every living thing there's a prayer taking shape—

If you show us where to dig, sister, we'll tend to the rest.

JEREMY HALINEN

It Cracked

and from it slipped a bird's eye, no, two,
going dry, dull, nestled in a smaller skull.
Inside us also, hardnesses split; what we
thought were hollow held skeletons
yoked by wings. Perhaps we'll bury them
in the sky tomorrow.

Horse: 4 Frames

Luck is the pick-me-up, Luck un-resented,
For one of these days we'll be the ones.
From "Common Knowledge"
Michael F. G. Standen

The gate stood wide open when he got there. A man he recognized
but could never quite name waved him through. The man's gray Stetson was soaked
and water dripped from it where the wide brim sagged. A pile of wet snow
grew on its crown. He wore a frayed Fish slicker whose sleeves were bloody.
He had blood on his hands.

Strange snow still fell. It covered everything

He thought, "*It wasn't like that. No. It wasn't anything like that.*"

but the crumbling county blacktop. It melted there and he could see
the road ahead stretch out wet and black and shiny into the storm.

There are stories that end well, aren't there? This could just as well be one.
The monster from our childhood darkness will die in a spray of blood,
strong sword-voice of the shield-breaker singing him the chant of edges.
Someone will discover, won't they, that one-eyed bastard in the game,
notice those aces up his sleeve? Accused, he'll deny, take chances
through another hand or two—push his luck—draw to an inside straight,
say, or try to fill a royal flush. Caught out, he will try to bluff.
When pressed, out of bravado, he will skin his little hideout gun.
Surely, some game soul will topple this tinhorn from soda to hock.
From those squirming entrails then shall step wisdom, beauty, the winged boar.
Out of that torn throat, out of that heart, sword-split and shivering, shall
spring forth, hoof on stone, the stallion, his brother of the heavenly air.

The woman had been standing on the front porch, had seen him arrive.
She wore no coat or hat. Snow dusted her red hair, her hunched shoulders.
Her eyes, without expression, unreadable, were red from crying
but she was not crying now.

The truck's bald tires made a hissing sound

The man's horses had all moved away from the fence as he walked up.

on the wet pavement as he drove along.

They were wet and they steamed,
shivering in the cold. Their heads low, their ears flat against their skulls,
they had moved off, their hooves sucking at the slurry of snow and mud.

Where the blacktop ended, the road was gravel.

The mare stood quietly
her eyes closed. Weak, shocky, she trembled, her breath rapid and shallow.
Snow piled along her topline and gathered in her forelock. When it
melted, water coursed downward in runnels, striping her tawny hide.
She wore a trophy halter. Hanging from it, a new white lead rope
tangled in a little heap at her feet.

Snow covered the gravel,

He thought, *"Hell. It wasn't like anything."*

but in ruts and low spots
there were black pools of standing water.

Each pad of the pricklypear
beside the machine shed drooped under its own burden of wet snow.
The new tin roof of the saddle house had shed in one rough furrow
its whole load of cold slush.

Fence pliers on the dash slid to the floor
as the truck bounced along. Gravel rattled under the running boards.

He didn't think anymore. He saw it all again.
His father,
a frail skinful of bones still presiding over household quarrels,
plays solitaire at the kitchen table, aware the losing cards
he deals himself today will still be here next week when he is dead.

The hero has arrived, you know. The moon can see him and the stars
peer down as witnesses. Wisely, he has consulted oracles,
poured out generous libations. Fragrant smoke of his sacrifices
hangs yet in the air. On the altar, the dun steer and shearling lamb
are bones and ash. He sleeps alone and dreamless on the barrow floor,
his broad sword freed from stone. Soon he will buck the tiger, braced or not.

      Water splashed in the fender wells.

He bent to examine the wound.
A long sharp spear of bone showed white through the muscle of the forearm.
Her lower leg, though bent at the knee, rested at an odd angle,
fetlock, pastern and hoof wall of the toe all flat against the ground.
Dried blood had caked thick and brittle over the leg below the break.
Where the mare had stood there was a shadowy stain under the snow.

      The heater fan clattered in its housing. The wiper motor whined.
      Wiper blades squealed back and forth.

           He remembered the truck wouldn't start.
           The old man totters out there— everybody trailing after him,
           an odd cortege. He makes the grown boys fetch him his tools:
                screwdriver,
           3/8 wrench, an emery cloth. He growls then with his old impatience,
           for an instant that eighteen-year-old gunner's mate in Navy wool
           spoiling for a fight. He fixes the wrench on the battery clamp.
           He strains heroically toward that one small success. His hand
           trembles. Sweat seethes on his forehead. And he can't break it loose. He
flings
           away the little wrench. It chimes cheerfully—once, twice, then three
                times—
           as it bounces down the driveway. He goes inside. No one else moves.

He is faithful—Pia Fidelis. In fulfillment of his vow,
he has raised up shrines. He is dedicant of a dozen fanums.
With good reason, he expects the sword, shield, cloak, the golden bridle.
Though the gods grant him all, he will fold, cards on the kitchen table.

Wipers packed snow into ice along the bottom of the windshield.

He had taken a yellow grease marker out of his coat pocket,
marked then the suffering mare's face clearly with the necessary "X"—
from the base of the left ear to the right eye then from right to left.

It was still early. Up ahead the road was white. There were no tracks.

He fished three cartridges from his coat and chambered them in the pistol
then rotated the cylinder and closed it up. When he cocked it,
his first cartridge came under the hammer.

Sinking under wet snow
nearby mesquite thickets looked for all like calving glacial faces.

Two active shifts of firemen at the graveside. Scores of retirees.
Naval Reserve Honor Guard. Back to the old hometown one last time,
relatives and friends gone for more than a generation.

Gravel,
mud, ice slush roared against the floor. Wipers could not clear the
windshield.
He could not see the fence line on the far side of the borrow pit.

When he looked around he saw the woman had come down from the house.
A gust lifted her wet hair, made of it a nest of red serpents.
Shivering now, she stood silent by the corner of the neat barn
her grey eyes fixed on him. He nodded and turned back to his business.

He could not see the windrow of pines just a quarter mile beyond

He didn't get it.
Echoes of a bugle. Cordite in the air.

and beyond that he could not see the ancient peaks of the Franklins.

He faced the crippled mare and drew back the hammer, placed the barrel
a foot from the intersection of the yellow lines of that "X"
he had drawn on her forehead and touched the trigger and as the gun

roared and bucked in his hand, the bad luck mare coughed once and bobbed her
  head
and spoiled his aim and he saw as she fell that he had not killed her.

In the rearview mirror he saw the end of the blacktop recede

No, he didn't
   Great grandad's Elgin watch was home in a drawer.
   Uncle Eddie's old Ivor Johnson was on the seat beside him.
   Dad's twelve-gauge, the Zoli over & under, was in the closet.
   What the hell was that all about?
      He nearly spoke the thoughts aloud.

until it disappeared behind falling snow.

She lay there grunting,
unconscious. Her legs moved as if she were running. The broken leg
moved at the shoulder but not below. The ball had entered her head
below the base of her right ear, passed through and lodged in her shoulder.
As she thrashed there, hot blood pumped from her wounds and sprayed him head to
      foot.

Ahead of him, he watched a coyote trot out of the borrow pit,
   cross the road, watched where it slipped into the chaparral and vanished.

Sometimes all the temples are empty. The gods just slip away.
The mad Pythoness straddling her sacred abyss cannot riddle.
Epona's horses run mad; her mules and asses die forsaken.
Somewhere even monsters must take the time to eat and sleep and breed.
Then sling stones find their shallow angle of repose. Then mosses bloom.
Just when they do, Rick's smiling croupier drops the ball on 22.

He tried to draw back the hammer to fire again but it was jammed
so he had to break it open and fiddle with the cylinder,
work the hammer back and forth and after a while he got it fixed.
He cocked it, caught the mare's halter, put the muzzle to her skull, fired.

The *Lucky Lady* casino's sign loomed suddenly above him

He remembered
the grave was in the shade of some kind of green ash.
On an east-facing hillside close to the road. All the stones are flat,
all set flush with the ground for easy mowing by summer groundsmen.

and he hit the brakes.

For a little space, a broad stream of blood flowed
out of her wounded forehead, out of her mouth, her nostrils, her ears.
It pooled under her head. It steamed in the cold. Then it slowed and stopped.

The truck bounced and slipped a little sideways

When he looked, the woman was gone.

as he turned into the mud lot.
The motor dieseled for half a minute after he turned it off.
He sat a while using a shop rag to clear himself of dried blood.

He remembered the only war story he had ever been told.
On the tincan David W. Taylor, *battle claxons blare.*
A seventeen-year-old gunner's mate stands amidships at the rail.
He is watching two Japanese torpedoes approach from starboard.
He waits for the concussion, fire and smoke, sounds of the breaking keel.
He does not breathe. He feels the ship heel over too late. He watches.
The torpedoes pass under his feet and in the next two seconds
he knows they have been set too deep. He smiles and goes to his gun tub.
So solitaire was his game. He was always luckiest alone.

Dusty trophies hang in his great hall—captured arms, the monstrous claw,
jeweled dagger hilts (giant-forged), silver cauldrons from the World Worm's
    hoard—
his hole cards bestowed by smiling gods whose runes fade from standing stones.
Amen. By now, the gates of Paradise will have closed behind him.
Some divine psychopomp or other surely will have waved him through.
His heirs, who will cast lots for the blue wool, must one day cash in, too.

Lottery scratch tickets littered the floorboards of the truck. He laughed.

We all know the rough beast runs loose. Red, black, green, we've got his number.
Still we bet the Red Snake and let it ride. We are out of our minds.
We expect miracles but not ordinary things.

    He drifted:
He is ten. It is Deadwood or maybe Lead—some tourist snake pit.
In a cheap copy of Number 10 Saloon, Wild Bill Hickok sits,
eights and aces in his hand, his manikin's back turned toward the door
where the old man smokes a cigarette and studies the horizon.
Outside, dust devils swirl. Route 85 is melting in the sun.
Across the road a farmer swaths a field of ordinary hay.

Soon our new ring-giver comes. Some bold Battle-bringer among us,
some longshot, our poker-faced Raven-lord, that grim pistolero,
will risk all and ante up, call the one-armed bandit's bluff. Or raise.
He will hit the jackpot, mark with red the feet of raven and eagle.
Should he fold, it is no matter. The same king comes time and again.
Wild rumors are abroad already—stunned virgins swell with saviors,
Kings and Knaves and Queens and Bulls. We shall have us much of anointing.
It will never end. Every day more new Grendels outgrow their fens.

    The little bell over the back door jingled as he went inside.

The one poker machine in the place has blown its breaker again.
He sits at the bar alone all afternoon and drinks good whiskey.
He bets recklessly on simulcasts from Sunland Park and for hours
he wins and wins and wins.

DONNA D. VITUCCI

Nothing Stops Us

I.

I want me a palomino. Horses' manes and tails look like pretty girls' hair streaming when they run. I could brush shoulder to forelock. That's all I know of horses. And that they are hands high. The measurement is in hands. Which is odd, but nomenclature unique to the field of animal husbandry. Which is further weird, the term "husbandry." Husband. Horse. My list of wants.

II.

Navigating to the cellar, fully loaded arms erase my feet, so I proceed with trust, and instinct as to breadth and depth of step. The clip clop emanates from my horse sense. How does the brain know? Memory. How does the body know? Practice. How does the heart know? It doesn't. It wants a tumble.

III.

The implied cruelty in this arena fells me. Lasso, my love. Lasso and spur. You'd think by now some of this would be rote, but it isn't. Riding a horse, you should feel it in your bones, he told me. In the saddle, you are horseflesh, you are one. His instruction buzzed past my ear with the flies. My palomino swished his tail while afternoon jostled the brain under my hat. I flicked the reins the way I'd been taught. His nicker thrummed my lower half and I recognized him wanting to have his way, but we had to hit the trail. I dug in my heels, and turned him otherwise. My direction. Forward.

蓝蓝

火车, 火车

黄昏把白昼运走。窗口从首都
摇落到华北的沉沉暮色中

. . . . 从这里, 到这里。

道路击穿大地的白杨林
闪电, 会跟随着雷
但我们的嘴已装上安全的消声器。

火车越过田野, 这页删掉粗重脚印的纸。
我们晃动。我们也不再用言词
帮助低头的羊群, 砖窑的滚滚浓烟。

轮子慢慢滑进黑夜。从这里
到这里。头顶不灭的星星
一直跟随, 这场墓地漫长的送行
在我们勇气的狭窄铁轨上延伸

火车。火车。离开报纸的新闻版
驶进乡村木然的冷喋：
一个倒悬在夜空中
垂死之人的看。

LAN LAN

Train, Train

Dusk carts away daytime. The window trembles down from the capital
to the dense twilight of northern China

. . . . from here, to here

Roads penetrate the earth's aspen forest,
lightning would follow thunder
but our mouths are safely muffled.

The train crosses open fields, this page erased of heavy footprints.
We tumble. We won't speak again
to help the lambs with lowered heads, thick smoke from brick kilns.

Wheels slowly slide into night. From here
to here. The inextinguishable stars
follow this long procession to the cemetery
stretching along the narrow tracks of our courage.

Train. Train. Leaving the news in the newspaper,
entering the countryside's stupefied shiver:
hanging by his feet in the sky
a dead man watches.

Translated by Eleanor Goodman and Ao Wang

胡续冬

圣若热

石头听说了石头，瀑布洗净了瀑布，
二十多个瀑布下来，太阳一泻如注。
犰狳出洞的时候，山大了、水累了，
水里婀娜着的大好的青春凉透心了。

整个峡谷的热都转移到了村子里边。
此地吊床林立，大麻香飘三十里远。
格瓦拉装束的鲍勃·马利叫住了我，
邀我同去，点黑姑娘肚皮上的篝火。

HU XUDONG

São Jorge

Stones hear talk of stones, waterfalls wash waterfalls,
twenty-some waterfalls run, the sun pours down.
When the armadillo emerges from his lair, mountains swell, the water grows tired,
the water's sensual, promising youth is cold through and through.

The heat of the whole valley is brought to the village.
Here is the hammocks' forest, the fragrance of marijuana floats thirty *li*.
Bob Marley dressed like Che Guevara stops me
and invites me along, lighting the bonfire of a dark girl's belly.

Translated by Eleanor Goodman and Ao Wang

ERIN MURPHY

Word Problem

Monica runs an errand for her neighbor,
Mrs. Sandoval. She skips to the store
and buys 12 pieces of fruit. She purchases
three times as many oranges as bananas.
How many fist-sized oranges does Monica
hurl at the man on the sidewalk who
grabs her pigtail and hisses *Pretty girl?*

JENNINE CAPÓ CRUCET

Just the Way She Does the Things

The day I got my Honda Civic Del Sol—almost two months ago, for my 17th birthday—Osniel was over that night. And yeah, he talked to me, sang happy birthday and ate cake and pastelitos and whatever, but I caught him later, talking to my dad about what else but Hialeah's Finest. Papi's the reason Osniel ever even talked to me way back in the first grade, because Papi had insisted—*insisted*, Mami says—that they name me Mercedes (*If God won't give me a son, the least he can do is give me a Mercedes!*—he tells the story all the time and without fail on my birthday, like a present I can't return), not realizing that I'd get picked on by boys, the first one ever, after Papi of course, being Osniel.

The night of my birthday, my little brother Carlos had put himself in charge of the car hype—he smiled, opened the doors and ran his hands over the frame like trying to sell it to my cousins and friends. I was letting him do all the talking so that he'd feel like a boy, even though it was my car; even Papi told him, when Carlos had asked when *he* could drive it, that first Carlos would have to ask him, then me. When my brother tried to get everyone to lie on their backs and look underneath the car at the suspension (all my girl cousins refused, but Lazaro from across the street was unbuttoning his shirt), Carla elbowed me and whispered that Osniel wasn't out in the driveway with us anymore, so I went inside.

I found him sitting across from Papi at our dinner table, a little less than half the cake still between them, Papi picking at it straight from the box with a fork. As he chewed, he stared at Mami, who was still at the sink rinsing plates. Her back was to us; her waist looked narrow compared to her butt, which was kind of huge, square-shaped, jutting toward us like a shelf. I could tell Papi only half listened to Osniel as he watched Mami from his grin, betraying himself and showing a few crooked teeth. Papi didn't have a shirt on, just his blue shorts, and yellow crumbs sat in the wires of his chest hair. I brushed them off for him, onto the floor. He looked down at my hand, stared at his big stomach for a second, sucked his teeth, then just kept eating cake and running his tongue over the whole fork, licking off frosting while Osniel talked.

"Señor," he said, looking down all shy (and calling Papi *sir* in Spanish because Osniel's *such* a suck-up), "Señor, you know how it is—it's not just about cars—it's la comunidad, Señor."

My dad had been in a car club when he was our age—Osniel knew that, as did everyone in our neighborhood. A lot of other people's dads had been in some sort of car club or gang before we came along. Osniel had heard enough stories about it from Lazaro's and Danny Garcia's dads (who, between the two of them, made up almost one whole dad for Osniel, whose dad nobody—not even Osniel—had ever seen or met) to figure out he could get to my dad if he does it through cars. But Hialeah's Finest is as local as a car club can get, basically just this neighborhood— nobody from *East* Hialeah is even in it yet. The guys who founded it (Lazaro from across the street, two houses down and Danny Garcia, my girl Carla's boyfriend of eleven whole months) have no aspirations to go countywide. I joke to Osniel that Hialeah's Finest is made up of guys whose cars aren't hot enough to get them into Miami E.L.I.T.E. or Xplicit ILLusionz (Osniel's right that they're tacky, but still, they're big, and picky, even if it's in a tacky way). But to be fair, Hialeah's Finest doesn't have those mad fees that the other ones do, so members can put that money into their cars instead. At least that's what Osniel says, but if you ask me, Osniel talks *too* much, especially to my dad.

"Forget it, Osniel." I said, smiling.

"Girl, you don't even know what we're talking about." He leaned back in the chair and winked at me because Papi was focused on his frosting. Mami warned Papi three times a day that God would send him diabetes if he didn't watch him-self. She'd said she would *not* cry when God sent him a heart attack; what else could God do with a heart full of fried platanos? Papi would just laugh and ask for more of whatever he was eating, and Mami would bring it. And if it was dessert, she'd bring two spoons.

I said, "What else do you talk about besides Hiale—"

Papi put his hand up flat in my face, stopped me from finishing, didn't even look at me. Then he leaned forward, his belly pressing onto the glass tabletop, and carved out another hunk of cake too big for the fork. He sat back in his chair.

"You think a Honda Del Sol is car club material, mi'jo?" Papi said toward the surviving cake. "Ha, shit!"

"Come on, Mr. Reyes. Seriously, Hondas are hot right now. They're *sporty*."

If I'd been allowed to talk, I would've agreed with him. The Civic Del Sol is a '95, used but in good condition, black on black with red trim. My dad had spent weeks looking through Auto Traders to find one with decent miles. Papi finally picked out a hard top convertible, super cute, and he told me it was fun to drive— he test drove it while I rode shotgun. The car definitely *looked* sporty. And accord-ing to 95 percent of Hialeah High, Osniel's car was supposedly the shit; he'd been bragging about his Civic since tenth grade, even before he got his learner's permit. When we were in driver's ed. together, he'd talk up his new hi-gloss paint job, or those chrome spider rims, so much that he'd miss when the teacher called for his row of drivers to drive. He *never* paid attention and failed the weave twice.

"That's a four-cylinder engine, Osniel. What type of sporty is that?" Papi laughed, and so did Osniel.

"It's all about looks now. And with that loud-ass muffler? Besides, Hialeah's Finest doesn't race."

They don't do much of anything, I wanted to say.

Papi laced his fingers behind his head. Little flakes of deodorant coated the ends of his armpit hairs. It looked like powdered sugar. Osniel raised his arms and did the same thing, but his sleeves didn't let me see if he even had armpit hair.

"A car club that *doesn't race*? Well, shit," Papi said. "At least it's safe then."

Yeah right, I wanted to say.

"I'm just putting it out there, Mr. Reyes. No fees or nothing."

Osniel leaned forward and stuck his finger in the yellow icing at the corner of the cake and pushed a whole big chunk of it in his mouth, pulling his finger out slow. Then he looked at me and said, "But I guess it's really up to Mercy, right?"

Papi kind of snorted and said, "Sure, sure. But I'm okay with it, mi'jo."

Papi pushed his chair back and stood, taking another forkful of cake to go, and said to me, "Is Carlos outside?"

"Yeah, showing off," I said.

"Sounds *sporty*," Papi said.

He put his hand on my shoulder and squeezed it as he passed behind my chair to go outside, leaving me there with Osniel. Papi's flat feet made little sucking sounds on the tile on his way to the front door, and he held his lower back like it hurt, or like he was pregnant. He yelled for my mom to come help him get rid of all the party people.

"Mami! Come help me get rid of all these people! Jesus Christ already!" he said.

She dried her hands with the bottom of her t-shirt as she walked over to him and said, "It's not even ten o'clock yet!" When she got close enough to him, she wiped her hands on his chest even though they were almost dry.

He said, "Hey, C'mon!" and slapped her butt.

She pretended to squirm away from him, saying in a fake squeaky voice, "What? What I do?"

Osniel came around to my side of the table, dragging his pointer finger right across the top of the cake this time—right through the word Felicidades—scooping another finger-full of frosting. He sat down next to me in Papi's chair and looked at the fluff of meringue balancing at the edge of his finger. Then he smiled at it.

I grabbed him by the wrist and said, "Don't you even think about it." He wrestled with me, and I screamed high like a stupid girl. Then he pulled the frosted finger away from me, getting his hand as far from me as he could.

"Okay, okay, you baby," he said.

I smoothed out my hair in case it had gotten messy just then, tucked it behind my ears. Osniel's shirt said Polo Sport in graffiti letters and I was trying to think of a joke to keep him paying attention to me. I had known Osniel since before I could talk, but now in high school we were in different levels of English class, so I had to be careful not to sound too nerdy.

Then he said, "A'ight, I'm out, Mercy."

"Huh?" I looked up from his chest.

"I'm gonna take off, girl." He stood and leaned toward me, kissed me on the top of my head while I sat there. "Happy birthday," he said. Then quick, he slid away but moved his hand in close and smeared the frosting on my nose—almost up my nose—and he stuck the rest in his mouth as he ran towards my front door. And before I could even get up to try to catch him, he turned back around and cracked up, pulling at his belt with one hand to keep his baggy jeans from sliding down as he ran, the finger from his other hand still in his mouth.

Since then, Osniel messes with me every day at school about Hialeah's Finest. He makes this bad joke about me doing my *Civic duty* every morning in homeroom—he's not even *in* my homeroom, he just comes by to tell me before showing up late to his. The only class I have with him is Spanish. We're actually in Spanish II, which is where they put people that *already* speak Spanish but are stuck because the county requires you to take a language to graduate, but our school *only* offers Spanish. We sit next to each other and ignore Mrs. Gomez hardcore. She's super old and yells all the time about us speaking Spanglish and that everything's being lost. But she's got enough kids in there that are right off the boat to keep her happy—I swear most of them got here like last week, their Spanish is so perfect.

Today, during Mrs. Gomez's class, I super-casually asked Osniel to grab food with me, just us two (though my Del Sol only fits two people, so I don't know if he knows that I *want* it to be just us, or if that's just the way it is because it's not like there's *options*). But once we were in my car, he started up with the same noise about Hialeah's Finest. The car did look amazing—my dad had detailed it himself. He'd even cleaned parts of the display and the ridges on the stereo's volume knob with a toothbrush, all before I woke last Sunday.

"Damn, Mercy," Osniel said running his hand across the black Armor All-ed dash. "When are you gonna hook up with us?"

I felt my hands get really sweaty on the steering wheel because he said hook up but I had a decent joke ready that time.

"Why do I have to hook up with anyone? Why can't I just be independent, like in politics?"

He blinked. Then he said, "*What?*"

"Like the parties—political ones—when you register? To vote? The Democrats and Republicans—because there's sides—not that there's sides with car clubs, but I mean, you gotta pick. You gotta register as something, but you can be independent, too—or, I mean, instead."

As I said this, *explained* this, I wanted him out of the car so I could whack my head against the steering wheel until I blacked out and forgot how to speak. He looked at me with his eyebrows scrunched up and his head tilted sideways, like either *I'm* the biggest idiot in the world, or *he's* the biggest idiot in the world. His mouth kind of opened a little and I'm thinking, *Please just don't say anything please don't please.*

"Oh. Kay," he said. He was trying not to laugh.

He turned completely in the seat, looked at me. He had the longest eyelashes. I was so close to his face I could see the dark brown dots of hair growing in thick all around his mouth and on his broad cheeks and I had to clutch the steering wheel so tight to keep my hands from rubbing up and down the hairless blank lines between the mustache and chin, like my fingers could make the connections grow somehow.

"Taco Bell? For lunch?" he asked.

Whatever you want, I wanted to say. *I love you*, I wanted to say. I wanted to grab his face, kiss him so hard right there in my car, and then never get out of the driver's seat—sleep there, even, to keep him kissing me in my head.

I smiled—I think—shrugged, and backed out of the parking space.

We hit the Taco Bell drive-thru.

"For $2.99 you eat like a king," he told me. I laughed even though he says this every time we get Taco Bell.

Power 96, the only hip-hop station that also plays Spanish hip-hop and some trance, plays my favorite Freestyle song "Love in Love" every day in the Power Lunch Hour MegaMix, and it came on just as we pulled into a spot to eat our food. I convinced him the dining room was packed with people we didn't want to deal with, but really I just wanted us to be alone. I covered it up by warning him that he better watch my interior and handing him, like, 50 napkins. Then he did the kind of thing that keeps me watching his house from my bedroom window all the time, one of those moments that I replay in my head so many times that it makes me cry because I start to worry that I made it up, it's so perfect. One of the things he does that makes me go, This *has* to be more than hanging out, more than just my car.

The song came on and Osniel, half-way through his first burrito, grabbed the second one still wrapped up and started *singing* into it like a microphone, doing this jerky side-to-side dance that looked like one guy doing the wave by himself.

Love in love, we are so on fire. Love in love, yeah I'm talkin' 'bout me and you.

He was really singing this to me, opening his mouth wide to show me his food and making gagging noises in between the verses. I had to pretend I was all grossed out by the ball of beans and cheese and sauce and spit he made dance on his tongue.

Cuz you're just the way I want the thing, because I know my girl is you.

These were not the right words (Osniel's got the words mixed up—the main guy in the group sings, *Cuz it's just the way she does the things, sometimes I worry love's untrue*), but I didn't care, because I liked Osniel's words better anyway. I didn't want to point out that he sang the wrong thing because then he'd tell me, so what, he was just joking. He started scratching an imaginary turntable and shoved the wrapped burrito in my face for me to sing the back-up echo parts (*On fire, on fire, in love*).

The song ended (we both yelled *Miami Freestyle in the house!*—the very last words) and we laughed big time—the kind that's so hard you don't even make a sound—and he smacked the dashboard a couple times, leaving a sweaty print of his whole hand on the Dad-cleaned dash. I grabbed a handful of napkins and tucked them under the bar of the emergency brake, so that I remembered to rub the hand off before my dad could notice.

I wiped under my eyes and said, "Thanks for the serenade—that was beautiful."

"All for you," he said. He winked and reached over towards my arm and at first I thought he was trying to put his arm around me, or maybe tickle my side. But instead he pinches me, hard. I swear he twisted the skin—it made my eyes water. He did this as he took another bite of burrito. Some red sauce dripped from the corner of his mouth.

I still have the dime-sized bruise on my arm because I saw it the day after, and I thought, *that's what he's like on me.* And when it starts to fade, I pinch myself in the same spot just as hard or harder. I don't stop twisting that soft spot on the back of my arm until I cry from how much it hurts because that's the only way I know I'm doing it hard enough to make it colorful again. Every day before getting in the shower, I stand in front of the mirror and lift my arm over my head and stare at it—a greenish yellow kiss. I press into it with my thumb to make it throb.

I close my eyes and let my hand fall, tracing the rest of me, imagining my body covered with all these little spots, watching Osniel push them into me one by one.

Once the song finished, once I'd parked and locked the doors, he said to me, "Mercy, for real, when you gonna come around to me?" and I swear I almost died right there until I realized he really meant joining the stupid-ass car club. But I was good—I threw my keys in the air and caught them (very smooth) and when I tucked them in my back-pack, my hair tumbled down over my shoulder all dramatic like in some Spanish soap opera. He even reached over and tugged on it.

"Whatchu getting into this weekend?" he asked.

"Whatever," I said. "No real plans—I have to call Carla."

My backpack started to slip off my shoulder, but he was looking at the ground right then and didn't notice how it pulled my tank top weird across my chest, shifting my boobs so that one looked higher than the other. I hoisted my bag up before he noticed.

"We should hang out," he said.

Like on a date? I wanted to say. But I just kind of nodded, the car between us.

"A'ight, I'll call you then, to see wassup," he said.

He jingled his keys in his pocket.

"Yeah, okay," I said. But he had started walking away to his car.

He had parked a few spots down, but still in the part of the lot close enough to the school to be safe. Get too far into the public lot and your ride will be on blocks when you come out. Lazaro used to park out far to keep people from keying his Integra. I told him the best way to stop that was to quit pissing people off, but he just laughed and made fun of me for trying to be on everyone's good side all the time. (Carla didn't talk to him for two days for saying that to me). And then one afternoon, we came out for lunch and the back two rims—I swear he had them on the car for like an hour, they were so new—were just *gone*, just two concrete blocks holding up the ass of the car. He wanted to beat the crap out of the school security people, but even *they* know better than to mess with people *that* set on getting some rims. Osniel told my dad about it, and ever since, Papi warns me every morning while I'm backing out of our driveway to park close to the school. The safest place for the car, Papi says, is in our driveway, locked behind the chain-link fence. Which is where it will sit all weekend, while I watch the phone.

Mom jokes I'm praying to the cordless, I'm so all over it. I carry the receiver to the bathroom with me, resting it on a towel on the toilet while I shower.

"*No one* uses this phone," I announce to my family Friday night at dinner, pointing to the cordless sitting between the picadillo and the congrí on the table.

Papi has no idea what's with me and says, "What's with her?" to Mami. Mami shrugs and then winks at me when Papi looks back down at his food. Carlos ignores the wink and launches into his list of reasons why Ricky Alviar's bullying might force him to drop out of sixth grade. Through the glass table I see Mami's toes wiggling, tickling Papi's ankle. He smiles at his rice then stomps on her toes with his heel. She stomps right back.

They keep playing this game until Carlos says, "Listen! He's trying to destroy me!" and moves around to their side of the table to show Mami what he claims is a pencil lead stuck in his palm.

I tell myself that if by nine he hasn't called, he's not going to. So at nine-thirty, I *really* give up and go to my bedroom, to my window. I shut the door and turn off the lights, and at the window I close the blinds but leave them raised about two inches from the bottom. Then I crouch down on my knees to look, my fingers and nose pressed to the cold tile on the windowsill. This is where I watch him from.

If I push my face into the window and look hard to the right, I can see the back of his house. His is the corner one, three down and across the street, facing the opposite side of the road that intersects mine. I know which room is his, and I can see his window—it faces my house. I can see when the light goes on and off. It's off right now, so I stand up again and get the notebook with the red pen hooked into the spiral from under my mattress and write on the next line, *Friday, 9:30. NOT HOME (?)*.

And then I wait. And I watch, and I don't move just in case he's looking back from the bottom of his own window (even though I *know* he's not).

This was how I got Osniel to drive me to school back before I had my Del Sol: I'd get up early in the mornings—way earlier than him—and watch for when his light would turn on (because he was awake) and when it would go off (because he was leaving for school). I'd get up early enough so that I was all the way ready—dressed, eye-liner on and not smudged, hair smooth, books in my bag—so that all I had to do was watch and figure out when he'd be coming outside so I could walk by at that exact minute and he'd offer me a ride. Too early and I was on the bus. He made me work for it too, because he went through some stretches last year where he'd just skip all the time—two, three times a week—and I'd have to give up and go because I hadn't seen his light *at all* and I wouldn't make the bus if I waited any longer. But I took good notes and got down even his skipping patterns eventually.

Kneeling there in my room, my knees and calves start to burn, so I shift forward and lean on the sill. Osniel's got to be out with Danny Garcia, because Lazaro's car (a lot easier to see from the window than Osniel's place because he's basically across the street) is in the driveway, and the kitchen light is on, so they got to be eating dinner. His dad's work van is there, too, and that means Lazaro's *got* to be home. Carla had not called me, but I knew she was home; impossible as it sounds, her parents are stricter than mine, so on Fridays she can't go out with Danny Garcia unless I go as a chaperone. Which just leaves Danny Garcia—unless Osniel's out with someone I don't know, which can't be it because we've always rolled with the same people.

Whenever I watch and I start to get tired, or feel my chin go numb from pressing it on the sill, I think about just getting into bed. But I know better. I can't leave the window because the minute I leave, the next second, I know the light will go on in Osniel's room and I'll miss it.

His Civic's engine works like an alarm for me, and I don't know what time it was, but he had finally passed by, home from wherever he was. I lift my head up from the windowsill in time to see him turn onto his street, and maybe two minutes later I see his bedroom light go on and then off again. So I cross out the question mark behind *NOT HOME* in my notebook and draw a dash and write *Gets home LATE—in bed FAST*. I shove the pen in the spiral and stuff the notebook back under the mattress. I can hear Carlos watching TV in his room—something with a heavy-duty laugh track—and my dad snoring down the hall. My mom interrupts the steady, smooth rumble when she half-yells, "Papi, Please! Roll over! Dear God!"

Then I hear Papi grunting back, "I'm not snoring, that's you." Then Mami laughing, then the smacks and thumps of their pillows as they pummel each other with them to figure out who's right. The snores stop for only a few minutes, and when they come back, they're muffled.

Flopping on my stomach onto the bed I think, *If Osniel is drunk, he's falling asleep face down, just like this.*

He never calls that weekend, though I watch him from my window do something—can't tell what—to the engine of his car. It takes him a while, and he keeps having to knock on Lazaro's door to borrow tools from his dad.

In the afternoon, I go out to our driveway where my dad's just changed the oil on the Del Sol even though I've barely put any miles on it. He's put in some new windshield washer fluid that's supposedly better than whatever was in there. I can't see Osniel's house at all from our driveway.

I stand next to my dad and lean over the engine. He's cleaned it up; replaced the original hoses with braided lines—the kind that have steel reinforcements— and he's put in these chrome valve covers and header tubes. The whole thing shines. I think, *who's even going to see this other than him and me?* Looking at all that chrome, hidden to everyone else when he closes the hood, I shift a little closer to him, but after a second he moves to keep the space between us the same.

"You like it?" he says.

It isn't really a question—he takes the towel tucked in his back pocket and wipes around where the washer fluid goes.

"It's *sporty,*" I say, but I laugh and so does he. And because he seems okay with my joke, I say, "Papi, I think it looks cool, but no one's gonna see it. I'm afraid to even open the hood cuz what if I don't close it right? What if I scratch up the paint?"

He wipes his hands with the towel and says, "Then don't open it. Even though, I already showed you how to make sure it's closed, you just listen for it to click—but don't open it, if you're scared. You shouldn't need to open it anyways. And the less you open it, the less chance you have of scratching the paint. The paint people see."

He shuts the hood, letting it slam, so that any click it made I didn't hear. He rubs the towel over the edge of the hood, over scratches that will never be there.

"You just have to be careful," he says. "You won't scratch it if you don't play around—it's not a toy. I didn't buy it for you to play games."

He swirls the towel over the same places he's just wiped. He leans down close to the hood, squints, blows at some speck, squints again, then wipes at the spot with the towel wrapped around his pointer finger. He presses so hard it sounds like a squeegee. I fold my arms across my chest even though it's very hot and we're both sweating.

I say, "I'm careful. I'll be careful."

I worry he thinks I don't like the engine, so I add, "You want some water or something?"

He grabs my arm, so hard he might bruise me, his rough hands scratching my skin. He kisses me on the top of my head, a loud smacking kiss. Then he pretends to bite my head, making fake growls, and I can feel his crooked top teeth digging into my scalp.

"Let go," I pretend cry.

He holds me out away from him, squeezing my arm even harder, grinning and growling at the same time.

When he finally frees me, I can make out every finger of his hand, glowing red on my upper arm.

"Yeah, water," he says, and he pushes me on the shoulder towards the house and I pretend to stumble. "Tell Mami to make me café," he yells when I grab the doorknob. I look back at him, and he wipes his hands with the towel again and smiles.

As I pull the door closed behind me, there on my outstretched arm is Papi's handprint, still clear but starting to fade. The red parts had turned white; now it looked like all he'd left was an outline. I stare at it for a second and then decide not to shut the door all the way. I leave it a little open so I can hear him, even if he'll yell later that I let mosquitoes in the house.

Mom is already walking into the kitchen.

"People three blocks away can hear when your father wants café," she says.

She hugs me and gives me a kiss on the cheek as she walks past me to the sink. I grab a clean glass from the cabinet and stand next to her, waiting for the water to run colder so that I can be lazy and not have to refill the ice trays.

We watch my dad pace around the car from the kitchen window. He looks hard at all four tires, then opens the driver's side door and reaches in, and the hood of the car pops up a little. He comes back out, leaving the door open, and grabs the edge of the hood with his hand, which is draped in the towel to prevent finger prints.

"Is that one of my *kitchen* towels?" Mom says. "Dear God, give me strength."

I watch Papi open the hood, then close it, softly, bending down a little with his ear to the car. Then he goes back to the driver's seat and pops the hood again. He does the whole thing over again. As Mami keeps staring, I say, "Let me make the café, huh? I can do it." But even though the car's hood barely makes a sound, Mami doesn't hear me.

"What is he doing? Mom asks. "Your father and his games."

She packs the coffee into the cafetera, fills the bottom with water, and sets it on the stove. I fill the glass with water, and when I look up from the sink, Papi is on his fourth shutting of the hood. From outside, he gives me a thumbs-up. He even winks and says, "It clicks—you barely hear it, but I hear it—click!"

"Clickclickclick!" Mami says like a bratty kid. "I bet you that glass of water he loves that car more than us."

But she doesn't know what Papi is talking about, and he doesn't let her in on it, at least not then. Right then, me and him are the only ones that know what he means.

I yell through the crack I left in the door, "Hey Papi, how much ice?"

On Monday, Osniel talks to me in Spanish class like nothing happened, like it's not a big deal that he said he'd call but didn't. I went to bed the night before so pissed that I didn't even bother to wake up early to watch his light come on that morning.

"What's up your ass, Mercy?"

I don't even look at him.

"Nothing. Why?"

"You so quiet with me today, I dunno."

"Hmm," I shrug.

I curl my fingers around the edge of the desk, *into* the desk—my nails could cut the fake wood (if I *had* any nails). I grind my teeth and I almost listen to Mrs. Gomez. But I can't take my hands and teeth feeling so tight, and a minute later I turn towards him and ask him what I want to ask him.

"Osniel?"

"'Sup?" he says, pointing his chin at me and smiling.

"How come a guy says he's gonna call you but then doesn't?"

He sits up and looks around our classroom. He squints at Danny Garcia, on the other side at the back of the room, who is trying to get Carla to sit on his lap. He squints at Lazaro, who's asleep on his desk.

"Who said they were gonna call you?"

He sounds almost mad. He leans forward in the desk quick, like a reflex. He holds himself there, his eyes darting around my face, just inches from me. He's closer to my mouth than the day we went to Taco Bell together, closer than he's ever let himself be to me. I smile and look down so he can't see me trying not to smile.

"I'm just asking," I say.

He shakes his head No. "Mercedes Beatriz Reyes," he says. "Mercy. You know how we do. It's all part of the game, mama."

I say like an echo, "The game."

He just has this big-toothed grin on his face. I let go of the desk. I look down at my hands—my nails chewed on and weak. They're so short, pushed so back into my fingers, that I bet it would hurt to open the hood of my car. There isn't even any white part left to bite off. Something clicks for me, in my head—I can barely hear it. So I ask.

"Osniel," I say, "Hialeah's Finest? Is it really about the car? Or is it about me?"

He sits there quiet for one second too long, and then says, "Pshh," and forces a laugh. He leans back in the chair, yanking his face away from mine. He puts both arms out, his palms flat on the desk, raises his shoulders a little, and locks his elbows. He doesn't look at me, but looks straight ahead like Mrs. Gomez had just called on him. He wrinkles his eyebrows like he did that day we went to lunch and he sang to me.

Osniel finally looks at me straight in the face.

"Why would a car club be about anything other than cars?" he says.

I turn back towards the front of the class and I hadn't noticed until then that I'd been holding my breath. From across the room, Carla says, "Danny, stop it," and up at the board, Mrs. Gomez yells, "Por Favor! Atención, mis hijos." And I stare at her to keep from looking back at Osniel. When I start breathing again, I *know* I'm going to puke or cry, so I grab my bag and go up to Mrs. Gomez and ask for a pass to the bathroom. I don't even wait for her to fill it out all the way. I tear the yellow slip from her hands and rush out of the room, and Carla's screaming, "Osniel! What the fuck did you say to her? What the fuck is wrong with you?" The door shuts behind me, and down the hall I still hear Mrs. Gomez—"Asientos! Todos—take your seats!"

I run past the girls' bathroom, past the lockers and down the stairs, out past the portables where the freshmen have classes, out to the parking lot. I walk up to Osniel's car. It's *so* red and he has the perfect rims—complicated webs of chrome, almost impossible to keep clean, every right to brag—and he's got the official Honda seatbelt shoulder padding on both the driver *and* passenger sides.

In all the time I've known him and this Civic, I've never seen the engine close up—no clue what it looks like, what he's done to it. I wonder if there's any chrome under the hood, whether he'd show it off to me or not. I didn't need him to see it; I could break into his car, lift up the hood myself—my dad had taught me to pick locks when I was little, in case I ever lost my house key. When he was Osniel's age, my dad could hot-wire anything. Mami still tells stories about Papi siphoning gas from cars parked in front of house parties, about showing up at her school—ditching his own classes—so they could sit together in his Chevy Challenger during her lunch period. He'd refuse to unlock the doors and made her late to fifth period so many times that the teacher had called her house. Once, in the middle of the night, Mami's neighbor caught Papi pouring sugar in his son's fuel tank, just because the guy'd sat next to her in the cafeteria three days in a row. Mami never admits how all this hurt—or helped—Papi's chances with her. She *says* she tells me these stories to warn me about guys like Papi, to stay away from them because they only do damage. And when I said, "Yeah, but you married that guy," she said, "Mercy, please, Papi is different. He's your father, he loves you." And from the way she avoids looking at me when she says this, I sometimes think she's bragging.

I reach into my bag and get closer to the car. I pull out my keys, hold them firm, out from my thigh, and walk past the car, down the length of it. The metal scraping metal sounds quieter than I'd thought it would. I scrunch my eyes at the screech anyway, a skinny ribbon of red paint peeling off, then turning to flakes as it falls away from the car, away from my keys. I don't look at the car as I do it—I can't—because I don't want to get caught like Papi did with the sugar. So I wait until I'm done keying Osniel's paint, and a few feet away, before I look back at the damage.

The line is a thin, crooked path from the front bumper straight to me. The rims and wheels looked wasted on his car now, like he knows his car is sad and he's trying too hard. A pinstripe done by a blind guy—that's what I bet my dad'll call it when he sees Osniel's car pass our house later. And maybe that's what I'll tell Osniel, if he ever asks what I was going for.

I can finally breathe right once I slide into my front seat, but my hands won't stop shaking. I hold them out in front of me; shiny red chips stick to the sweat on my palm. I don't brush them off on my jeans—I keep them on me, the stubborn flakes itching a little and sparkling. After curling my fingers over the specks to protect them, I stick the key in the ignition with my other hand. I throw my Civic in reverse and steer out of the spot, doing it all one-handed, riding out like a pimp or a gangster. And even though Papi has told me a million times this is *not* the safe way to drive—that God gave me two hands and won't think twice about taking one back if I don't keep both on the steering wheel *at all times*, Papi says—I do it anyways just to keep Osniel's fist shut. I drive home going way faster than I should because I need to beat Papi home—I don't want him to catch me acting stupid, with only one hand on the wheel after everything he's told me. Maybe—if I have enough time before Mami asks, "And school?" and Papi asks, "Any car problems?" like they do every day, talking over each other because they know they're asking the same thing—maybe I'll even wash my hand.

MICHELLE REALE

If All They Had Were Their Bodies

Fat girls sit on the low, crooked wall smoking slow and disinterested, the same way they do everything. They are brilliant in their tattoos and jewel-colored hair. The fat girls sit on the low, crooked wall and smoke slow and disinterested, the same way they do everything. Their too-small t-shirts boast philosophies they really don't believe in, like "Live and Let Live." They rarely say a word to anyone.

The good-looking boys roam along the wall in groups, nearly identical: lank hair, drooping over eyes that roamed with the abandon of the confident. They shove their large hands, with veins like ropes, deep into their pockets. They are tough. They kick whatever is in front of them.

The fat girls follow them with their eyes, the softer among them hazarding a smile.

The skinny girls watch. They let themselves feel the thrill of expectation. They hold the fragile scaffolding of their wraith-thin bones in their own arms, rocking gently as if they were their own babies. They are concave and vulnerable, dressed in the colors of sickness.

The boys taunt them for showcasing their weakness. One tosses a dollar: "Go eat something!"

It pleased the fat girls to no end. They grin and high-five one another. They stuff French fries into greasy, red mouths. They blow smoke in thin streams and great gusts.

The boys swagger, lighting each other's cigarettes. They talk of things they know nothing about, like what a woman wants.

They hold their backs straight and strong, well aware of the longing of those watching them.

A fat girl on the wall crosses thick thighs, revealing a musical note tattooed on the puckered skin at the back of her knee.

A skinny girl spots this, tracing the form. Her eyes become bright. She closes her eyes and sings the note aloud. She thinks of the possibilities there. She takes small, wobbly steps toward the fat girl, who is so surprised that she makes room for her on the wall. They sit silently, side by side.

The other girls take a second look at one another across the divide. On everyone's mind was what the two might say to one another when they finally speak. They contort their mouths into familiar positions of envy. They are glad for the stories there would be to tell. The speculation thrilled. The fat girl places her heavy arm across the shoulder wings of the skinny girl because it feels right. She looks at the backs of the good-looking boys who are now even farther away. They'd be sorry to have missed something so momentous. That not one among them would be worth waiting for.

COLIN LOCKARD

Ordering Drinks *en Español*

For some reason I don't understand,
words like "shot glass"
had not been covered
in my intermediate college Spanish class,
evidently considered less relevant than
"scuba diving"
"cucumber"
and "post-impressionist art."

So I had to guess as I stood
at the bar at the nightclub
that first night in Barcelona:
"Una copita, por favor,"
A little glass, please,
"de Jack Daniels,"
(in my best Spanish accent
the Tennessean's first name
now a Himalayan beast of burden).

I knew my guess was wrong
when I was asked if I wanted ice
but I didn't let my mistake show.
"Siempre," I responded,
Always,
Always I want ice
in my little glass of whiskey
when at bars in Barcelona.

PATTY SOMLO

Even with a Stack of Dollars

Blanca Peña needed a pair of blue jeans and there was no place to buy them but the Dollar Store. This infuriated Blanca, whose skin was white as a *gringa*'s, but what could a woman do in this son-of-a-whore country? Blanca would have to ask that *flaca* reporter from the United States, so skinny the bones in her shoulders stuck out, to take her. Even with a stack of dollars earned from letting *gringos* eat, sleep and shower in her three houses, Blanca couldn't get into the Dollar Store on her own. Only foreigners had permission to enter.

It was bad enough that she rented a room to the *gringa*. She hated to have to sweet-talk her but there was no choice.

"*Buenas dias*, Anita," Blanca said, when the *gringa* reporter came out of the kitchen carrying a cup of coffee.

Blanca silently admonished herself not to bring up politics. Otherwise, they'd get into a fight.

"Did you have a good sleep?" Blanca asked, as if the *gringa* were a friend or lover.

The *gringa* hadn't anticipated such concern from Blanca. She had learned to steel herself for the endless complaints and pointed jibes that steamed out of Blanca's mouth. In truth, the *gringa* hadn't slept well at all. She'd been in the country for two months but was still having trouble getting acclimated—to the dripping hot climate, the mosquitoes whining in the night, the overly salted, oily food, the lack of even the most basic necessities, the phones rarely working, the difficulty of catching a cab, and the impossibility of renting a car. All of it slowed her down, to the point where she had trouble doing her job. As a freelancer with no regular paycheck to rely on, the *gringa* needed to hustle to beat the staff reporters to stories.

"It was very hot," the *gringa* named Ann Cameron, who went by the name Anita in this country, finally answered.

"Yes, the heat," Blanca said, and picked up a sheet of the government-run newspaper from the table and began to fan herself, as if to agree.

"I have a technique," the *gringa* went on. "I take a shower and leave my hair wet. That keeps me a little cool. If I'm lucky, I will fall asleep before my hair dries."

Blanca smiled at this. She knew she should say something pleasant and reassuring, sympathize with the *gringa* about the heat and the mosquitoes, and try to be agreeable and nice. But the familiar anger and resentment was beginning to bubble up—the feelings that gave Blanca heartburn, right underneath her breastbone. *If we didn't have these son-of-a-whore* Comunistas *running the country, people like me might be able to have air conditioning.* That's what Blanca wanted to say but she knew right off that was wrong. The *gringa*, like the other foreigners here, was in love with the revolutionary government. No matter how right Blanca might be, the *gringa* refused to see any fault on the government's part. And that would all lead to an argument.

"The heat," was all Blanca could say now, and picked up the makeshift newspaper fan and batted it back and forth.

Blanca Peña was forty-five years old. Anyone could tell that only a few years back, Blanca had been a beauty. She was blessed with classic Spanish looks—long, black, thick hair and pale skin, like porcelain. In her younger days, Blanca had been crowned Round-Up Queen three years in a row. She'd grown up in the Eastern part of the country, the daughter of a rancher who owned so much land, it took an entire afternoon to drive around all of it. Her father never dirtied his hands but still liked to dress in jeans, pointed-toed boots and the large felt hats worn by cowboys.

Blanca had dreamed of one day leaving this country, spending part of every year abroad, shopping for clothes and jewelry in America. She had married Gilberto Diaz, a rancher like her father, and he agreed right off to move to the capital, which was livelier, in hopes of pleasing his beautiful young wife.

That, of course, was what happened before this son-of-a-whore revolution, when a bunch of scraggly students and poor farm workers took over the country. They didn't steal all of Gilberto's land, thanks be to God, but did hand some hectares over to the poor, as if the lazy bastards deserved any of it.

And now, to make matters worse, a war had begun. Blanca secretly supported the forces fighting to overthrow the government, though she wouldn't have whispered a word of that to anyone.

Blanca tried to get control of her mind, which was starting to meander into territory she needed to avoid. It was so hard these days not to complain. What she really wanted to do was get up and shake this little *gringa*, yell at her to open her eyes, look around and see what had happened to Blanca's beautiful life. She wanted to tell the *gringa*, as she often did, how impossible it was to get new tires for the car. More than anything, she wanted to throw this too-thin, smug woman out of her house. How would she feel, Blanca wanted to know, if she woke up one day and found she had to let strangers live in her house, just to get by?

Of course, none of this would get Blanca what she wanted most at this moment, which was a brand new pair of blue jeans. So she bit her tongue. She couldn't go to the Round-Up wearing last-year's style, which was all she had, and it was impossible to wear anything but jeans to the opening night party.

Blanca knew she'd better try and soften up the *gringa* before she asked. Just as she was about to complement the *gringa* on her hair, Marta, the cook, walked into the dining room.

"*Buenas dias*, Anita," Marta said and beamed warmly.

The *gringa* touched the cook's fat arm and said good morning back. Watching them made Blanca start to seethe. She knew the *gringa* spent time most mornings hanging around the hot kitchen talking to Marta. In this country, Blanca wanted to tell her, we don't chat with the servants. Blanca also wanted to remind the *gringa* that she paid Marta to work, not to socialize. It was bad enough that these *hijo-de-puta* Communists kept putting funny ideas into Marta's mind. Marta no longer apologized when she arrived for work late. Instead, she blamed the dictator, for having stolen all the people's money meant to replace broken buses, so that now the system had to operate with vehicles that constantly broke down.

Marta had even gotten the nerve to demand higher wages and threatened to walk out in the middle of the busy lunch rush if Blanca didn't agree to pay. Blanca, who by that point had a popular *comedor* in her house, serving lunches to scores of government workers—the only people in this country with any money, Blanca liked to say—couldn't afford to lose customers and that's why she agreed to Marta's outrageous demand for higher pay.

Everything had been turned upside down with the Communists in charge. Now, people from the bottom like Marta—workers and peasants who didn't even know how to read and write—felt they deserved to be on top.

Blanca knew that the *gringa* and Marta had gotten chummy. One morning, the *gringa* even had the nerve to talk to Blanca about her treatment of Marta. It wasn't direct, Blanca might have been willing to agree, but Blanca knew that the *gringa*'s sympathizing with Marta was meant to punish her and every other person in her class.

"Marta works so hard," the *gringa* said to Blanca that morning. "I'm surprised she doesn't pass out in that hot kitchen. No air conditioning, no ventilation. With the oven going and the stove, it must be a hundred and ten in there or more."

Anyone could see that Blanca was the person who deserved the *gringa*'s sympathy, not her fat slob of a cook, who should have been grateful for a job in such a lovely house. But once again, Blanca reminded herself that the arguments running through her head were fine every other day of the week but not today, because she needed to get on the *gringa*'s good side.

Marta hustled back to the kitchen and returned with the coffee pot and two poached eggs in a bowl. *The little bitch thinks she's too good to eat like the rest of us,*

Blanca silently told her girlfriend Elena, whose husband had been smart enough to pack his family off to Miami the minute the *Comunistas* took over. The skinny *gringa* wouldn't touch anything fried. She even had the nerve to complain that the food was cooked with too much oil and salt.

In this goddamn country, Blanca wanted to say, *it's a miracle a person can even get the ingredients to put a decent meal on the table*. If Blanca didn't have a stack of dollars from renting out rooms, she wouldn't be able to go on the black market and get eggs. Period.

The *gringa* took a bite of the eggs while Marta stood there and waited.

"*Perfecto*," the *gringa* said, looking up at the cook and beaming. She'd made a little circle with her thumb and index finger to be sure her pleasure with the way the eggs turned out was even more apparent.

The cook patted the *gringa* on the shoulder and said, "*Gracias*," before heading back into the kitchen.

Blanca was tempted to scold the *gringa* about the way she had just treated Marta, warning her that coddling the servants would only lead to more demands that couldn't be met and then trouble. But she remembered her goal for the morning and understood that such warnings would have to wait.

"I was wondering," Blanca began. She placed one of her dark crimson painted nails up above her top lip and took a breath.

Across the table, the *gringa* noticed the collection of silver bracelets that suddenly slid down from Blanca's wrist and the rings on nearly every one of her fingers. She noticed the red lipstick that Blanca had applied a little too high on her upper lip, the heavy dark blue eye-shadow and her thick hair piled on top of her head.

"I was wondering," Blanca said again, "if you might need to go to the Dollar Store today."

Blanca held her breath, her hands in her lap, the fingers woven together in a tight embrace. What if the *gringa* said no?

The *gringa* took another bite of her egg and chewed slowly. Blanca hadn't brought up the government once during the entire time they had sat together at the table. She must want something—the *gringa* felt certain. But what?

"No, I don't," the gringa said a few seconds after swallowing.

Blanca let her breath out now and the fury once again began to burn in her belly. She thought about the last time she spoke to Elena, before the phone, as usual, clicked off. Elena had just come back from the mall.

"A hundred stores," Elena breathlessly reported to Blanca. "Jewelry, clothes, shoes. Dishes, silverware."

Elena paused for a moment before going on.

"And so much food. Every kind. Whatever you want. I must be careful here not to get too fat."

Blanca hung up the phone and tried to imagine how it would feel to go to a place like that mall, with such bright lights, Elena had said, even if all Blanca did was look at the merchandise. Before Blanca knew what had hit her, she started to cry. Midway through what had become an almost daily session of weeping, Blanca heard the voice of her husband Gilberto, reminding her that life in Miami wasn't all that wonderful.

"Do you know what Mario has to do to keep food on the table?" Gilberto would have said. "Mario washes dishes in a restaurant. And Elena? When Elena's not walking in the mall, she's cleaning people's toilets and washing their clothes."

In her lowest moments of despair, Blanca would tell Gilberto that she would rather clean people's toilets and at least be able to buy a few things she needed than stay in this son-of-a-whore country and watch her life go down the toilet. Gilberto would rub her hand and then her shoulders and back and say, "Blanca. You don't know what you are saying."

Now, Blanca realized, she would have to ask. She hated to ask for anything but if she didn't get a new pair of jeans, going to the opening night party at the Round-Up would be out of the question.

She bent the fingers of her right hand and studied her crimson nails for a moment, as if the answer she craved was waiting for her there. Then she opened her mouth.

"I need a pair of blue jeans to wear to the Round-Up. Would you take me to the Dollar Store so I could buy a pair?"

Blanca felt the blood race to her cheeks. She turned her head away from the table so the *gringa* wouldn't see.

"I would be happy to take you to the Dollar Store, Blanca."

The *gringa* patted Blanca's hand, as if to assure her that everything was going to work out now.

A driving rain came down that afternoon, turning the streets into rushing rivers choked with brown mud. The rain lasted less than a half-hour and then the sun came out. Steam rose in lazy whorls from the rivers of water and deep puddles.

Blanca picked her way across the muddy field, her wide feet crammed into a pair of backless, gold lamé heels. The *gringa* stepped carefully behind her in a pair of flat brown comfortable sandals.

After a few minutes, they reached a spot where someone had dropped a thin plank to serve as a bridge over a narrow canal of rushing water. Blanca teetered her way across and the *gringa* followed.

It was crazy, the *gringa* thought, how underdeveloped this country was, even here in the capital. The dictator, whose family had stayed in power for years, had pocketed all the revenue that should have gone to build and repair roads and sidewalks, phones, electricity, water pipes and sewers. Instead of roads in many places, there were dusty lanes that, after the short hard rains that came down every afternoon, turned into churning rivers of mud. The sidewalks were the same.

They finally reached the paved road that led the rest of the way to the Dollar Store. The *gringa* showed her passport to the guard, a young handsome soldier, and explained that Blanca was accompanying her. The *gringa* and Blanca both knew the rules. Goods in the store were only for consumption by foreigners—diplomats, reporters and the staffs of nongovernmental organizations. Everything had to be paid for in dollars.

The place was brightly lit, and the shelves were stocked. Even the most basic items, such as toilet paper and soap that were hard to come by in local stores, were here in abundance. Blanca followed the *gringa* as she led the way through the cleaning supplies and dried and canned food over to the clothes. Blanca's heart began to flutter the minute she spied the racks of blue jeans ahead of her, in the far corner.

The *gringa* was surprised to see Blanca begin to look at jeans in the same small size she wore. The *gringa* couldn't imagine how Blanca could possibly get a pair of that size jeans on. If asked, the *gringa* would have guessed Blanca to be about three sizes larger. At least.

Blanca draped the jeans on their hangers over her arm. The gringa grabbed a couple and held them. Then Blanca looked over at the *gringa* and smiled.

"I think I'm ready to try them on."

The *gringa* stood outside the dressing room and waited. On the other side of the beige curtain, she could hear the jingle of silver bracelets and what sounded like Blanca doing sit-ups.

The curtain parted and Blanca stepped out. She hadn't managed to get the jeans zipped all the way up but that didn't seem to matter to her.

The jeans clung to Blanca's thighs like a whisper at the edge of an ear. Blanca stood atop her gold lamé heels and slowly spun around. Her normally downcast eyes were lit up and she was beaming in a way the gringa had never seen her do before.

"How do I look?" Blanca asked.

The *gringa* let her eyes run down Blanca's hips to her crotch, where the pants were so tight, they gathered up flesh on either side and pinched it into two matching balls. She studied the bulges that poked out the front of Blanca's thighs. And when Blanca turned around, the *gringa* couldn't help but see the unsightly dimples that formed thick rolls underneath both sides of her buttocks.

A moment later, an ache of sadness seized her, right in the center of her gut. The last thing she'd expected was to be feeling sorry for Blanca.

Blanca turned around. Her eyes briefly caught the gringa's gaze, and then dropped down to the floor.

"You know what you look like?" the *gringa* was finally able to say.

"What?" Blanca said, and began to chew on her crimson-painted lower lip.

"You look like the Queen of the Round-Up."

TANYA CHERNOV AND LAURIE JUNKINS

What a Poet Can Bring: Juan Felipe Herrera

The final poem in Juan Felipe Herrera's new and selected collection of poetry, *Half of the World in Light*, begins with this simple request: "Before you go further, / let me tell you what a poem brings." Juan Felipe Herrera knows art; he knows community and struggle, and he knows something about making a literary life over the span of several decades. But what Juan Felipe Herrera is absolutely certain of is what a poem has the power to bring. Herrera has watched poetry enhance multi-cultural awareness, education, and community ties. And more than anything else, he has watched as poetry has brought, and continues to bring, urgency and social change.

Juan Felipe Herrera was born in Fowler, California, in 1948. The only son of migrant farmers, Herrera moved often, living in trailers or tents along the roads of the San Joaquin Valley in Southern California. Throughout his childhood, he attended school in a variety of small towns from San Francisco to San Diego. In a 2004 interview at California State University Fresno, Herrera remarked on the impact that his home state has had on his life. He spoke of the different Californias he has known: the small agricultural towns of the San Joaquin Valley from his childhood, San Diego's Logan Heights, and San Francisco's Mission District. Herrera has carefully examined how these locations have influenced his work: "all these landscapes became stories, and all those languages became voices in my writing, all those visuals became colors and shapes, which made me more human and gave me a wide panorama to work from."

In addition to working as a musician, an educator, and a painter, Herrera has for decades been recognized as one of the most influential poets in the Chicano Literary movement. It is because of his multi-faceted approach to art that Herrera has been able to break new ground in the field of poetry. New York Times critic Stephen Burt lauded Herrera as one of the first poets to actually succeed, where so many other poets have floundered, at creating "a new hybrid art, part oral, part written, part English, part something else: an art grounded in ethnic identity, fueled by collective pride, yet irreducibly individual, too."[1] In creating his own brand of "hybrid art," Herrera has contributed to the phenomonon Luis Leal and Manuel M. Martín-Rodríguez describe as "the creation of a new type of books that transcend the barriers of genre to contract

---

1 "Punk Half Panther," *The New York Times*, 2008.

deliberately hybrid texts; their hybridity, in turn, becomes metaphoric of . . . continuous 'border crossings.'"[2]

With this merging and crossing of boundaries, Herrera's writing matured, and his focus shifted from his own personal sphere to the interests and concerns of others, finally taking him back on the road. Herrera's interests in indigenous cultures inspired him to lead a formal Chicano trek to endangered Mexican-Indian villages, from the Lancandón rain forest of Chiapas to the mountains of Nayarit. Herrera's experiences on that journey greatly changed him both as a person and as an artist, instilling in him a newfound passion for representing the voice of those who are oppressed, marginalized, or ignored.

His artwork, which includes video, photography, theater, poetry, prose, and performance, has made Herrera a leading voice on the Chicano Civil Rights Movement as well as in the Chicano Literary movements. Herrera's role in working for civil rights has, at times, immersed him in the turmoil, tension, and urgency inherent to social change, and those sentiments and experiences have surfaced in his poetry. His work is abundant with themes of displacement and exile, violence, war, and a sense of helplessness; these themes often evoke a nightmarish quality through the piling-on of images and action with few breaks. The poem "Night Train to Tuxtla," the title poem of his 1994 collection, illustrates this nightmare motif, as well as Herrera's willingness to use whatever form suits him at the moment of composition. "Night Train to Tuxtla" is a prose poem largely composed of sentence fragments within a single block paragraph, and is one of the best examples of Herrera's ability to write as if describing a dream, a painting-in-words, or even a film loop. Like so many of his poems, it reflects the plight of the immigrant, a sense of panic, powerlessness, and ongoing discomfort:

> Blurred gate at La Central in D. F. This is where you bring your bags and cardboard, leave behind a sack of viscera. It's not going to help you cross over. La Central: the wooden hub of brown exiles dressed in rubber; bound south. Some prefer the East. Prefer the South where you can breathe in broken pieces of sweat music. Billie Holiday and her velveteen dress waves from above, frocked in a Virgen de Guadalupe shawl. Stars, marimbas, sex, and moon shafts. She drops it on the man ahead of me, the guy with a herringbone comb in his hip pocket, the guy, with a newspaper jammed in his short sport coat, flying. We are all running. No one looks up . . .

---

2 "Chicano Literature," *The Cambridge History of Latin American Literature: The Twentieth Century*, 1996.

While this poem and many of his other early to mid-career works deal heavily with his own history and the Chicano experience, in his more recent work, Herrera serves as a recorder of human suffering, exploring loss and destruction in a world of little beauty. The cynicism that many feel with the relentless war, poverty, and suffering that make up life in so many parts of the world is the scaffolding on which these newer poems are built:

> I forget to mention the blasts, so many things flying,
> light, existence, the house in tins, a mother in rags.
>
> It is too cold to expose her tiny legs,
> the fish-shaped back—you must take these notes for me.
>
> Before you go. See this
> undulate
> extend
> beyond
> the pools of blood.
> from "Enter the Void"[3]

These social commentary-based poems are full of graphic reminders of what conditions are like beyond the sanitized American experience, painting a dark, almost post-apocalyptic world. "Rubble" is used relentlessly, a refrain of destruction, illustrated in the poem "I Am Merely Posing for a Photograph:"

> My face to one side.
> Listen to gray-white bells of rubble, the list
> goes on—the bones, hearts, puffed intestines,
> stoned genitalia, teeth, again I forget how
> to piece all this together, scraps, so many scraps,
> lines and holes.
>
> The white gray rubble light blinds me,
> wait, I just thought—what if this is not visible,
> what if all this is not visible.[4]

---

3   from *Half the World of Light*, University of Arizona Press, 2008.

4   Ibid.

Herrera admits to focusing heavily on the plight of the oppressed and victimized and says, "sometimes I say to myself, 'This stuff is so bleak, unrelenting.' I take a breath and re-work a bit, sometimes leave it as is—because, to paraphrase one of my favorite anthropologists, Sherry Ortner, there are always the unpredictable forces of individual and social response." Never one to take lightly his role in the ongoing dialogue of social response, Herrera doesn't allow modern-day villains to be let off the hook in the poem, "A Percentage Will Survive:"

> . . . you, and the commedia, the infernos,
> or shall I say the Cabinet, the Advisors, the Board,
> satellite screws ajar, corporate investment bankers
> with their hand down my groin, the accountants
> with Picasso Avignon faces, I mean
> the re-writer apologists, the agribusiness
> pump pesticidal wave, the plague powders en route to you,
> forgive me . . .[5]

When asked whether there is room for hope and optimism in the midst of all the brutality in our world, Herrera says, "there is more than hope. There is the power of the present where all is possible. I take my poetry to as many social spaces that come to mind and to as many literary forms that I can find . . . (although this takes a little time, here and there, since the idea is to de-rail yourself, your tight self and your tight work and sometimes it is good to add a dash of research)." Because Herrera moves in and out of so many artistic mediums, he allows each genre to inform the next, using each form as research for whatever obsession has grabbed hold of his attention. He lists exercises such as writing while watching a Fellinni film or while viewing a photo exhibit at MOMA in San Francisco among his repertoire of research practices. He says of these free-flowing habits that "all of this moves my writing one way or another; nothing stays neutral. I do not protect my poems from influences—instead I yield to them with Aztec delight."

Herrera has had a great deal of practice in allowing the artist inside him to dictate where his focus will settle, in both his literary work as well as his work as a teacher and mentor. He currently teaches in the Creative Writing Department at the University of California Riverside. Herrera attributes his comfort in the role of teacher to the many mentors he learned from in his own life. Reflecting on the work of a teacher, Herrera writes, "It is good to leave your poetry behind. If it is really yours it, you won't lose it. My books and literary accoutrements move to the

---

5   Ibid.

margin. When I do this people cry, students who had never said a word begin to speak, people sing a song that they carried in their heart for years. Parents, too."

As a member of the Chicano Civil Rights Movement vanguard throughout the '60s and '70s, Herrera views the current landscape of racial issues in our culture and in literature with the same drive to reflect on this landscape in his writing now as he did then. He believes that there is "no center, no preferred demarcation or paradigm." He claims that "maybe the poet who can meet this whirl of perspectivism is the one to follow. Follow fast because, yes, race issues have picked up since September 11, 2001. What to do or say or write? The writer, the poet, all of us needs to assess all this cautiously; it is not a Manichean world—it never was." Herrera accomplishes the difficult task of creating a sense of all-inclusiveness within this racial "whirl;" instead of railing against a particular racial group for injustices or misdeeds, he pulls his readers into the perspective of the group he is writing about. Juan returns to simplicity of form and language to place the reader into the minds of his subjects rather than bombard his poetry with intricate formatting or complex language. In the poem, "A Percentage Will Survive," for example, he writes about "the mother under curfew/ en route to a hospital in Bethlehem," effectively humanizing the struggles we see on the news or hear of on the radio. Repeating this technique in many of his social commentaries, Herrera creates a sense of all-inclusiveness by consistently putting a human face on the tragedies of the world. This forces the reader to identify with that mother heading for a hospital and insert his or her own emotional response inside the perspective of what Herrera views as a global community. Herrera reaches out through his poetry and invites his readers to join him in viewing the pain of others, even as he questions his ability to do so without labels, as illustrated by the final lines of "A Percentage Will Survive:"

if only I could write without the Nomenclature
in between my teeth, the ideology lapel stuck
to my chromosome lines

of afro-indian-hebrew-mestizo-arab-muslin-moorish dancers.
Forgive me.

Perhaps one of Herrera's most admirable poetic traits is his ability and desire to comment on the suffering of those outside his own heritage with both intelligence and compassion, ferocity and tenderness. Gloria Anzaludúa discusses the connectivity between Chicanos and other oppressed peoples in her book, *Border-lands/La Frontera: The New Mestiza*:

> The struggle is inner: Chicano, *indio*, American Indian, *mojado*, *mexicano*, immigrant
> Latino, Anglo in power, working class Anglo, Black, Asian—our psyches resemble the
> bordertowns and are populated by the same people. The struggle has always been inner,
> and is played out in the outer terrains. Awareness of our situation must come before
> inner changes, which in turn come before changes in society. Nothing happens in the
> 'real' world unless it first happens in the images in our heads.[6]

Herrera often voices that responsibility to recognize or represent groups other than his own— groups who have also suffered at the hands of oppressors. His approach to the world's downtrodden is democratic. Reflecting on this responsibility and echoing Anzaludúa's insight, Herrera claims that "every poem is a poem about all of us whether we like it or not." In "Giraffe on Fire," the title poem of his 2001 collection, for example, he makes a conscious attempt not only to include "many peoples such as the Ilongot of the northern Philippines and the Tallensi warriors of Africa but also to collapse time-space so as to have peoples come together that were historically dispersed by the intractable powers of time and place."

In "Memoria(s)," from the same collection, Herrera remembers the conflicts of the peoples of the Middle East and North Africa—Turkish, Moorish, Egyptian, the Jewish, and Arab alike. "Letter to the Hungry Students of Berlin" is written for the victims of Hitler and Stalin; even Mexicans and Vietnamese make a brief appearance. In "Simple Poet Constructs Hunger," Herrera writes:

> One of the boys deserted his military unit in Chechnya. They too are
>   hungry;
> I can tell by their stiff fingers. The war is over, one says.
> Forgiveness or bread?
> Punishment or wine? Five thousand march in the iciness, in the ruins.[7]

Herrera's position regarding all suffering people of the world can best be summed up by these lines from the aptly-named "We Are All Saying the Same Thing:"

> She is the sky you were after, that immeasurable breath
> in every one of us.

---

6   Aunt Lute Books, 1987.

7   from *Border-Crosser with a Lamborghini Dream*, University of Arizona Press, 1998.

We are all saying the same thing, Yeti.
We lift our breast & speak of fire, then ice.

We press into our little knotted wombs,
wonder about our ends, then, our beginnings.[8]

Herrera has overcome many of the obstacles that the publishing industry thrown in his path, defying the standards of what is popular or conventional in favor of expressing his voice however it comes to him. He has similarly surpassed any creative boundaries in his literary work, due in large part to his self-proclaimed determination to never think of his own limitations, much less of needing to break down any limitations. He says that in considering one's own limitations, a writer will "lose time when doing that. Most of all, you lose the powers at your fingertips. As Victor Hernandez-Cruz said decades ago, 'You gotta keep your tips on fire.'" When other writers can only manage this in ways that come off as forced or contrived, as with Ginsberg, Herrera possesses the rare ability to craft poems without revealing the work behind the curtain. One of the most profound ways in which Herrera has implanted this determination lies in his ground-breaking ability to weave Spanish into his English poetry. Merging his dual identities as both a Latino and an American man, Herrera succeeded in publishing poems that seamlessly blend the two languages and cultures. He has created work that does not need to be only English or Spanish, only performance-oriented or for the page alone. Susan Bassnett writes in "Bilingual Poetry: A Chicano Phenomenon" that "the poem can be read . . . across boundaries, and there is a new kind of interlingual process . . . the poem offers an illustration of the different dimensions that can be obtained when the same lines are written twice."[9] Herrera accomplishes this very brand of boundary-crossing in his bilingual poetry, connecting his readers to the respect he has for the beauty of each language.

Several of his poems appear in English and are correspondingly translated into Spanish, such as the experimental poem "Grafik" and poems from his 2000 collection *Thunderweavers/Tejedoras De Rayos*. In the latter, the English and Spanish occur within each poem, translations appearing section by section, as in this excerpt from the first section in the poem "Xunka":

So many huipiles on fire,

---

8   Ibid.

9   *International Studies in Honor of Tomás Rivera*, ed. Julián Olivares, Arte Público Press, 1986.

Torches without end and mother Pascuala
Her small hands, her eyes of lights and
This forest that crashes
Over my breast

| | |

Tantos huipiles en llamas,
Antorchas sin fin, y mi madre Pascuala
Sus manos pequeñas, sus ojos de luz y
Este bosque que se derrama
Sobre mi pecho.

Herrera views the process of wandering far away from the established poetics as ways of speaking and writing cultures as an art form. He describes this "collective poetic process in search of a new expression" as a social movement. "It does not have to involve different 'languages,' it can merely take into account different orientations, moods, sonic templates, terms, arrangements," he says. "Then, there is the publishing world that rarely accepts bilingual work. To make matters worse, given the national 'conservative' leaning toward a frozen monolingual cultural monolith, writing in multi-vocal forms is most challenging." When asked what advice he would give to young writers wishing to establish new ground in this vein of literature, Herrera continues, saying, "... you need to be bold, for them to be bold; be luminous—then they will see you."

Herrera is the epitome of boldness. Not only has he broken ground with bilingualism in his work, but he has shattered virtually every known poetic form, often creating new forms. If one can imagine it, Herrera has likely written a poem about it. His poems come in all permutations, including nightmare-style sequences, journal entries, lists, experimental free verse, l=a=n=g=u=a=g=e poetry, letter poems, and even a theater-like choreo-poem with a variety of speakers. His attitude is one of ultimate creative freedom; Herrera has found great artistic satisfaction and success in allowing a poem to create itself in whatever form arises subconsciously. He says "the form meets the moment I am in, the road I have traveled, the voices I am moved by, the thing of the ocean when it trembles in blue-greens and French blues or a micro-moment such as a baby hummingbird floating in front of me, then drinking from a leaf, half a drop of water, then leaving." When asked what the process of creating such boundary-less work is like, Herrera says it is "a mind process. A letting-go process. Reckless, in heat, feverish.

Tobacco and Expresso. Columbus Street, North Beach, Provolone and blistering Chinese mustard on a hard French. Never outside the writing, inside, inside. Devouring it, smelling it, rubbing it on your face and running outside into the shoulders and faces and winds."

Herrera encourages his students to free themselves, as well. He says to young poets, "Start where you are. Go from there. Make radical leaps. Mess yourself up. You can always step back to your cubbyhole. Also, get down to the detail of things. If you want to take a leap, first you must muddy-up your pants." As the concept of creative writing education changes and evolves with low-residency courses and the digital era, Herrera applies his undeniable open-mindedness to the discussion over the legitimacy of the teaching of poetry. When asked about his teaching methods, he advises us to " . . . turn the workshop upside down, so everyone has to scramble out, find a way to create an authentic collective. Finally, it is healthy and perhaps necessary to embrace a global family of writers, an international scope. We are not here to write around ourselves, for ourselves. We are here to merge with the planetary pulse. Kerfuffles and donnybrooks come and go, but the poet continues." Herrera strives to teach, to learn, and above all else, to represent those voices that might not otherwise be heard. In his role as a mentor and teacher in the arts community, he still encounters surprises, beginning anew each day.

Juan Felipe Herrera continues on as poet, teacher, and vanguard, providing an artistic beacon for us to look toward and be guided by. In a world of racial conflict, cynicism, and brutality, Herrera uses his creativity and passion to show us that there is indeed reason to hope. He shows us, through both his writing and his contagious outlook on life, that above all other things a poem can bring us—social awareness and change, creative freedom—a life of poetry can also bring great joy.

ARIONÓ-JOVAN LABU'

Como Mí

Negro . . . Negro como medianoche—

Negro como una sombra dentro de una sombra.

Jorobadas y nocturna con
manos juntas, ojos bajos
sentado un montaña de basura
en las rincón de Mission y Van Ness.
vestido en harapos, olientes de alcanfor
vómito y basura caliente.
Zapatos sucia de barro y excremento,
rota con dolor, mordido por los vientos de violencia.

"¿Tiene usted un cigarrillo?" él pregunta

"No"—digo

Poco después, como intoxicó
por el que es Santo, perdido a la luz de vino
himnos como si el esclavo- estación central.

Y miro este retrato abstracto de un hombre,
sin hogar & marchitando en este frío/
cruel y mundo criminal.
En esta ciudad de hambre y moho
con el mismo derecho de vivir como el rico.

Negro . . . Negro como carbón—

Negro como mí.

ARIONÓ-JOVAN LABU'

Like Me

Black . . . black as midnight—

black like a shadow within a shadow.

Hunchbacked and nocturnal,
hands joined, eyes downcast
sitting on a pile of debris
at the corner of Mission and Van Ness.
Clothed in rags, smelling of camphor,
vomit and steamy trash.
Dirty shoes of clay and excrement,
broken with grief, mauled by the violent winds.

"Got a smoke?" he asks

"No" I reply.

Shortly after, like poisoned
by that which is Holy, lost in the light of wine
hymns as if the slave-central station.

and I look at this abstract portrait: a man,
homeless and wilting in this cold,
cruel, and criminal world.
In this city of hunger and rust
with the same right to live as the rich.

Black . . . black as coal—

Black like me.

SARAH BLAKE

The Men

The men on the main drag want to give me
the pretty-girl special. The men on the bus
love me, too. They ask me to touch their scars.
They want to run me around the parks.

The man, whom I love, who lives in my house
like an American Cockroach, got lost
looking for water and I trapped him under a glass
until I liked looking at him.

But a man is always a man—unless
he's a bird, and then he's a grackle.
And even the grackles fan their tails
and throw back their heads for me.

SARAH BLAKE

The Heat Has Us

The bus is blasting the air conditioning.
The bus driver's real fat.

Across from me, a woman has goose bumps.
Her lips look blue.

Next thing I know, she jumps up, screaming,
Where is the warm air? Where is it?

The driver yells right back,
It's in me! All the heat is in me!

The boy in front of me turns
and says, *I think it's all in you.*

What could a girl say? I kiss the boy
and think about the driver.

It puts the Texas afternoon
right inside me.

Анны Ахматовой

Муж Хлестая Меня . . .

Муж хлестая меня узорчатым,
Вдвое сложенным ремнем.
Для тебя в окошке створчатом
Я всю ночь сижу с огнем.

Рассветает. И над кузницей
Подымается дымок.
Ах, со мной, печальной узницей,
Ты опять побыть не мог.

Для тебя я долю хмурую,
Долю-муку приняла.
Или любишь белокурую,
Или рыжая мила?

Как мне скрыть вас, стоны звонкие?
В сердце темный, душный хмель,
А лучи ложатся тонкие
На несмятую постель.

Осень 1911

Anna Akhmatova

"My husband whipped me . . ."

My husband whipped me with a decorated
Doubled-up belt.
I wait with a candle lit in the small half shuttered
Window for you all night.

Dawn. And over the blacksmith hut
Black smoke unfurls.
With me, ah, once more you could not visit,
Mournful prisoner.

For you I have accepted a fate of sadness,
A fate of anguished dread.
Does the one you love have blond tresses?
Or is her hair red?

In a heart, drunk with dark suffocation,
How can you, my groans, be hid,
And then thin beams of sunlight lie down
On an undisheveled bed?

Fall 1911
Translated by Don Mager

ALEX DIMITROV

Begging For It

He crosses the dead avenue,
walks toward you, and loosens his ring

the way you imagine your father once did
on some night he still hasn't returned from.

Men you've lived with
and men you live on.

Whose scent will your knuckles keep?

His jaw clenches because your blood mixes sweetly
with the flower under his tongue,

the marquee's cheap glint,
each cab that passes and won't stop.

It's the night before Easter.
You do not forget it.

How the body becomes a cage you can't feel your way out of—

how God rips through the skin
of every man you know,

on a quiet evening,
in a city already done for, like this one.

RACHEL MCKIBBENS

Into the Dark and Emptying Field

I'm sorry, he said, *I'm afraid*
you love me too much.
You're making a mistake, she said,
I don't love you all the way yet.

If she stood still, she could hear it coming,
could feel it knocking at her organs
like blood piñatas. She turned around
and parted her hair,

revealing a peephole at the base of her neck.
Go ahead and look, she said,
I don't mind. He took off his coat, and leaned
toward the round glass portal and squinted.

The love inside her was astonishing,
too many horses to count. Clydesdales, Palominos,
Stallions, and mares roaring through a field
of deep and luscious grass, their hooves crashing
against her bones as they passed the man's eye,
thunderous and full of meaning.

He pushed the woman down to the floor
and straddled her, his desperate eye
pressed hard against the peephole.
Is that all there is? he shouted,
ripping her dress open. *How do I get*
a better view? he begged, banging his fists
against her back. *I need a closer look!*
He screamed into the dark and emptying field.

R. A. ALLEN

Cancellation

Atlanta Hartsfield is fogbound. Delta flight #1459 delayed, then canceled. The whole inconvenienced lot of us is trying to get from Memphis to Charlotte by way of Detroit or New Orleans or Beijing. We hate airlines, the FAA, the TSA, price-gouging airport vendors, each other. At the Delta desk, belted crowd-control stanchions cordon us into a switchback maze where we wait our turns with one of their agents.

Deadheading is how I would describe this leg of my commute, dragging back home to Charlotte. I sell a line of high school textbooks (the only job I could land with a new BFA from Appalachian State). The board of education in Memphis wasn't buying, and now I have nothing but a slacker's excuses to hand the Southern district sales manager.

Stuck in line, your opportunities for entertainment are limited. I try people-watching but realize that this is a time-killer better practiced while with your buds in a trendy bar or at a sporting event, preferably while rating women. My dank mood has turned everyone into a flotsam of dumpy, potato-faced dullards. Boredom sets in. But then:

"I can*not* believe how rude you were to my father," I hear her say to the guy in line ahead of me. They are a couple about my own age and they have been quiet up until now. I immediately realize that this is about a "meet the folks" visit. Like my own, an optimistic trip gone bad.

"But darlin'," the guy says, "He thinks Bush should go down in history as the last great American political martyr since General MacArthur. Couldn't agree to that."

"You could have shown some respect for his age by keeping your mouth shut."

"Age? He's, what, 45?"

"I just wanted everything to go smoothly," she hisses.

Audibly, they are staying just within the haute bourgeoisie limits of causing a public scene; I have to take a step closer in order to eavesdrop. Looking over his shoulder, I'm intrigued by the girl. She is petite and has a fair-complected, oval face wreathed by brunette ringlets that are somewhere between Shirley Temple and Bob Marley. Her eyes are intelligent and unruly.

"I thought it went smooth," he says.

"You kept looking at my mom's boobs."

"What?"

"Don't try to deny it, Randall. My little brother took a phone picture of you staring at them—right there at the dinner table."

"That thing she was wearing was really low cut. She had them right out there."

"You didn't have to gawk."

"I wasn't 'gawking,' and anyway, if I did look more'n once, it was because I was thinking how they reminded me of how great yours are," says Randall, shucking for a smooth-over.

"Don't hand me that crap, Randall. Daddy saw you."

"Jesus."

"He was going to pay for a big wedding," she says. "Now he's not. Ever since I was little, I've dreamed of a fancy wedding."

I notice her eyes glisten. And, like that little girl of yore, she stamps her little foot.

He says, "Aw honey, we don't need a big wedding. We've got each other. Everything will be fine. You'll see."

"While I'm on the subject of dreams, I woke up from one in the taxi on the way here: I don't know how I was stupid enough to go out with you, much less waste four months of my life, much less get engaged. You're a windshield-crack repairman. Your concept of men's fashion is straight out of a cubist painting. You drive a clown car. Illegal immigrants wouldn't live rent-free in your filthy, dope-reeking apartment. And, frankly, you bore me. We're finished, Randall. Kaputski!" She turns away to check a bank of flight monitors.

The heatforce of her wrath is enough to drive him backward, and he steps on my toe.

He says, "But . . . "

She spins back around and shouts, "And what's more, YOU'RE A LIMP-DICK!" Again, she gives him her back.

Randall disappears.

Disappears not in he ran off or slipped away. He disappears on the molecular level—as in he vanishes completely. Poof! Gone.

Stunned, I look around to see if anyone else has noticed, but they're all lost in their private reveries or involved in conversations with travel companions. Corporeal reality has just been defied. I pass my hand through the space where Randall once stood.

Nothing.

Not even residual body heat.

The girl senses my presence. Over her shoulder, she shoots me a what-do-you-think-you're-doing look.

I feel a certain unease. But then she takes me in, and with a smile more whole-some than Disneyland, says, "Hello, sailor."

MELISSA HART

Who's Looking

I was searching for my Spanish audio-course in my boyfriend's backpack when I excavated a video from among the spare bike tubes and Bob Marley cassettes. *Hot Latinas at Play*. The cover depicted a bevy of dusky beauties in skimpy bikinis, voguing beneath a volleyball net in the sand. A buxom raven-haired vixen held out a white ball with a fortune teller's portentous smirk.

My cheeks burned and my heartbeat hammered in my ears. My self-image shattered. I was neither Latina, nor hot. Acne scars riddled my sunburned cheeks. My hair frizzed in the damp salt air that pervaded our seaside college town. My skin hung white and flabby on awkward bones. But Tony and I made love often and loudly. Up until that moment, I'd believed him to be closing his eyes in ecstasy.

Now the truth slammed into me and bounced off my head. My boyfriend, while astride me, had been picturing Penelope Cruz.

When he biked home from his job at the Alzheimer's care home he found me vengeful and simmering. "This is *porn*." I held the video aloft in my left hand, my right fist clenched.

"It is not." He grabbed the tape and lobbed an explanation my way. "It's a sports video."

The shot went wide, out of bounds. I volleyed it back to him. "Don't their double-Ds get in the way of their serve?" I snarled.

"Okay, so once in a while a girl's top falls off . . . accidentally." He rolled his eyes, but his voice rose. "It's not like they're having *sex*."

Tears sprung to my eyes, an automatic forfeit. I wrung my hands and wailed. "You told me you liked art films!"

Tony flashed his crooked, charming smile. "Sure I do. *Like Water for Chocolate* kicks ass. Is that porn?"

He had me there. A soldier doing it horseback with a bare-breasted woman in the context of a Mexican Revolution epic seemed suddenly suspect. To cover my confusion, I cried harder. "It's because I'm white!" I sobbed. "Your sister told me all about your ex-girlfriends Marisol and what's her name . . . *Catalina*."

"That's an island," Tony protested. "Anyhow, this has nothing to do with you."

"I'd prefer not to see that video again," I stammered.

He shouldered his backpack and walked out. "You won't."

Thus, we incorporated a "don't ask, don't tell" policy. I avoided Tony's backpack and tried to focus on my Latino Literature course. But even my students' enthusiasm for Amaranta's passionate affair with her nephew in *One Hundred Years of Solitude* failed to distract me. All I could see were the lovely dark-skinned faces and the tawny curve of breasts barely contained on our TV screen. And I wondered, *what's wrong with me?*

That weekend, I shut myself up in the bathroom. "I'll have a surprise for you when you get home from work," I told Tony over the phone, embracing my newly purchased bottles of spray-on tan and Clairol's "Nice and Easy Blue-Black." But when he knocked on the door three hours later, I refused to open it.

"C'mon! I have to pee!" he called.

I slumped on the toilet seat, despondent. My limbs glowed an alien orange. My hair hung coal-black and crispy. "I can't open the door!" I cried. "I'm hideous."

In desperation, Tony turned to Billy Joel. "I love you just the way you are," he sang. "And I really have to pee, so open up!"

Slowly, I unlocked the door and turned the knob. Tony gazed at my dayglow arms and legs, my gothic hair, my cheeks streaked with tears and black dye. "It'll fade," he said and turned to the toilet.

I fled to the one person I knew who could give me insight into my predicament. "What should I do?" I appealed to my great-grandmother. "It's not like I can change my skin color."

My granny laughed and laid her arm against mine, identical in tone except for the liver spots. "It's a pity," she agreed and glanced at a photo of her long-ago circus beau, Pedro Morales, his scallop-edged photo tacked up on the refrigerator next to a recipe for stewed prunes.

She reached into the tote bag affixed to her walker and produced a tattered copy of *The Thorn Birds*. "Forget Pablo Neruda." She tapped the book's fiery orange cover with one arthritic finger. "*This* should be at the top of every girl's reading list."

She was right. The novel was a page-turner. My cheeks flamed as I studied graphic accounts of red-headed Maggie getting it on in the Australian outback with a Roman Catholic priest. She commanded her lover's attentions so completely that he never dreamed of dropping his knickers near another bush. The erotic scenes were titillating—the sort of stuff you wanted to read alone in your bedroom at night instead of out in the den with your great-grandmother grinning from her easy chair.

"What'd I tell you?" she chortled. "Thanks to this book, Tony won't care if you're white, brown, or purple."

But the image of other people making love on page or screen failed to impress me for long. I felt about pornography the way I felt about craft and travel shows on TV—why watch Martha Stewart or Rick Steves doing something when I could go out and do it myself?

A few weeks later, I turned on my computer to research Spanish immersion programs. A school in Mexico promised two weeks of free lodging and lessons for students willing to participate in a study on anti-diarrhea medication. I moved my mouse up to Yahoo's address bar to type in a URL. For the first time ever, I noticed the pulldown menu off to the right of it and clicked.

In an instant, a new world opened up to me. Slack-jawed, I scanned the browser's history. *Latinababes.com. HotChicanas.com. BurritoBabes.com.*

Tony sat on the futon playing Tetris. I called to him, forcing my voice to stay steady. "Where'd . . . where'd all this come from?"

"Where'd all what . . ."

He approached my monitor with its unanticipated capabilities for tattle-telling, and his amiable grin faded into a practiced vacancy. "I don't know how to use your computer," he said. "I never even turn it on."

I narrowed my eyes. He met them with his own hostile stare. "Someone in the manufacturing department must have loaded those sites onto your server as a joke," he snapped. "I can't believe you thought . . ."

My trigger-finger clicked on the mouse. At once, beautiful dark-skinned teens frolicked naked on a beachside volleyball court across my monitor.

"Did you download these sites?" I whispered.

"No!"

Silently, I walked into our bedroom and shut the door. I sat on the mattress and closed my eyes. Now the pieces fell into place. While I labored at teaching college students how to use a semicolon, my boyfriend had mastered the study of female anatomy. But why?

The full-length mirror bolted to our door hinted that I'd grown more attractive. I ran three miles a day. I straightened my frizzy bangs with a blow dryer and a round brush. My skin had cleared. But Tony's fascination with nude Latinas brought back all my old feelings of inadequacy. I opened my eyes and stared down at my pale, trembling hands in despair.

Tony found me crying when he shuffled into the bedroom. "Okay, you win," he mumbled. "It was me. But this isn't about you. My dad, my brothers, my uncles, we all look at girls. We like what we like, you know? It doesn't mean I don't love you."

I looked into his inscrutable face. "We need to go to counseling," I said.

"What's your problem with pornography?"

A white-haired counselor in a royal blue caftan leaned forward on her couch. Her tiny blue eyes bored into mine. Tony had discovered her under "Couples Counseling" in the yellow pages. "She specializes in sexual issues," he'd mumbled.

"I'm . . . I'm not sure porn's healthy," I stammered.

Above my head hung a framed drawing of ancient Greek men carrying an enormous effigy of a penis through city streets. On the coffee table stood a marble sculpture of a couple elegantly engaged in simultaneous oral sex. The rug, which Tony had been surveying so intently, depicted outlines of a man and woman wrought nude from the hair of some luckless alpaca.

"How often do you view erotic images together?" she asked.

"N . . . never."

She smiled, revealing sharp canines.

"But he lied," I wailed.

My boyfriend slumped with his eyes downcast on the area rug. The woman smiled at him. "Of course he lied. You made him treat you dishonestly by suppressing his natural urges. You have vanilla sex," the counselor concluded.

"There's no need to get racist!" I said. Despair caught in my throat. I'd believed our sex life to be satisfying. Movies, internet images, silicone rabbits with pearls—none of these had struck me as integral to intercourse. I fumed. I wrote a check for fifty dollars, thrust it into her hands, and stumbled outside.

In my Honda, I burst into tears. "I'm sorry I made you lie," I wailed to Tony. "I'll try not to repress you. I'll try not to be inhibited. Let's go to the video store *right now*." I pictured the dingy curtain separating the art films from those vague others and burst into fresh tears.

Beside me, Tony stared straight ahead. A train clattered across the track in front of us. I suffered a Tolstoy-esque urge to throw myself onto the track. "We don't have to see that counselor again," he muttered. "I won't touch your computer. Stop crying."

After our therapy session, I no longer called home on class breaks. When I discovered how a search engine's task bar may be cleared with a swift right click, I said nothing. I ordered a catalogue from Xandria and left it on Tony's pillow. The next day, I found it in the recycling bin, still wrapped in its brown paper shroud.

At thirty-one, I moved in with a photographer who printed large-format shots of sepia-toned skulls and bones. His elegant photos compelled me to look with new appreciation at what I'd previously disregarded as unsettling and gross.

One night, we sat on the floor with a bottle of Riesling between us and pored over a book of fine art photos. Marcus paused at his favorite—Dieter Appelt's black and white image of a nude man standing on a cliff with Icarus-like wings. "Amazing," he said.

I turned the page and studied Robert Maplethorpe's photo of a man in a three-piece suit cropped to reveal a semi-erect penis. "Is it . . . is it pornography?" I hid my embarrassment by draining my wine glass.

Marcus shrugged. A faint blush stained his pale cheeks. "Depends on who's looking, I guess."

We flipped through the book and paused at Edward Weston's iconic nude stretched face-down on the sand, her body outlined in shadow. "That's art," I said. "Right?"

He turned away from the page and kissed me, the wine sweet on his tongue. "You're that beautiful."

I stared at him. "You've gotta be kidding. I'm so white."

He tapped Weston's photo with one finger. "So's the model."

I took another look at her, and then at his slender hand, pale as mine. "Do you ever take nude shots?"

My question surprised both of us. He shook his head. "Not my style. Besides, who would I get to model?"

"Well . . ." I smiled coyly. "Me."

I longed to see how my new lover would depict me. Could he render my image as graceful and compelling as those he'd wrought from cow femurs and the clavicles of white-tailed deer?

"I guess we could try it . . ." He averted his eyes and looked down at his book.

Then I whispered the most sensual words I'd ever spoken. "Go get your tripod."

Tipsy and laughing, we stumbled to the attic of the dim garage behind our rental. A ratty red throne of an easy chair slumped among the cobwebs. Marcus set up his Nikon and peered at me in the shadows. "Don't take everything off, love," he protested. "It's cold out."

But I threw off my clothes and slipped a Mardi Gras feather mask over my face. Marcus extracted two vulture feathers from a dusty vase in one corner and handed them to me. I reclined across the chair. The upholstery smelled of cat piss. Pallid winter light crept in from a broken window, and goosebumps marred my skin.

Across from me, Marcus fired off shots with his camera. "These probably won't even come out," he said. "The light's not right."

After three rolls, he ran out of film. He wrapped his wool peacoat around me and we reconvened in the bedroom.

The next day, he came home from the university and handed me a flat box. "I hope these aren't offensive," he said. "They're large-format, black and white like Weston's work."

I knelt on the floor and lifted the cardboard cover.

The photo revealed nothing of goosebumps, of cat pee or cobwebs or worried protestations of cold. There was only the soft-focus presentation of a lovely nude woman in a feather mask lying regal across a throne, light streaming across one perfect ivory breast as she gazed with new comprehension into the camera's lens.

I couldn't look away.

TORY ADKISSON

Oracle & Ecstasy

The moon's frail rictus failed to move
beyond the shadows cast by the teacher's tents,
strategically pitched to keep boys
and girls separate. Deep within the cave
behind our tent, we reached into each other's pants
(his callused hand beneath my briefs,
mine between his boxers' vertical slip)
trying to keep focus on Kelly's ruddy lips,
April's olive eyes, or even Ms. Buchanan's
massive tits. We felt each other prick
and rise. Glowworms dangled above
like limpid strands of tumescent
drool from the stalagmites:
a row of stone fangs poised
to gnash through our sudoric bodies.
But the flashlights suddenly bobbing outside
forced us back under canvas
before that maw could snap. Maybe an hour passed.

Next to me, Jake snored too loud
to be convincing. Ever so gradual, his hand drifted
over a pile of his sullied Levis, a pair of weevils,
our compass, into the collar
of my partly-buttoned Henley.
His fingers grazed my nipples. They grew sharp.

And he murmured low
and prophetic into my ear:

this is how it's supposed
to happen.

JAQUIRA DÍAZ

Malavé

Today we're going to play our version of Cowboys and Indians: Españoles y Taínos. I like this game best, because I get to be the Taína princess who is always in my father's stories of Puerto Rico, back when the island was called Borinquen, before the Spaniards came to conquer. I follow Levy as he heads outside to meet the rest of the boys. Whenever my brother is headed somewhere, I follow. Pequita, Edgar, and Azael are already waiting on the sidewalk in front of our building. As we approach them, Pequita's lips turn into a mischievous smile.

"Are you ready for war?" he asks, tossing a pebble back and forth from one hand to the other.

Pequita is always the boss. He's in the sixth grade, but reventa'o, smaller than most of the other street kids, with a short afro and a face full of freckles, which is how he got his nickname. We usually play Cops and Robbers in the streets of El Caserío, but Levy and his friends don't want girls around, so I have to beg them to let me play. And they do, but I'm always the robber, always the one to get shot by the cops. Because they're all boys, they get to carry the guns, they get to do the shooting. They show no mercy, shooting me six, seven times, and I have to lie on the sidewalk, pretend I'm dead. I don't have a gun, because according to the boys, girls don't carry guns, so I must always play dead. How am I supposed to rob a bank without a gun?

I'm desperate to be more like my brother, to be with him and his corillo of friends, to be the boy my father wants.

I'm tanned from the summer sun and days spent running around the streets of El Caserío. Levy looks nothing like me. I'm slender, since I spend my days climbing the tangled branches of the flamboyanes, riding my bike in the street, or if there are no boys around, playing Double Dutch with las vecinas, the triplets who live in the next building, singing along to their Spanish version of The Jackson Five's "Rockin' Robin." Levy is chubby, and has my mother's blue-green eyes, blond hair, fair skin. I am just like my father, dark eyes and wiry curls that turn into an afro when you run a brush through them. I'm the wild one, always longing for the outdoors, always dirty, sweaty. Levy is blue-green, light, beautiful. Golden. I'm brown. Like tierra.

Pequita decides that we're all Taínos, and we must defend our island from the Spaniards who come to conquer and enslave us. If Pequita says climb a tree, we climb. If he says break into the neighbor's apartment, we break in. So when he says, "Today we make war against El Viejo Malavé," we run around El Caserío looking for rocks and pieces of broken glass to use as bullets and grenades. The streets and sidewalks of El Caserío have plenty of ammunition, enough to take down an entire army of rotten Spaniards like Old Man Malavé.

El Viejo Malavé is usually sitting on his second floor balcony, staring out over the lawn in front of his building. Across from his yard is the largest tree in El Caserío, a twenty foot ceiba, thick with bunches of long, green leaves, and a trunk thicker than my torso, covered in prickly thorns.

Pequita says El Viejo Malavé is tosta'o. Toasted. Says he killed hundreds of Taínos in Vietnam, that's what made him crazy. And now the rotten Spaniard has to pay. Pequita stuffs the pockets of his jeans with rocks and glass. His younger brother, Edgar, taller, less freckled, does the same. Levy doesn't have any pockets, and neither does his best friend, Azael, a skinny trigueño with thick straight hair, just like a Taíno's. Levy and Azael fill every one of my jumper's pockets with their ammunition, forbidding me to throw any rocks, since everyone knows girls can't throw.

When Pequita says, "March," we make our way across the narrow, cracked sidewalks, cutting through patches of weed infested grass and moriviví. El Caserío is made up of clusters of two-story concrete buildings, each with four apartments on the first floor, and four on the second. Each apartment has two balconies, one facing the front yard, and one facing the back. Some buildings, like ours, face the street, some face the plaza, the basketball courts, the elementary school at the end of our street. We make it all the way to the other side of El Caserío, to the yard in front of Old Man Malavé's building. El Viejo is sitting on his balcony, just as we expected, looking out over his yard at the ceiba tree, which stands right behind us.

Pequita throws the first rock, which lands in the middle of the yard. Malavé doesn't move.

"Attack!" he commands.

At once, Pequita and Edgar start flinging rocks toward Malavé's balcony. Levy and Azael follow, taking rock after rock from the pockets of my jumper. One after another, the rocks land in the lawn, in Malavé's balcony, or the first floor balcony below.

Pequita shouts at the old man. "Get up you filthy Spaniard! Come down and fight!"

But Malavé still doesn't move.

When Pequita runs out of ammunition, he scans the lawn for more rocks, picks my pockets, but we're all out. He searches the ground behind us, near the ceiba tree, until he finds exactly what he's looking for: an empty beer bottle. He picks it up, and without a word, he throws it toward Malavé's balcony, where it lands and shatters.

The old man rises slowly from his chair and steps off the balcony into his apartment. We wait, anxiously expecting him to come back out, maybe with his own ammunition, or his own bottle to throw at us.

Pequita's eyes widen, his jaw hangs open, and then he takes off without warning, running in the same direction we came from, toward Abuela's apartment.

I don't know who sees it next, but I finally realize what Pequita was running from. Old Man Malavé is crossing the lawn, headed toward us, a machete in his right hand. We all follow Pequita, but then Azael peels away to his apartment, which is much closer than my grandmother's. I cut through the same spots of patchy grass and morivivi, paying no attention to any of the boys yelling "This way!" and "Faster!" I follow Pequita's route. I don't know exactly why. Maybe I know that once we reach the safety of Abuela's apartment, she won't let El Viejo Malavé get me. Maybe I think Pequita knows what to do.

Or maybe because I'd prefer Malavé to chop his head off instead.

After all, Pequita's the boss. I'm only a princess.

A few weeks after Malavé comes after us with the machete, they find him in pieces. Limbs, torso, head severed. His body is found in a saco, inside a dumpster. They say he's been dead at least a week.

Edgar is the one who tells me the story, his eyes glowing with excitement, as if he's retelling the end of *Star Wars*, or *Jaws*.

Some say El Viejo Malavé owed money to one of the hustlers around El Caserío. Others say he was just a crazy old man who must've chased the wrong tecato with his machete. Abuela, who knew the old man, suspects his wife. I suspect Pequita. After all, I know Pequita is capable of anything. He may be reventa'o, but he's strong, smart, foulmouthed.

People go around El Caserío relating their stories of El Viejo Malavé, as if somehow wanting to be connected to him in death, if they could not be connected in life.

"He sprayed me with a hose as I walked out of my building" and "I knew him before he went to Vietnam."

Even we kids, "He almost chopped my head off with his machete!" And Levy's favorite, "You can still see the marks his machete left on Abuela's front door!"

I never see any marks, and according to Abuela, El Viejo never even made it to her door. But that never stops any one of us from backing his story. "Si, he almost killed us all!"

After a few weeks, we go back to climbing the flamboyanes, back to running wild in the streets. We forget about Malavé, the machete, the saco. We disregard the stories about Vietnam, about the dangers of war. Our parents set us free without the slightest warning about not talking to strangers, as if they can't imagine a future in which the street kids in El Caserío are no longer pointing toy guns at each other, but real ones. When the boys are no longer boys.

TOM LARSEN

Southpaw

I was at a family gathering when I heard the name. After forty years it still stops me cold. Not symbolic of the game like Mays or Mantle, but apart from it and shrouded in mystique. The nigglers claim greatness is measured in time, that five or six seasons do not a legend make. The believers let it pass. We know that greatness is measured not in decades, but in moments. When you're talking best ever, you're talking Koufax.

Koufax.

The name spelled out in my head. Those jagged consonants fitting together perfectly, as they always did. At first I thought my brother-in-law was just trying to get my attention. Those who know me know of my devotion. Then I realized he wasn't talking to me at all. He was telling my mother about *seeing* Koufax. In a bar! Nearby! That Koufax was, more or less, a regular, that he favored this bar because they left him alone. Could this possibly be? My brother-in-law is a joker, but would he go this far? A man's heroes are nothing to trifle with.

I could see my mother gauging my reaction. She'd witnessed my obsession first-hand, even played a role in the seminal event—the tape-recording of the first game of the 1963 World Series. Koufax vs. Ford and the hated Yankees. I'd planned to stay home from school and tape it myself, but my dad nixed that deal. Desperate, I enlisted my mother, drilled her on my primitive setup and prayed she'd get it right. She did, by God, and for weeks thereafter suffered the replays, Ernie Harwell's increasing hysteria as Koufax blew it by them, striking out the first five, 15 in all en route to a World Series record and a four-game sweep.

I can quote every stat from the Koufax years, but I knew little of his life since then, couldn't say for sure where he lived or what he was doing. I'd seen exactly two photographs of him in the intervening decades, one taken at a celebrity golf tournament a few years back and just recently, a shot of him with Billy Cunningham at the NBA finals. After his untimely retirement in 1966 Koufax did color commentary for a few seasons, then simply disappeared. Had he resurfaced here, as so many do? Was my brother-in-law a reliable source?

"What bar is this?" I butt in, trying not to sound anxious. He mentioned a place we'd passed on our way over. A rundown roadhouse with a row of pickups parked out front. I looked to my sister for verification.

"I wanted to get his autograph but Bill wouldn't let me," she handed me a beer. "You should see him. He looks fantastic."

In the photographs he looked smaller, but trim and tan. The hair turned silver, the smile, unmistakable. I tried to picture him perched on a bar stool, shooting the breeze with some yokel. It wasn't possible.

"You're sure about this?" I pressed her.

"Oh yeah," she nodded, "it's common knowledge."

I have doubts about my brother-in-law but my sister wouldn't lie to me. Not about this. My head swam with visions of Koufax peering in for the sign, the high kick, graceful and fluid, more ballet than baseball. He whiffed 382 in a single season, a hundred more than the runner up. In 1963 he won 25 games, eleven by shutout. For four straight years he led both leagues in ERA and strikeouts. By any measure Koufax owns the '60s.

But we go back further than that, Sandy and I, before the no-hitters and MVP's, before the curveball that would set him apart. To Ebbets Field, the Bums beloved, when "potential" dogged him like a curse. Years when he'd lose as often as not, unschooled, inconsistent, but frightening— even then. It was his line in the papers that caught my eye. 12 Ks, 10 Ks, and gone by the fifth. That he walked just as many didn't matter to me. They might beat him, but they couldn't hit him. I knew only one thing could account for this. Simply put, the kid threw smoke.

"I remember you up on the roof with your radio," my sister snapped me back. "Every night I'd hear you up there."

"Every fourth night," I corrected her.

Koufax always credited a seldom-used catcher for his dramatic turnaround. The story goes that while warming up in the bullpen, the catcher, Norm Sherry, suggested he take a little off the fastball. A sure ticket back to Triple-A for most pitchers, but even at half-speed Koufax's heater was a blur. With less velocity came a lot more control. Once he started throwing strikes the hitters were forced to swing and the line scores show it was rarely a contest. Sherry's career never amounted to much but his impact on baseball is immeasurable.

The fastball set him apart but it was the curve that put Koufax in a class all his own. Coming over the top it looked like a fastball. Halfway home the bottom dropped out and the batter's knees buckled, even in photographs. Like rolling off a table, Mel Allen used to say. He could throw it belt-high so it broke at the shoe tops or drop it right down the letters, and he would throw it anywhere in the count. The heater made the hitters flinch. The curveball took their breath away.

For me a Koufax win was a foregone conclusion. The rare defeat left me stunned and befuddled, more often the result of his own team's deficiencies than the prowess of the opponent. The Dodger's offense was anemic, at best. Had he pitched against them he might never have lost. If the other team's ace was on his game the zeroes could stretch across the scoreboard. These were the match-ups Koufax fans lived for. Marichal, Gibson, Spahn, Bunning. A lead built around a sacrifice fly, an errant throw, a stolen base, then rows zeroes on into the night.

Those nights on the roof are my fondest memories. Towards midnight the local stations would shut down, clearing the airwaves for baseball. With a good radio and the right weather conditions you could cover three time zones and half the night's schedule. Mine was a Philco with a grille like a Buick and dials as big as doorknobs. I developed the touch of a safecracker, pulled in St. Louis, Pittsburgh, Cincinnati, and New York. Lost in the crackle of East Coast lightning, fading out and fading in. A summer soundtrack of crickets, crowd noise, and play-by-play. If I could relive one moment it would be flat on my back on those still-warm shingles, staring up at the stars with the Philco to my ear.

Koufax's startling rise led me to suspect I had something to do with it. Not directly, of course, but in the untraceable way one thing affects another. Until I signed on he was just another pitcher. Good stuff but no clue. Our first year together he went 14 and 4 before a circulatory ailment ended his season. Coming back the next year he shut down the league. Coincidence? I think not. A third-string catcher may have pointed the way but blind faith and radio waves have powers beyond measure. We were in this together, Sandy and I. To a certain extent I feel this way still.

I pressed his clippings between the pages of a World Atlas until it bulged like a pillow. I sent away for obscure magazines worth a fortune today. I kept a framed triptych of his delivery that never quite captured the essential grace. I considered winter a waste of time and counted the hours until opening day.

I slept to visions of Koufax and often dreamed I was playing behind him, the twelve-year old phenom in center field. I wanted a dog so I could call him Sandy. When my parents refused I made my friend call his dog Sandy. My mother worried that it was unhealthy and at times I had to wonder myself.

My brother became a Yankee fan just to spite me. In my heart I pitied the fool.

Koufax retired in 1966 at the age of 31, lost to an elbow injury that would be minor today. A class act to the end, he turned his back on a guaranteed contract and walked away without looking back. With no Koufax, my interest in the Dodgers waned and by the late 60s baseball, like everything else, had taken a back seat to sex, drugs, and rock and roll. My disaffection lasted until a guy named Carlton started piling up Koufax numbers for a Phillies team that would draw me back. The resemblances were uncanny. Both stylish left-handers, both fiercely private, both possessed of uncommon stuff. Many of the records Carlton would go on to break were set by Koufax and many of those still stand today. But where Koufax was shy and accommodating, Carlton was sullen and incommunicative. For most of his career he refused to talk to the press. When the end finally came he couldn't see it, bouncing around both leagues until no one would have him.

In one of those ironies unique to baseball, my last rooftop vigil would feature a two-hit, 10-strikeout Koufax masterpiece just good enough to win, Dodgers 1, St Louis 0. Losing pitcher, a rookie named Carlton.

In 1974, seven years after his retirement, Sandy Koufax was voted into the Hall of Fame. The vote was unanimous, a first for Cooperstown, and he went in as the youngest member ever elected. For a single week he was back in the limelight and while most in attendance had seen him pitch, his numbers spoke of a different era, a time when pitching was the name of the game and every fourth day might bring something special.

I've been to Cooperstown only once. The setting was impressive enough, but the Hall of Fame was a disappointment. The plaques were smaller than I'd expected and the place had the overblown look of a theme park. But the names still resonate greatness and to speak them again is to step back in time. I'm not one of those who say the game was better then, but I wouldn't argue the point.

A few years ago the Museum of Radio and Television History opened in New York City. Their goal is to preserve all that remains of the medium's message. I'm of the first generation to grow up with television and the concept struck me as long overdue. I thought of the programs I'd loved as a kid, *Captain Video*, *Ding Dong School*, *Andy Devine* and *Flash Gordon*. That I might see them again at this late date seemed nothing short of miraculous. Visual contact with my own past, as close to time travel as I'm likely to get. Then I thought of Koufax.

Though our strongest connection was via radio, I'd watched Sandy pitch countless games on TV. I'd grown up within broadcast range of the Mets and Phillies and the World Series was a network event even then. Memories of Koufax's high-kick delivery were as clear as ever, but my eyes hadn't seen it since Johnson was president.

My wife and I were in New York with friends not long ago and I suggested we go to the Museum of Radio and Television History, but the only one interested was my friend's daughter Caitlin. She wanted to see the first *Simpsons* broadcast, ancient history to a 15-year-old. We searched the museum's data base and, as would be expected, *The Simpsons* were well represented. But when I punched up Koufax a mere three listings appeared; one of those listings was his admittedly dismal acting stint on an old episode of *Rifleman*. The preservation of baseball games is apparently not a museum priority. Pity.

The second listing was a short news piece on the Hall of Fame induction ceremony and the third, a profile on a fairly recent NBC program called "The Fifty Best Athletes of the Twentieth Century." His inclusion surprised me. Koufax's relatively brief reign usually relegates him to the second tier of immortals—understandable, given the longevity of some, but mystifying to those who fell under the spell.

I selected this second listing.

We took our program numbers to a room full of closed-circuit monitors and settled into adjoining cubicles. I slipped on my headphones and punched in my numbers.

The first face to appear was that of Johnny Roseboro, Koufax's old battery mate and forgotten victim of the infamous Marichal bat attack. Nicknamed "Gabby" for his taciturn manner, the old catcher's eyes lit up as he spoke of Koufax.

"I played with Sandy for most of his career, but I didn't even know where he lived. The man was private and so was I. All I knew was that every four days him and I were gonna kick somebody's ass."

Perfect.

Roseboro was followed by Ernie Banks of the Cubs, one of the most feared hitters of the '60s and a perennial fan favorite. Banks on Koufax's perfect game in 1963:

"What can I tell you? It was *the* perfect game. I came to bat three times, saw nine pitches and went home."

Yessss!

The profile told the whole story: his boyhood in Brooklyn, his early struggles with the Dodgers and then the glory years. The Dodgers, famous for nurturing pitching talent, stuck with their prodigy, and their patience would pay off handsomely. I watched the montage of newspaper clippings, the young left-hander's sporadic moments of brilliance, an 18-strikeout game followed by a 13-strikeout game, his first no-hitter, his heart-breaking 1-0 defeat in the '59 World Series. And then photos gave way to film. A chill brushed me as the screen showed Koufax prowling the mound at Wrigley Field. Ninth inning of *the* perfect game, crowd hysteria and shrill play-by-play, it was an innovative camera angle for the time, ground-level, just outside the catcher's right shoulder. Catching the strain on the face of a man about to release a hundred-mile-an-hour fastball. Then a tailing streak of white and a visibly late swing and miss. This was more than I dared hope for. Not only could I see him, once again, at the very top of his game, I could see him for the first time as the hitters saw him, majestic and terrifying, not of this world.

The last pitch, the last hapless swing and Wrigley went crazy, the first perfecto in 35 years and my man making baseball history. But the best was yet to come. Somewhere in the dim recesses of my consciousness I could hear Homer Simpson ranting and Caitlin chortling but I was no longer with them. I was across town in Yankee Stadium watching in disbelief as Tony Kubeck stepped in. It is a fine September afternoon and the scene I am about to witness for the first time, some 30 years after the fact, is the very game I badgered my mother to tape-record. Arguably the most profound start to a World Series in the game's history . . . and here it comes. Kubeck takes two fastball strikes then whiffs on a rainbow curve. Richardson watches a strike three called, Tresh swings through three straight fastballs and it's on to the second. The mighty Mantle takes two rips then watches the curve drop straight down from heaven. Then Maris, fresh off his Ruthian chase flails away in frustration. I sit transfixed, seized by a swirl of emotion. It is Koufax and me, 1963 and the whole world bears witness to the legend.

My wish, to see him pitch once again has been granted in full. I never thought it could really happen, but now it has and I am unprepared for the impact. The image corresponds so perfectly to the one I've been carrying around in my head. It's disarming. The pull of the past tears me loose from my moorings and reels me back to a place I can never forget—where I come from but no longer belong. If there's a word to describe this feeling I don't know what it is. Caitlin shouldn't see me like this so I look away for a moment, to McCartney and Lennon on the Sullivan show, to Chevy Chase and the Weekend Update, to a bank of TVs taking us back. None going nearly as far as me.

Then it's back to the job at hand. Bob Costas, looking a few pounds lighter and a few years younger telling me exactly why it is Koufax is included in "The Best Fifty Athletes of the Twentieth Century." When the money was on the table it was always lights out. In 51 post-season innings he posted an earned run average of 0.83! Less than one run per nine innings. Check Clemens, check Ryan. There is simply no better way to measure greatness.

For the purist, pitching is a science and setting up the hitter, the essence of baseball strategy. The savvy pitcher is one who can spot a tendency and exploit it to his advantage, whether it's nibbling corners, changing speeds, or preying on a weakness. Cooperstown is full of pitchers who kept a "book" on hitters and could consistently throw what they couldn't hit. A handful made it on talent alone.

The rest are variations on a theme: good stuff, fierce determination, and ungodly durability.

The science of pitching was of no interest to Koufax. They couldn't hit what they couldn't see or didn't believe.

The news that he lives nearby came as a shock, but also confirmed the notion that we are somehow linked. The cosmic connection that saw us through the 60s had somehow endured. Looking at it that way, it's not surprising he'd settled here, though it might surprise Sandy. Just the sort of thing he was hoping to avoid, if I had to bet.

This summer I turned 60 years old. In recent years the town where I live has gone from working class to local resort and most weekends the place is packed. I like to sit on my front porch in the evening and watch the couples on their way to the newest restaurant or gallery opening. If there's a game on I'll have my radio with me and occasionally someone will ask for a score. More often than not he will be my age and more than once I've felt the spark of kinship. For the briefest of moments the air is charged and it's all I can do not to speak the name.

Koufax.

JASON MCCALL

Because Black Kids Can Read

comics too, I'm the conscious colored, dark
and wise, the suntanned wingman. Like Iron Man,
but with more guns and less
brains or the Green Lantern who willed
himself out the ghetto. I'm bursting
through the wall when the hero needs me,
carrying the cliffhanger of War Machine

vs. Doctor Doom! Falcon
vs. Red Skull! Steel vs. Darkseid! No, I won't
save the day, only keep the action going,
keep the message boards warm while the man
on the cover recalibrates his armor or finds
out why his powers didn't work the last issue.
Either way, I'll be found in a pile of rubble
with a villain standing over me making jokes
about Jesse Owens. The real hero

will return to avenge me, and then it's back
to the mansion until it's my turn
for the special issue that shows me cleaning up
my neighborhood and saving my siblings
from the street gang led by my childhood
best friend. I'll show the brothers
drugs and thugs are as bad as a Lex Luthor lovechild
with Lady Deathstrike, and, if they stay in school
and follow the rules, they can be second class
superheroes, just like me.

TIMOTHY L. MARSH

How to Make White People Happy

Way over there on the Asian side of the Earth, on the saddles of two or three tectonic plates that buck like spooked mustangs every couple of months, sits the island republic of Indonesia—a shifting, fractured, shattered dish of a dominion with roughly 17,000 bits and pieces of itself spilled across the eastern equator. Some of these pieces are unchartably small, some are quite large. Some are greatly inhabited, many are not, but all of them, regardless of size or population, share at least this one thing in common: they are all fairly poor, even the ones where white people go.

One of the more charmed and chosen of all these archipelagic morsels is the island of Bali—an island famous round the world for its pampered tourism and shameless Anglo indulgence, largely less famous for its native penury, and the setting for a story that makes me all white and writerly every time I think about it.

When I knew Ketut Sutapa he was 37-years-old with a rotten front tooth that never gave him any pain or stopped him from smiling. He was the definition of a self-made man, but always denied it because no man made himself without the help of others, and because it made other men who weren't self-made a little sad and irritable.

Like a lot of Indonesians, Ketut's life began with the kind of cards that couldn't easily beat a fold. At the age of five or maybe six his mother took him to the busiest road in Bali, gave him five packs of sticky rice wrapped in banana leaf, and left him. She got on one knee and told him without tears or memorable grief what she had to do and why: that the family was too poor to care for so many children, that sooner or later someone kind would come along and give him a better life than she ever could, that this was a good road to be left on because white people with money used it all the time.

Two days later Ketut was picked up by the Salvation Army, fed, clothed, inoculated, sent to an orphanage and never adopted. The orphanage was like a tinted glass aquarium where hundreds of eager young fish swam in hope and pining behind a one-way veil of no demand.

Once when Ketut was little a beautiful white couple came to the orphanage and took him for something like a test drive. The couple took Ketut for a walk and bought him an orange juice and afterward took his best friend to Melbourne.

"His hair was combed and mine wasn't," Ketut would always laugh. "Now it's the first thing I do when I wake up."

At 18, the orphanage evicted Ketut via a work placement program that placed him as an apprentice cook at a three-star resort for one US dollar a day, seven 13-hour Indonesian workdays a week. Within a year Ketut had vaulted from apprentice to master, and within a few more years he had mastered the entire cuisine of his culture. He cooked for all the tourists and by and by learned enough English to teach other orphans how to say hello to white people and tell white people their names so that their best friends wouldn't be taken to a better life instead of them, even if their hair wasn't combed. English was a comb toward a better life.

The years passed without occasion until one day when a fat Dutchman checked into the resort.

The Dutchman was so rich and important that he'd never learned how to drive. He'd also never booked his own accommodations before and had booked a three-star resort by accident.

The Dutchman was inconsolable when he arrived at the resort and saw his $400 villa without all the lunatic luxuries of an $800 villa, and ordered a heap of Indonesian food as a way of sulking. "Things can't get much worse," he sighed. He was at a place in life where ordering Indonesian food was proof that things couldn't get much worse.

The Dutchman ordered many traditional dishes like seafood nasi goreng and soto ayam. The dishes were a new and complicated enjoyment like Russian ballet dancing down every part of his pallet and afterward he was so utterly fulfilled by the performance that he stormed into the kitchen and demanded to meet the cook and take that cook back to his restaurant in Holland.

Ketut could hardly believe it. He was very excited and a little afraid.

He went out right away and bought a bag and some new clothes to put in the bag. He'd never needed new clothes for a bag before, but he was going to Europe now and in Europe people had things in their bags like new clothes and sometimes watches and nice soaps.

He bought two shirts and a pair of pants and immigrated to Leeuwarden to work for the Dutchman. The Dutchman gave Ketut a car and a nice apartment, plus a big kitchen in his restaurant where Ketut created all kinds of simple rice dishes that white people called exotic and were more than happy to overpay for.

The Dutchman was so tickled at how much everybody was overpaying that he offered to send Ketut to university just to keep him around for another four or five years. The plan worked perfectly until it came to an end. Four years later Ketut had a degree in hospitality management and enough money to come home and have children and actually keep those children.

The Dutchman was inconsolable. He offered Ketut anything he wanted to change his mind. He even learned to drive just to drive Ketut to the airport. "I've never driven or driven anyone to the airport in my life!" the Dutchman begged. "What do you say?"

"Ik wens jou veel geluk en voorspoed," Ketut said.

Along with English, he could now speak Dutch.

• • •

Ketut had departed Bali with one language and one bag of clothes and now he was back with three of each plus some very nice soaps. He also had a nice watch.

The watch was German and kept the time in places nowhere near to Germany like New York and Bogota. It looked very nice but made other people feel bad about themselves, so he didn't wear it. How would he like it if somebody impressed him?

Ketut went back to work at the same resort where the Dutchman had found him. The resort had grown two stars since Ketut had last worked there. It had grown marble floors, bigger rooms, and a unique and premium taste that included a 50-meter pool with several tinier pools around it. But most of all it had grown white people. The white people were like lullaby daisies that grew around the edges of the pool and swayed back and forth from one end of the resort to the other. They were very pretty and delicate in their swaying and all the native staff worked and smiled hard to ensure their easy rock-a-bye remained at the resort and was free of aggravation.

One day Ketut was talking to one of the guests and mentioned that he'd gone to school in Europe. That afternoon, he was called to the General Manager's office and told to take a seat.

The General Manager looked terribly serious like maybe one of the guests had died from Ketut's cooking.

"Is there a problem?" Ketut asked. He wondered if the guest had an allergic reaction.

"Did you tell one of our guests that you went to school in Europe?" asked the General Manager.

"Yes," said Ketut. "I'm sorry."

"Did you tell them in English?" said the GM.

"I did," said Ketut. "I'm sorry."

"Is it true?" said the GM.

"It is," said Ketut. "I'm sorry."

"Congratulations," said the GM.

"Thank you," said Ketut. "For what?"

"You're my new assistant."

Ketut thought it was a joke. There was no reason to think that it wasn't. He could hardly believe it when he came to work the following morning and found a furnished office just for him. The office had a leather chair on wheels and flowering plants and an old Indonesian woman who wouldn't leave him alone until she made him coffee and watered the plants. Ketut liked everything except for the woman. The woman was like his German watch and made him feel bad whenever he saw her on the wrist of some menial duty he could've done himself.

At any rate, Ketut took on all the duties of Assistant Manager and after a few weeks all the duties of General Manager, too. The General Manager had a problem. The problem had to do with prostitutes, but mostly it had to do with paying prostitutes with resort funds and sleeping with prostitutes in the Presidential villa.

One day the General Manager didn't show up to work and that afternoon Ketut was called to the owner's estate and told to take a seat. The owner looked terribly serious like maybe someone had been paying for sex with his money.

"Did you know our General Manager was paying for prostitutes?" asked the owner.

"Yes," said Ketut. "I'm sorry."

"Did you know he was paying for them with resort funds?" said owner.

"No," said Ketut. "I'm sorry."

"Do you sleep with prostitutes?" said the owner.

"I don't," said Ketut. "I'm Christian."

"Congratulations," said the owner.

"Oh, no," said Ketut. "For what?"

"You're the new GM."

Ketut had absolutely no desire for such a promotion because he was absolutely sure he'd screw it up. He pleaded with the owner to reconsider but the owner was convinced that not paying prostitutes with his money was the direction his resort needed to go. The next day Ketut became the interim General Manager of a five-star Bali resort, and the next week the interim part fell off the title like a dead leaf that had been on the wrong plant.

The resort flourished under Ketut's management. It didn't matter that he'd never quarterbacked a front office or controlled an F&B department, for it seemed he'd mastered the most important knowledge a person in Bali could master: what white people liked.

He was seemingly so educated on the matter that banks and businesses hired him for seminars to teach the great art of Anglo satisfaction. Ketut went to the seminars and got dozens of different questions all asking the same thing: How do you make white people happy?

Ketut had no idea how to make white people happy. It wasn't anything he'd ever worried about. But it was true that there was a lot of money to be made in making white people happy and he felt obligated to offer the best answer he could. The answer usually went something like this:

"Good afternoon. My name is Ketut and I am here today to talk about making white people happy. I do not know what makes them happy all of the time, but I will tell you what happened with me and maybe that will mean something to you.

"When I was very little I had much less than any white person had. I had almost nothing. I was left on a road and a group of white people took me from the road and gave me a home and food. They did not ask me for money or work. They gave me these things even though I was little and dirty and could not give them anything in return, and that made them happy. But when I was older my teeth went bad and my hair wasn't nice, and that didn't make them happy. I was still very dirty and poor but they didn't like that anymore. I didn't see them for a long time. Then I got older and learned their language and they were happy again. I learned how to cook the food of my people and they loved the food and gave me an education for it. They traded their education for my cooking, but when I got my education I took my cooking away and that made them unhappy again. So when I came home to Bali I went back to the kitchen, but that made them the most unhappy. They didn't want their education in the kitchen. They made me leave the kitchen and put me in charge of making them happy. I didn't do anything special. I talked to them and smiled when they asked for things and when they asked about my life I told them the truth, and they were happy again.

"In conclusion: I speak to them in their language, I have less than almost any of them, and I smile when they ask for something, and they are happy. Thank you."

The audience almost always left Ketut's seminars looking for a refund. It didn't seem like Ketut knew anything about white people. He might've known less than they.

Ketut didn't care. He didn't know what white people wanted. He didn't care what they wanted. There was only one thing Ketut wanted, and that was to find his family and start a family and keep a family happy and together.

He went back to the road where his mother had left him over thirty years before. He wanted to find his village and then his mother. He wanted to show her his diploma which he kept folded in his wallet. He wanted to show her the fine paper it was printed on and the elegant European language that was printed on it. He wanted to hold her hand and tell her things like:

"Now this family has money and can take care of itself. It does not have to leave its children by the road for white people to take them to better lives. It can give them those lives itself. And we will be proud and have nice soaps and raise our children well, because I have made people with money happy, and it will take us from nothing into anything."

Ketut searched all afternoon. Finally he found an old man who remembered his family and even a little about him.

"You look different," the old man said.

"I'm not poor anymore," said Ketut.

The old man took Ketut to his babyhood home, but it wasn't his home anymore. There were other poor babies and another poor mother there now. The mother had a grove of children and three jobs that had nothing to do with taking care of the children. She didn't know where Ketut's family was. She didn't know where the father of her children was. Two of her children had diarrhea. None of them had shoes. "Take this," Ketut said, and gave her a card with his name and number. Two days later her eldest son had a job at the hotel and was talking to white people.

Ketut never went back to that road again, not even to drive on it. The road was like his rotten front tooth. It never stopped him from smiling, but it was always somewhere on his face, dead and disregarded, permanently divorced from sensitivity.

That was as far as Ketut's story had come at the time that I knew him. He made his money and ran his resort. And on nights when the kitchen was short-staffed he got behind the burners and worked his old magic with fervor and joy. He married a girl he'd met at his orphanage and had three children, and he loved going to work because he loved providing for and coming home to children. His face had the life and youth of his children, and looking into it you could not detect any of the poverty or strain of obsequiousness that takes a steel pipe to the spirits and energies of others born to the soil of identical circumstance. Everything that could've been gained from the content of white people, he'd gained.

They'd made him happy.

• • •

I've lived in a lot of places and been to a dozen more, but my memory of my travel life almost always begins and ends with the evening Ketut told me that story, the two of us trading culture on his terrace, his baby daughter asleep on his lap, slumped and drooling against his chest.

I remember the easy way it arrived to me from across the wreckage of a neglected childhood, amid a concerto of nearby field frogs and the rich sunset tones of a Muslim prayer chant rolling a cappella across the murmurous warm eve.

I remember the white color of the moment—the color white bleeding ink-like from off his words, leaking over us, the color of my skin eating me like the mosquitoes, and in the moments directly and long afterward, humming above the head of his dreaming child, that white 1,000-watt smile sending its light far into the past, farther into the future, one burnt-out bulb that only made the others brighter.

CLAIRE MCQUERRY

Inexhaustible, the 24-Hour Grocery

The doors sigh open in their tracks (so glad
you've come) because you are a body
moving forward. You're wanted. You're in.
The deli smells love you, the waxed floor
loves you, the shelter of strawberries loves
you and offers you cream. Card swiper,
cart pusher; *choose, please choose*
from our plenty. You're sufficient. Take your
pick because you can. Canned chilis, canned
olive halves, can of red-fleshed salmon. Loaves,
cheeses. *My aisles are open, my baskets*
are light. Luminous florescence, oh windowless
walls, clockless as a casino. *Special on grapefruit,*
cake mix, mixers, cigarette special, you're special.

ANGELO NIKOLOPOULOS

www.daddyhunt.com

I.

Like the sweetness of our coffee, the firmness
of our poached eggs, there are preferences.

Here, there is body type, dick length, sexual role.
You want *daddy* or *hunter*, average or horse hung,

top or bottom—sometimes versatile. You can search
by age range, body hair, and *looking for*: blue collar,

bear, ex-smoker, within five miles of [enter zip code].
You send *gropes* to members to say, *I'm interested. I'm looking.*

In the top left corner, my yellow mailbox blinks:
TopDad4U types, *Horned verbal jock—hosting.*

II.

To host, to receive, to entertain guests.
To host means to live alone, probably,

so you *travel* to the Upper West Side
by red line express, through wet underground,

by erection in the lap and blind faith,
to apartment 1E, where you are rewarded,

this time, by handsome face, height-weight
proportional—a leather harness. *On your knees, boy,*

he commands, and you obey in silence,
in reverie, chin up to receive the host—

as in wafer, as in holy Eucharist, the cold marble
of your childhood beneath you, but this time

the language more reciprocal—the jeans parted
down to the thighs to give, and to be given, the body.

III.

On the subway ride home, it is not guilt
that hangs overhead, not regret soiled

in the folds of the shirt, in the torn buttonhole.
It is wonder, instead—and lineage.

I imagine the long row of men before me
in their muslin shirts, their trimmed beards,

and Nixon is president. I think of
Bloody Thursday in Berkeley, the paisley,

blue handkerchief in the back right pocket,
the pebbled hill of the Castro.

And then the Christopher Street piers
in the lull and glow of the Hudson,

how they'd feel their way around the darkness,
over damp planks, until they hit body—

chest, torso, legs—and that was that:
You—I'm so happy to have found you.

But I'm surprised how they managed
to find each other at all

in that heavy secrecy, wet veil,
until I am brought back to sixteen

where I stand at the foot of a ladder,
and there is a man, a worker, halfway up—

the sweat moving down the bicep,
where we were left in our own clothing,

bare and in person—that I understand.
Having had nothing but our eyes,

we said in our honest silence:
Whatever you want, I'll give you.

Whatever you want, it's yours.

BEN NICKOL

The Rising Cost of Baloney

Late one night at a bar, I turn to my friend Chris and challenge him to drive with me through the night to Colorado. We will climb some mountain and sleep beside a fire. Six hours later, we're rounding Salina, Kansas, onto I-70. Dawn gathers over the empty prairie and we're sober now. We wonder what has happened to the goodness of our idea.

It's a bad town, Salina. Its buildings are spaced at awkward distances, facing whatever direction. When we stop, it's at Hays. Hays is an hour and a half past Salina, and although I don't like relating distances as units of time, in this case that seems appropriate. The land separating Hays from Salina is so flat, so barren and changeless, that crossing it seems to happen only on the clock. The speeding car goes nowhere. Salina merely falls away, then Hays rises. It feels generational, one town succeeding the other on the same plot of soil, like Mexico City on the site of Tenochtitlan. Only not quite, because Hays is a derelict place of grass shoots pushing up through cracks in the municipal slab.

We eat breakfast at Long John Silver's.

Back on the interstate, Chris drives while I read him articles from the paper. Nothing is getting said about our hangovers, or about the goodness having drained from this idea to drive to the mountains. It seems important, somehow, not to mention these things. It is because we're hungover, and because there is no more goodness, that we need fuel wherever we can find it, any kind of onward propulsion. The refusal to blink is a good source of it.

Now it's my turn to drive. Chris pulls into a rest area and we each walk a wordless little arc around the hood to the other side of the vehicle. The sun bangs down from the east. Then we're back on the road. The rear window of the truck in front of us is hammering my eyes with glare. Somewhere near the end of Kansas, we enter the Mountain Time Zone. I'm thinking I need more of that, more hours stripped off the clock, until I am standing again at that bar in Fayetteville. I want a second chance at not suggesting this awful trip. Of course I'm not suggesting we go back, either. No, sir.

Eastern Colorado is a gentle, westward ramp. Chris has been asleep, but snorts awake now and slides up in his seat. He looks confused, unsure of his whereabouts. But then a few miles later I glance at him again and he knows where he is. He knows what's happening.

I see his jaw muscles dance around.

We exit the freeway at Limon and head north on a two-lane highway. When a cloud passes over the land, Chris says it looks like a manta ray.

"What?"

"It looks like a manta ray swimming along the ocean floor."

"Oh, a manta ray."

"Yeah."

Then we're silent for miles.

With the exception of one eastward blip, this highway runs straight north to Brush. I see the blip on the map (on a road this straight it is hardly dangerous to spread a map across the steering wheel and trace things with your finger), ten or 15 miles north of Limon. With no indication why, the road hits a 90-degree corner and shoots east, then hits another 90-degree corner and continues north. We wonder: what is it doing? Is it avoiding some gorge or ravine? Some rookery of endangered birds? When we get to it, we don't see any obstructions at all. The road just bends hard right, then after a few miles bends back left. Whatever the reason, it does not appear to be natural. More likely, I think, it was a man in a broad hat, bolo tie, and belt buckle, who years ago ran his tongue under his lip while some agent of the state explained eminent domain.

The West is full of these people. I don't mean cowboys, I mean people who are stubborn and only happen to be cowboys. Their great-grandparents arrived on trains from Minnesota. They tried their hands at dryland farming, failed at that impossible venture, but then kept doing it, kept failing and failing while their neighbors disappeared into town or bought (on credit or charity) passage back east. They had kids, and those kids had kids, and every generation the unstubborn of them left. In fact, my father is first generation unstubborn. He left his family's dryland farm outside Ledger, Montana to attend college and live in a town. Not that he isn't stubborn. His veins carry the blood of generations of tight-mouthed men shaking their heads. My brother and I have got it, too. It is the refusal to abandon, once initiated, any gesture.

We come to a town called Last Chance. It is not on the map.

Chris says, "Last chance for what? To turn back? Where would you go?"

He's right. If you're going anywhere and have ended up here, then it's too late to turn back. I think about the man in the bolo tie squinting past the bureaucrat, or my grandfather, in World War II, refusing to carry a weapon. Is the name of this town, this little no-town of six buildings, along those lines? Is it a squaring of the shoulders, a spitting in the dirt? To whom are such gestures ever addressed?

Because even the cartographer, whose job is to acknowledge towns, failed to notice the hardened stare of Last Chance, Colorado.

West of Greeley, the prairie stands on end. The horizon grows rugged, irregular. Twelve hours ago, drunk and under cover of darkness, we slammed home the doors of the car and pulled out into the street. The mountains then were a romantic idea, a figment, some notion of beauty for us to rush at. Now they are mountains.

We pull into Fort Collins, where we will stay the night with our friend Bridgette. I am still driving. Long stretches of highway have dulled my sense of the car as a piloted thing, and in the first mile of city blocks I blow two stop signs and have to slam the brakes for a man on a bicycle towing his child in a wheeled pod. There's a sense you get, arriving on a weekday in a town where you have no legitimate business, of harboring some secret or shame. Or else being invisible, that you could wave money in the faces of pedestrians and they would walk right on by (though the man on the bike, releasing his handlebars to flip bird with both hands, certainly did see me).

Bridgette lives in a small house on the west side of town. We find the key and go collapse inside. I am tired enough that certain synapses have ceased to fire. In each of my hands is the aglet to a shoelace, but I can't make the thing happen. There's a way this works where you tug and the knot falls out. In fact, that is how it works. Only I can't do that.

I leave the shoe on and get up from the couch to snoop through the rooms. Chris has landed on a recliner and is gape-mouthed and snoring. I look at Bridgette's pictures, test her light switches, inventory her refrigerator. I flush her toilet, pull curtain chains, flick the thermostat.

This is a place of adult normalcy. By making our trip, Chris and I are in violation of that normalcy and its rhythms. We were driving after we had been drinking, awake when we should have been sleeping, are at play while others labor. We meant to do this, it is part of the gesture. But to find ourselves here, in the empty home of a woman out participating in the workday—we lose the luxury of abstraction. Now the emptiness of our surroundings testifies to our backwardness. It pushes against our gesture like the wrong end of a magnet.

That night, we're at the Trail Head Tavern in the old part of town. Our hamburgers are finished, red baskets stacked to the side. Bridgette spreads a map of the Cache la Poudre Wilderness across the table. She hunches over it, involves herself in the terrain, points out roads and geographical features. By this stage of the night, we've had beers in whatever quantity and she has decided she's coming with us. It won't be for the whole weekend—she has teaching tomorrow and things to do Saturday—but she'll be out there off and on.

Clapping shoulders, ordering more drinks, saying jocular things to strangers at nearby tables—beyond the fact we like Bridgette, there's something affirming about adding a member to our party. It gives our trip trajectory, a sense of gathering momentum, really just some basic forwardness. At the very least, another person has gotten drunk and altered the course of her near future. We'll take it.

Friday morning, I awake on my side on the couch with a styrofoam cup of gas station coffee hovering near my nose. Chris says, "Let's go." I take the coffee out of his hand and collect my wakefulness while he paces through the room looking for our map.

Bridgette has already gone to work. She plans to meet us after. We're not sure where our camp will be, but have agreed on a stretch of road where we'll leave the car. The plan is to leave a note on the windshield telling her where to hike. It seems like a surefail plan, but so also does it seem like what we should do. Not to be careless now would be ridiculous given the ridiculous extent to which we've been careless thus far. Yes—what we are doing has become also the tone of our doing it.

At Safeway, we each take a cart. We rip in half the list of provisions and set off tunneling the aisles. It is the first time since the trip began that each of us is sober and alone with his thoughts. The energies that have sustained us—alcohol, pride of gesture, toughness in one another's company—are unavailable now, and each must devise his own reasons for going on. I walk the aisles, dropping items into my cart. The beauty-threat of wilderness, the mystery of what can happen in a place not oriented towards any specific happening—these are reasons to forge ahead, but mostly what I think about is the distance we traveled yesterday. Of course that's a dumb way to think. A sunk cost should never determine future spending. But I just dropped a pound of baloney into my cart, and if I go home now then I came 800 miles for that. My heart is not capable of such a reality. So: onward ho. As long as I move forward, then everything that happens, everything I see and everything I accrue is still the gathering of some eventualness. No one item must justify the items that preceded it. We all know Indian boys were told on vision quests not to return until something happened. This could be why.

I turn down some aisle and there's Chris coming my direction. We pass like strangers. Somehow it's clear that conversation at this juncture could be fatal.

Then we're back in the car. West of town, the shade trees fall away. The mountains ahead stand clear and etched, and with the sunlight at our backs they are textured in a way they were not when we saw them yesterday. Yesterday, they were the horizon-wall, blue and monolithic. It had seemed possible to walk up and bang on them like a sheet of tin. Now they are ground a man could stand on. Grass, bushes, trees, rocks. He could walk up there and stand.

We make camp about 200 yards from the car. That's not much of a distance, but we're at 11,000 feet and on top of whatever else we have two full coolers of beer. We lug them up the hill. Every hundred feet or so we stop and sit on the coolers and look out east at the lower and lower grade of mountains, and then the boxed-off plain stretching flat out into a haze. Then one of us starts going again and the other follows.

We throw down our stuff in an open patch of ground near some bristlecone pines. We find rocks and make a fire pit, then collect wood and stack it nearby. Only Chris thought to bring a chair. He sits, and while he gets lunch together I drag into camp a log I can use as a backrest. We eat sausage and cheese on Ritz crackers. We drink beer. Then each of us takes a styrofoam cup, scoops it full of ice from the cooler and pours in whiskey. We spend the rest of the afternoon in and around camp, refilling our drinks.

At one point, I walk up through the bristlecones. Their trunks and branches are gnarled and drawn, have an almost arthritic quality. Months later in an in-flight magazine I will read that these are the oldest living organisms known to man, and it will seem like I already knew that. Just looking at them you see the centuries that wanted passage but got tangled in the limbs. Just what are these trees trying to prove?

Farther up the hillside is a scattering of boulders. I pick my way onto the highest and sit. Everything is visible from here, every direction unobstructed. To the east are the plains, to the west are the snowcapped fourteen-thousanders of Rocky Mountain National Park. Camp is downhill and north, with the river way out beyond running a seam around the plateau.

None of it is less than I imagined. What I closed my eyes and saw two nights ago is here right now when I keep my eyes open. I lay on my back with my hands behind my head and look at the sky. God, I think. We haven't been disillusioned at all. Now what the fuck are we going to do for two days?

Bridgette appears in the hour before dusk, coming up the trail with her sensible and efficient backpack. Chris and I have been working on a fire. We straighten up and wave our arms like castaways. She waves back and starts off the trail at an angle.

It is the waning part of a Friday. For Bridgette, this is the end of a workday at the end of a workweek, which means one wheel of responsibility has completed a revolution at the same time its containing wheel has completed a revolution. In other words, she is happy. She wears it like a flag, too, dropping her pack near the tent and grabbing a beer from the cooler. So Chris and I get beers of our own and everybody lifts their cans at each other before they drink.

This is a good feeling, the three of us drinking beer with the fire behind us beginning to spark and pop. We're lucky Bridgette showed up. Our being here spurns the rhythms of her life—that is true. But her being with us, and being happy, somehow sanctions what we're doing. And isn't that why we spurn in the first place? To impress the spurned? Why else would the word 'sanction' have two essentially opposite meanings?

Dinner that night is hot dogs skewered on sticks and held over the fire. I don't particularly like hot dogs, but something about food that only barely meets the description of a meal gives its eater a very intimate sense of what that description actually is. It's like clothes that only barely cover the body. When the hot dogs are finished, we use the same sharpened sticks to roast our marshmallows. I hold mine high over the flame, where the inside has a chance to melt before the surface catches fire. Sometimes it melts so completely that the stick falls through and the whole thing drops in the ashes. Part of me is rooting for this to happen. I find eating marshmallows flecked with debris more satisfying than eating them clean off the stick. Tomorrow, with boredom at its zenith, Chris and I will sit in camp and share our amazement at ever having passed (over there behind the bristlecones) this nonsense from our bodies. But for now it seems right. Needs are being met in a place not designed for that.

Out on the plain, points of light have become visible without our noticing when. You can still see a great distance, but things are growing blue, then darker blue. Chris walks out from the fire and comes back with an armful of wood. Then Bridgette and I get wood, too, and when we have more than we could possibly use (we will use it all), we sit by the fire, closer than we were sitting at dinner, and take out the whiskey. We tell stories about people we know. We hold our hands to the heat. After a while our boots come off and we hold our feet to the flame, too. It feels like we're getting away with something, staying warm at night at 11,000 feet in October.

On one of my trips out from camp to urinate, I look up and see that clouds have moved in. The clouds are still there when we spread our bags by the fire and wrap our boots in our clothes to use as pillows. But when I awake that night, shivering badly, the fire is long dead and there are thousands of stars.

The boredom starts Saturday morning after breakfast. Bridgette has already left. She will be back that night, but has errands to run in town. Breakfast is a process—I work on the fire while Chris slices cheese onto bagel halves, then sand-wiches them and wraps them in foil. We lean the silver bundles against the inside wall of the fire pit, then put more foil over a big tin cup filled with water and heat it for coffee. Every few minutes, we turn the bagels. We eat apples while we wait.

But when breakfast is over, there stretches before us a full and empty day. The mountains, the views, the ground under our feet—they hold the day forward as a challenge. What are you going to do with this? You've thought so much about getting here, you've spent effort and money and have ignored responsibilities. Well, here you are. Here we are.

Ways are found to pass the time. We play cards, we drink more coffee, we propose hypotheticals (at what distance would you feel safe spotting a cougar?). The hour before lunch finds us on the boulders and in the clearing beyond the boulders hunting crows and one robin with rocks we find on the ground. Neither of us would like to kill a bird, but the chances of hitting one seem low enough that if it happens it was probably meant to happen. Plus, dreadful as it is to wing stones at innocent creatures, it is either that or think candidly about the empti-ness of the day. Sorry, crows.

When a stone knocks the branch where one of these birds is perched, or sails past its beak, it takes flight and lights again on a different perch farther away. As long as Chris and I can see this new place where it has landed, there is no question of giving up. We find new stones and walk softly after it. It is only when they have all flown places we cannot see that we think about heading back to camp. If they had remained in view, though, I do believe we would have followed them on and on, wherever they wound up going. Part of me even wants to sit there right now and wait for them to come back. Or throw stones at where they were.

For lunch, we eat baloney and apples. With little to do that might distract us from the reality of having little to do, I ask Chris if he'll join me for a walk. He declines, which I probably expected. When it comes to deep, authentic boredom, and not just your everyday weariness, you're better off alone.

I set out towards the birstlecones, then cut across a grassy clearing to meet up with the trail. I follow it into a stand of bigger pine and fir, where it turns muddy and is stamped with deer and elk tracks. Off to the left is a fallen Ponderosa. Its enormous bulb of roots stands on end beside the crater it made. The trunk tun-nels off to a place farther up where it lies across the trail. When I come to it, I pull myself up through the branches and scramble over the top. On its side, it is still very tall. It takes me a minute to pick my way down. Then I follow the trail out from the forest onto a long saddleback with the big peaks way out west. They disappear behind some close trees, then farther ahead become visible again. Each view is as grand as the one that preceded it, and what I'm fighting is the notion

I've had since we got here, and really had even as far back as Salina—namely, that this is the view. I can go as far as I want down this trail, or farther, but this is what I'm going to see. And even if there is a better view, it will still be just that. It's just a view. It's not going to repay me for anything.

I sit on the nearest flat rock. There is a pebble in one of my boots.

That night, with the fire dying, Chris comes back from urinating and tells Bridgette and me to follow him. We huddle into our jackets and walk out to the edge of the clearing. Way out on the plain is a dense disk of light. Then farther south, less dense and closer, is another one.

Chris points south. "Fort Collins," he says, then swings his other arm north. He looks from one disc of light to the other, "I mean, that isn't. . . ?"

"Cheyenne," Bridgette says.

He drops his hands, "Wow." And nobody really has more to say. We sink to the ground and wrap our elbows around our knees.

Enough maps have come before my eyes over the last few days that I can picture the inch that separates Fort Collins from Cheyenne. But seeing that now as an actual stretch of earth, an actual differential between places, I finally understand the scale. God, we're far from Fayetteville. Tomorrow, at the earliest swell of dawn, we will climb out of our bags and drain the coolers. We will pack our things and walk out to the cars. Bridgette's headlights will be in our rearview until they aren't anymore, and we won't know when exactly she turned off. In a word, we'll go home. But for now, sitting in the cold grass with distances no longer the shrunken stuff of maps, it is easy to understand the person who does not go home, the person who reaches his destination, finds nothing to justify the hard trip getting there, and has no choice but to believe it has all been justified anyway.

GRAHAM HILLARD

Huntingdon, Tennessee: Age 20

The knowledge that we will do nothing
sits on the table between us, gets into the taste

of our eggs and toast, our discussion
of last night's movie and the things

we will accomplish today. And the wall says
I'll beat the shit out of you

if I hear that shit again motherfucker,
and the wall pulses for a moment, the wall braces for

the body it's come to expect, the force
of how much weight we don't know—we've

never seen either of them.
We come home late.

And we chew while the other side
of the duplex has its usual morning.

Forty-five minutes to Jackson by car.
Time to get moving.

JILL MCCABE JOHNSON

A La Tavola

Vince ordered the octopus. Karina could forgive a lot, but not swallowing god's most exquisite creature. The date might have progressed differently, if only Vince had ordered chicken or the steak. Even the squid would have been acceptable. Did he not see the aquarium when they walked into La Tavola? Surely he'd heard—unless he just ordered it to provoke her—the reverence in her voice when she told him how much she loved octopus. She had looked directly into the aquarium, stopped in front of it for godsakes, even put one hand on the glass, and sighed a little. Vince was supposed to be, well, at least according to the ski lift operator, her vet, and Jake the morning barrista at Broad Street Coffee and Karaoke House, the artistic type. They said Vince volunteered at the art museum once a month, though he only helped with the books, and only if they needed him, and only when it wasn't golf season. The point is an artist doesn't destroy beauty, an artist honors beauty. As soon as he got his food, Vince proffered a morsel, and as soon as he offered, Karina haughtily refused. Being a person of refined sensibilities, she had not ordered the lithesome octopus nor the squid nor any seafood, for that matter, but instead savored each tender bite of her filet mignon, extra rare, lightly seared, juicy and delicate, the way she liked it, with her bread soaking up blood where it pooled on the plate.

AMORAK HUEY

House of Sticks

The stories will label you lazy as your younger brother with his heap of straw, his hundred girlfriends, his meth addiction, but they're getting it wrong. There was no wolf. There was only mossy clearing, cool in the woodshadows, place to call your own, a cake soaked in rum. The stories will not say what you were leaving behind. They will seek to blame, point fingers, call names. Your priggish older brother with his over-the-top bricks, he's the one who started the rumor about the slobbering hell hound chasing the three of you, with his heaving and huffing and meaty breath. It's a lie. He will not tell the reporters that he failed to protect you from the start, that his weakness was why you all left your birthplace as soon as you could trot. The only wolf is the one within. Your sticks took shape over days, months, years: pagoda, temple, shrine, monument climbing toward bleeding sky. You never believed in magic but the word *home* is rough and brassy on the tongue like a coin.

DAN COSHNEAR

The Old Lizard and the Young Goat

A brown and gray and black lizard lies on a brown and gray and black rock charging his old battery in the late afternoon sun, once upon a time. Soon, considers the lizard, the sun will go down, as will my energy, my alertness, my zip. What is not going down is my hunger; I could eat a horsefly.

Once upon a different time, the lizard lived under a rock in a meadow not three hundred yards from the rock on which he sits. Now the meadow has a barn on it, surrounded by muddy pens and filthy pigs. Rumor has it a pig will eat a lizard if the opportunity presents itself. And with regard to lizards, which produce neither milk nor meat for humans, a farmer with a spade is unpredictable. So our lizard ventured on an enormous uphill journey; over wet and dry dirt, over short grass and longer grass, and under a fence.

Now from his rock perch, he looks down at the barn, the pens, the pigs, the wider meadow with cows and sheep and goats. One young goat in particular has caught his attention. He is not fifty feet away gnawing on a fencepost. More interesting even than the kid are the buzz of flies that accompany him.

"Psst!" Says the lizard.

"Bah," says the goat.

"Bet you can't get over the fence," says the lizard. "Not that I see any reason you would."

"Bah."

"You probably have plenty of delicious mushrooms right where you stand."

At this, the goat raises his head. The old lizard knows a goat will eat the upholstery out of a farmer's truck. Once, a goat ate windshield wipers—the lizard heard about it, such hollering. Why would this kid care about a patch of fall mushrooms, or a glistening little thatch of onions. Lizard raises the question in a tone one might describe as rhetorical, almost diffident, "I don't imagine clover holds any interest for you?"

If the young goat has learned anything from his nanny, it is this: everyone doesn't need to know how smart you are. She'd had more to say, something about holding something close to your vest, but that didn't make any sense. Nanny, it was frequently said, spent too much time waiting for slop outside the kitchen window. But the kid is clever enough, he got the gist of it. "Bah," he says.

The old lizard persists, but with a new tack. "I've never seen a cow leap over a fence. As for a pig, well, that'd be a sight, don't you think?"

The sound of chewing on a fencepost is interfering with the kid's thinking, and thinking seems suddenly like a good idea. He raises his head once more. He thinks: first an appeal to my appetite, now my vanity. I could jump over a pig or even a cow if I wanted to, but no one has to know about it. "Bah," he says.

The poor old lizard watches the sun sinking and with it, his spirits. A fly or two would sustain him, but he hasn't the strength to pull himself across the grass. What does a young kid care about these days? If not food? If not pride? Alas, considering his own youth, a strategy comes to mind. "I've often wondered why a farmer builds a fence. I mean," the lizard sighs, "if his stock is satisfied, why would they leave? As for me, I've known only freedom and could not imagine life any other way."

Once more the kid stops chewing and raises his head. Good food, improved status, now freedom: all very appealing and thought-provoking. Maybe it is Nanny's ego, but she's always said the fence is to keep dumb animals out. Real freedom might mean inclusion. In any case, one can talk about freedom to move about as one pleases or freedom from such oppressive worries as danger and hunger. The subject is quite complex. "Bah," he says, and he thinks, this might make a good topic tonight when he sits with the old lady in the dirt.

But there is something else—more intriguing, more puzzling, more disturbing. The young goat cannot resist. He clears his throat. "Are you a talking rock?" he says. "Because a talking rock is not something I've ever seen or heard of."

The old lizard stands (if you could call it standing) as still as any lifeless thing. Even a smile might give him away, so he doesn't smile. He waits and waits until the kid lowers his head and returns to his gnawing preoccupation. Then through a yawn, as if no subject could be more trivial than the one on which he is about to embark, he says, "A talking rock is rare indeed. I daresay, I've never heard of one either, excluding your present company, of course."

The kid's ears perk up at a perfect 45-degree angle, then that poor excuse for a tail points skyward. "A talking rock," he says. "Is that even possible?"

"Come closer," says the old lizard.

The kid looks back toward the barn. He looks up and down, left and right, then raises his front feet onto the taut barbed wire which connects post to post. Pushing down on the wire, he vaults himself over the fence without a hitch. The buzz of flies swarms in wider orbits, briefly, then funnels and keeps pace with the young goat.

The old lizard braces himself to strike. What this means is that he curls his tongue in the back of his throat. Braced, it is difficult for him to talk.

The young goat has plenty of time on his hooves, and this being the case, he has learned, or rather taught himself, how to walk coolly. Slowly—leg one, leg three, leg two, leg four, pause, repeat, pause, repeat until as if by pure coincidence he finds himself standing five feet in front of the brown and gray and black rock.

Now, without getting too detailed about the anatomy of goat, let me simply say that the kid stops approximately five feet in front of the rock because this is where his monocular vision is binocular. As he moves closer, he loses depth perception. Still, he continues, because, well, he's cool. He assumes a position beside the rock, facing the barn, and looks at the ground.

"What I don't see," he says, "is a single mushroom, or an onion. I don't see clover." There is a long quiet pause as both the young goat and the old lizard watch the farmer run from the barn to the backdoor of his house. Now the farmer is standing in the threshold of the back door. Now his wife is at the threshold, and the farmer is in his truck. He drives the dirt and gravel road to the gate and before the dust settles he is out of sight. The behavior of the farmer and his wife is endlessly entertaining, but the kid has not forgotten where he is and why. "A talking rock," he says.

Another long pause while both watch the farmer's wife heave a bucket of scraps into the pigs' pen. The pigs trot in her direction, grunting and snorting.

"I mean," says the young goat, "where is the motivation? Why would a rock—"

At this very moment, the lizard strikes, which is to say, he flicks his tongue toward the buzz of flies hovering around the young goat's hindquarters.

And at the very same moment the kid raises one of his two front hooves and sets it firmly on the old lizard's back.

The old lizard coughs out his meal. He gasps, "I have done you no harm," he cries. "Why do you treat me this way?"

Soon enough the farmer returns in his truck. The farmer's wife stands at the door, her hands in her hair, then returns to the kitchen. The farmer follows her into the house. Endlessly entertaining, really. What could they possibly be thinking? But that's another subject, perhaps another conversation with Nanny before bed. The sun sets. The poor old lizard expires. And still the young goat stands tall with one foot on the lizard's back.

Stories with morals: aren't they always a bit reductive? Character is characteristic, nothing more; motivation is always singular and self-interested. Extrapolate if you will, if you must, but know by doing so, the fabulous world appears, becomes, rather flat, rather grim. After all, what can we say? Just don't lie to The Kid.

AVITAL GAD-CYKMAN

The Bison

It was not until the incident with the bison that Sara Frishman started eating olives. Green, black—all kinds of olives, even imported ones. The bitter flesh rolled on her tongue like Arabic letters.

As soon as Ruben and the children left, she sat on the pile of planks in the backyard, sucking on olives, licking their slick brown skin.

When the neighbor's baby cried, ever so loudly, her tongue coiled in, and she held her breath, imagining the diaper's stench. She could smell it through the sweet aroma of the over-ripe dates falling off the tree. The air wraps a transparent layer over pregnant women, letting nothing out.

If she had inhaled that other day, the scent of the shepherd's sweat would have reached her, and her palms would have become wet.

The rough seed fell out of her lips before she took another olive.

She had never seen a bison in her life, hadn't imagined such an oppressed power possible. The animal seemed unaware of its own erection. She stared at it while the shepherd stood behind her, talking in Arabic.

He could have said anything. She barely felt the rhythm of the words, the languishing end, and she didn't turn around. It had been long since words played with her body like that.

She put another olive in her mouth.

That day, she had found she was pregnant. The baby was Ruben's, but she felt it could have been the shepherd's.

A wagtail landed on the palm tree, and a date fell on the ground, already rotten.

GIUSEPPE CARBONE

Push Me, Pull Me

I log into my eTrade account while the boss is at lunch. Maybe he wouldn't mind so much me being on, except that I am really *on*. That might rub him the wrong way. I mentioned to him that I am building a modest portfolio of sub-sub-sub-penny stocks, the ones with tiny little prices like 0.0004 dollars a share, and that I feel good about it because they are all stocks in green companies, you know, like Restaurant Oil Recyclers Inc (OTC:VEGG), and Solar Moon Corp (PINK:SOMO), and that I am going to hit it big and it would be good for the environment at the same time, and he just chuckles, calls me a chucklehead and goes on with his day.

So then I get this great tip. It isn't a tip that's directed at me exactly, it is in a newsletter about microcap stocks and the newsletter goes out to maybe 200,000 investors and me as well. The tip says that Aussie Wind and Whinge (OTC:AWAW) is now a BUY, that it has the combination of liquidity and volatility that we are looking for. I trust this newsletter. These guys aren't opportunists, you know, like, 'DAFT is a top 5 Market Mover for Tuesday, May 4!!' Of course it is. Because the move they're talking about, it already came up, like the day before. No, these guys at the newsletter can sense a change before it happens.

So the tip says BUY, so I buy. Not too much, they tell you right up front. No more than two hundred fifty on any one stock. At 0.0002, that'll get me one million two hundred fifty thousand shares. If it ever reaches a dollar . . . man! But I know it won't do that. I'm calm. I'm sober. I put up 250 clams. Sure enough, just like that it goes up. Eighteen percent in one day. Now it's a HOLD. Unless the newsletter says otherwise, it's a hold. That's their official recommendation. So I hold.

On the way home I lose my Philadelphia Eagles money clip. It's got just a couple of twenties and a few ones, but I kinda miss it; it had sentimental value. Next day AWAW goes up again. Nine percent. The day after that it rises forty-four percent. I go to Yahoo Finance, punch in 'AWAW.' There's no merger news or big new contract announcement or anything like that. Where do the newsletter guys get their information anyway?! It's not like they go visit the company. I mean, the headquarters got to be overseas.

Every day I look and every day it's going up. I would be on Easy Street if I put a pile of dough into this one. I don't have a pile of dough. But I've doubled my money and this one's a HOLD, so I'm holding.

My daughter's just got her license and she drives real careful. Parking, however: $237 in a handicapped zone. She ran into a store to have her iPod battery replaced. She thought it was okay to park there if she left the motor running.

What do you know, AWAW keeps going up after the appointment of Jack Ruddy as the new CEO. Until recently Mr. Ruddy was the chief financial officer. The company announces a huge government order for turbine monitor clips. AWAW doesn't build the turbines. It supplies the monitor clips that must be integral to the functionality of the turbine. At 0.00058 I've got nearly seven hundred fifty bucks in there. There is a God in the heavens.

I'm feeling good. Got something right going on just by picking up on this stock's vibe. My wife calls and says the Aveo needs a timing belt. $493.50 parts and labor.

AWAW climbs some more and then it's the weekend. Market's closed but the newsletter comes out before Monday's opening bell and sure enough it doesn't say anything about selling AWAW. In fact it congratulates me because AWAW's performance has ranged between 60 and 320%. After a slight dip on Monday morning my stock rises some more.

I dump all my other green stocks, they're not going anywhere. I can always come back. I dump the lot and pour the proceeds into AWAW. It cost $12.99 to sell each one, and there are ten of them valued at $30 plus-or-minus $20 each so that's $129.90 in fees. No, it's less than that because no one would buy HorseFly Maggot Bioconversion Inc (OTC:HFMB). It just sits there for sale. Good for the Day. Day after day.

I put everything into AWAW. Now I'm out on a limb here with this stock. It's not a BUY/HOLD you know. It's just a HOLD.

But it keeps going up. Up, up, up. My piece of the pie is worth well over a grand. On the way home I buy a bag of pistachios to celebrate, the red kind you can almost never find anymore. I crack a tooth on one that wouldn't open. I need a crown. With dental insurance, which, thank goodness I have, it's going to run me $1,167.

I'm sitting in the dentist chair during my second visit, the one where they chuck the temporary and fit me with the permanent crown. Today's the day my personal gold mine will probably top the 0.002 mark. Ten times the original investment, and no signs of slowing. I try to set up alerts by text-messaging but they won't do it for stocks under a dollar. Before the cement is even dry I rush back to my cubicle and log on. Yes! I'm holding.

I phone the wife to tell her the news. She's all upset. She came home to find the front door jimmied, furniture toppled, the flat screen gone. She sobs extra hard for her engagement ring, which she had left on the coffee table when she went to the gym. I do a little mental math: $2,350. I tell her they must have taken something else. Sure enough, my daughter can't find her iPod.

I can't afford all this prosperity. What's life like for the truly rich?

AWAW is through the roof. A big turbine manufacturer makes a play and Mr. Ruddy rebuffs it. My chunk of the company's worth over ten grand now. The wife borrows my car while hers is in the shop. Talking on her cell, totals the car. Thank God no one's hurt. I check the car loan on-line, everything's on-line, right? We owe nine thousand four hundred and fifty on the Cobalt and I had tried to save a few bucks by dropping collision with GEICO. What the hell was I thinking. Where am I going to get that kind of money?

I'm walking to work now, it's good for me. On the way in I take the stairs, I don't like elevators and it's peaceful in the stairwell, I can think about stock market strategy even though I have only one strategy and that is to hold AWAW and await further instructions. Between the second and third floors I spot a hundred dollar bill on the steps. I gasp. Oh no! I rush up the remaining three flights and log on in my cubicle. Sure enough, AWAW has slipped. Down 4% since the opening bell. The rest of the day fabulous things keep happening to me. I win the office salsa contest (roma tomatoes, not beefsteak; a dash of clove). I land a contract. I get a raise. I feel miserable.

The next week is a roller coaster. My stock takes a dive the day I get a big promotion from the home office. The boss is surprised, but hey, I've worked hard. I've got some financial acumen. The next day the promotion is rescinded. It was meant for somebody named Carpone, with a 'p'. In the Peoria office. A big mistake, an embarrassment. My stock rallies.

The Girl Scouts come through the office selling raffle tickets. A national campaign with a million dollar grand prize. What happened to hawking cookies? I avoid the scouts, I can't buy a ticket. What if I win? I shudder to think what would happen to AWAW.

I get the feeling that my fortune is tied to my fortune. Inversely. To test my theory (I swear I am not superstitious) I go outside to check the weather. It's July in California. When's the next rain expected—in five months?! It's drizzling and dribbling, and back home I had left my entire stamp collection on the picnic table in the backyard. Let the rains come! Things are looking up for AWAW.

My optimism is short-lived. Too many good things keep happening to me. Little things, but they are chipping away at my fortune. I inherit a rototiller from my great-uncle. My fig tree yields a bumper crop. My daughter lands a full scholarship to a graphics design school. When will it all end? My stock is not doing so hot now. Every day it sinks a little further. AWAW(E) is down to 0.00007 a share.

It long ago became a SELL, the day the extra letter (E) was added to its symbol when Mr. Ruddy got nailed for an improper filing with the SEC.

I've abandoned my strategy. I don't care. Life is great. I can't sell now. Yesterday we lounged around the house and read the entire Sunday paper, and it was a Tuesday. Today I trace a meandering wild grapevine from beginning to end. I find a nest with two amazingly tiny hummingbirds, the parents humming a diversion right above them. AWAW(E) has been in bankruptcy proceedings for a while now. It's in the tank. Even if it loses half its value each and every day, it just will not disappear.

I'm going to ride this puppy all the way into the basement.

Casserole

A dog gets hold of some leftovers. This produces a startling effect. After eating, the dog pads over to a wall of the apartment where it lives—and starts climbing.

It climbs past the tacked-up postcards and the calendar. When it reaches the ceiling, it barks. It starts across, upside-down with its tail hanging in the air. In the middle, by the light fixture, it stops. Alarmed and excited, it barks and whines.

This is how the owner finds it when he comes home. He gapes. He stares at the bowl of tuna-noodle casserole leftovers, which the dog has gobbled up. Normally the dog's unauthorized helping-itself would provoke a real scolding. But the owner has immediately put two and two together; he sees the amazing cause and effect going on here.

Presently the power of the casserole wears off. The dog tumbles down onto the sofa, which the owner has dragged over under it. "Good boy, good boy!" the owner says, patting away at his pet, trembling with excitement.

Can you imagine how much money you can make with a dog that can walk on ceilings?

Furiously the man rushes off to the store and comes back with armfuls of ingredients. He starts cooking up a storm of tuna noodle casseroles. But guess what? He can't seem to duplicate the exact recipe that fueled his dog's gravity-defying exploits. He just can't seem to get it right. He tries light tuna in oil, chunk white in water—solid albacore in water, in oil. He tries thick noodles, thin noodles, egg noodles, lasagna. Spaghetti of all kinds!

Every time, the dog barks and thumps its tail and gobbles the bowl down and rushes barking to the wall, and scrabbles away with its paws.

And then turns sheepishly, whining, and stares forlornly at its owner.

Finally the whole thing starts to drive the owner mad: the reek of tuna, the burned casserole pots. Not to mention the exorbitant cost of ingredients and the claw damage on the wall. The dog gets fat and refuses to eat dog food anymore. It waddles over to the wall and yawns and lifts a half-hearted paw, just for show.

So the man gets rid of the dog. He buys a cat instead.

Whenever the cat jumps onto a table and readies itself to spring up onto a bookcase—as cats love to do—the owner rushes in and squirts it with a water bottle.

"Don't you dare!" he hisses. His eyelid twitching.

And the poor cat finally just curls up all day at the foot of the couch and stares at the carpet.

JOHN CALDERAZZO

Cheeta Lives!

Yes, that yammering ham who stole the final scene of every 1930s Tarzan movie, jumping up and down in the no-longer-lion-haunted grass, then turning a back flip to make Jane and the grateful Natives laugh before throwing his arms around the swim champion shoulders of Johnny Weissmuller . . . well, the little guy has outlived them all. Hard to believe, but the newspaper clipping seems like proof: Cheeta spared from a research lab to live in an old age home for animals in Palm Springs. More than seventy-five now, a record for a chimp, but eons removed from the leveled jungle where "his talent was discovered." Still looking good, and spending hours every day painting. But painting what? His roommates over the years? Say, his evil cousins, the green-faced monkeys of Oz, though shorn of their creepy, wired-up wings. Or the gelding in *National Velvet*, pining for teen-aged Liz Taylor. Or Old Yeller, still fuming over the toad they must have made him lick before his big scene, as though they didn't trust him to foam up with rabies on his own. Or maybe, palette in his hairy, almost human hand, Cheeta reaches for his farthest-back memories, brushing in raucous parrots with un-clipped wings, re-creating extinct complications of green: Thunder tree, Euphorbia, Flame of the Forest. He leans close to his work, his breath moistening the drying grays and ivories of tusked giants, hauling themselves—and how much of their forest?—to the Secret Elephant Burial Grounds.

After *Doctor's Orders,*
a fused glass sculpture, by Tom Dimond

The man with the birdhead fingertips
feeds all the baby birds. He walks by gooseberries,
elderberries, his beak fingers clicking away.
He scans trees. Haunts skylines. Phonelines.
Searches for pink mouths. Tiny sharp tongues
to drop the berries onto. He knows only
three hundred more birds to feed, and he will
become one. He knows his bones are hollow.
He has felt the southern pull on him in fall,
the northern tug in spring. The feathers
are sprouting out of the wingbones in his back.
One day he will no longer be able to call in sick
to work. All that will come out is a squawk.
A caw. No one at the office will notice
when he soars away overhead. They will think
the enormous shadow just a trick of light,
another pigeon shitting on their concrete building.

TIMOTHY LIU

The Gift

—for Amy Gerstler

The joint must have come a long way
to be with us, hints of oregano
smelling of skunk. Didn't you tuck it
in your sock as you sauntered
through the airport security check?
Neither of us even sure we were high.
Last night, my cat came back to me
in a dream, her coat a darker shade,
still bony in the way she had become
in her last days—one shot from the vet
and she was out, two shots and her heart
just stopped. Still dreaming, I said
to her, *but I know you're dead!*
Even my own dream couldn't fool me,
heavy sobs stirring me from sleep,
a half-smoked joint left somewhere
in your room. Last night you said,
smoke as much as you want, and I
knew you'd meant it, the joint having
traveled far to be with us, no farther.

CHRISTINA ROSALIE SBARRO

If You Fall It Is Your Fault

"Please do not stand or walk until the vehicle has stopped. The camera is on. If you fall, it's your fault. We will be there in exactly 180 seconds," your driver announces sensationally as the bus lurches out into traffic.

People with black bags, and bags that are paisley, and also some that are Samsonite, ram their bodies and luggage into the narrow upholstered seats and hold on. They look at each other skeptically. Then you see him. He is sitting to your left, a few seats down and over.

You are heading home after a week of sales meetings, but here, across from you, the detour is sudden and plausible in a gray wool crewneck.

Look everywhere else: out the window at the Las Vegas skyline with its preposterous buildings, and at a woman in a puffy jacket waiting for a doorman to open a door. Then give in. Look straight at him. He is leaning back with his legs at wide angles. He knows you are watching.

This is what you know: the bus will be at the airport in three minutes and ahead of you, in a different geography, the man you married will have just gotten home from work. He will be standing at the back door, towel drying the dogs' feet as they come back inside from the muddy yard. His hair will be falling into his eyes, his jeans ripped at the knees, his feet bare.

The bus smells like diesel and air freshener and sweat, and beneath your feet and against your shoulders you feel the motor vibrating as it accelerates towards the airport.

You are sweating because you have just run from the rental car return to the bus terminal lugging an over-the-shoulder bag, two rolling suitcases, and a paper sack of cinnamon sticks. Your cheeks have turned the color of borscht.

You are a woman whose skin betrays you. When you are angry or nervous it prickles red at your neck and then blooms, mottled and bright up to your cheeks. You have freckles and sometimes acne. You dye your hair blonde. You take ibuprofen for cramps, sore muscles, toothaches, general ill ease. You are afraid of pain.

You do not like to show that you are afraid of anything, and to hide it you force yourself to do many things that terrify you but aren't painful, like climbing hundreds of vertical feet of rock with your husband. You do this in particular because he loves it, and because you feel like you owe him something. When you climb he cannot see that you are gritting your teeth, though your skin becomes blotchy. You can fake a great smile.

Contemplate his travel plans; if he has a loft in San Francisco or if he lives here in this godforsaken desert of fake palms and money. Ponder briefly if he is good in bed. At the red light consider offering him one of the doughy snacks you bought at the kiosk.

You want to touch his hands.

You know there will always be this. A hundred alternatives like holographs hovering at the fringes of these seconds that are your life.

As the light turns, you look up from licking sugar off your fingers and see that he is watching. For a moment you think your heart has skipped a beat, and then you think, damn, what a cliché.

You feel it: the future, snapping open or closed like a jackknife.

When you get home you will throw yourself full tilt into righting your life. You will walk the dogs and sort the mail. You will file the bills alphabetically, presort your husband's laundry, and remove his screws and spare change and pulpy receipts from the dryer. You will make soup from scratch; clean the kitchen with peroxide including the place at back of the faucet where the water drips and the counter grows scummy. You will wait for him to notice. But really what you will be doing is waiting for him to forget. He wants a baby.

When you get home everything between you will take place in short sentences like diced onions, tears always at the back of your eyes. You will ask, how do you think we can we possibly have a baby? We live in this shitty house in the suburbs, both of us working full time. You will put your hand on your stomach. A reflex. You are terrified of childbirth. Of the pain and the stretch marks. And also of the dark circles that will crowd under your eyes and of someone always counting on you.

You will say, you hardly even take care of the dogs.

He will shrug.

Then you will ask him what he wanted before he met you.

This, right here, he'll say with a slow grin. This and a bunch of kids running around in the yard.

There is one cinnamon stick left in the bag. Eat it. Get sugar and grease on your fingers and lips, and think about all the women he has probably slept with. Notice he has no wedding band and that his hair is just barely turning gray at his sideburns. His jaw is angular and tan. His pants are impeccably clean. You like this. You are a woman who keeps a lint roller in your glove box, a Tide pen in your handbag. You buy your husband pants because if you didn't, he'd wear the same ones—stains or no stains—forever.

Lick your fingers and close your eyes and remember: when you were first married, your husband took you skiing every weekend. After the last run, he'd build a fire at the slope-side cabin and peel your wet clothing from your body, layer by layer.

When you crane your neck you can already see the airport out the opposite window. He looks up at you again and smiles, slightly. His eyes are blue like yours, but bluer, like a high-altitude sky. When he stops looking, feel grateful. What would you say if he spoke?

For an instant you become distracted with the way he rubs his thumb and forefinger across his eyebrow.

The bus is already slowing. It takes a sharp turn to the left making you tilt until you feel gravity in your stomach. You catch a glimpse of your reflection out the window. You are flushed.

Maybe you want the same things.

In the autumn you convinced your husband to buy a new bed as an anniversary present. Before it, his college futon. But now it is winter and the understated Mission frame and the 400 thread-count sheets in persimmon mock you.

Birth control pills made your skin break out. They made your arms itch and at night you'd wake up in a cold sweat. When you decided to stop taking them to give your body a break you told him, it's your turn buddy, but he refused to buy condoms. Now the nights are wide between you. You go to sleep facing the wall, your legs and arms wrapped around the sheets.

When he tries to touch you, maybe all you say is "go."

You never imagined a baby. Instead you imagine cherry cabinets and granite and a house up on a hill somewhere where the dogs can run, and you can go hiking right out your backdoor.

Think of the circumstances of your disembarking. Pull your sleeve down over your rings. Put on some lip-gloss. Check your watch. If the driver is not bullshitting, you will be at the terminal in twenty seconds. Consider how you will attempt to make your awkward bags look easy to carry.

You watch as he drinks the last of his coffee from a paper cup with a plastic lid. He drinks it quickly, all in one gulp, like he has a reason, like he'll be staying up late. Then he puts the empty cup between his knees.

When you get back you will look at your house and see only what it isn't. You will look at your husband, lanky and content in the small circumference of the town he has known his entire life and you will feel compelled to ask again, what do you really want in the next five years?

And he'll say, like he always does, this right here, baby.

Your house is small, between two others, on a block with still more. Your roof leaks. Mold grows in the spring. Every year you sprinkle diatomaceous earth and borax around the foundation to keep the ants from invading your kitchen.

When you get home you will scrub the kitchen and then you will plant hops along the fence in the backyard because this is something you can maybe do together. On the back deck in the twilight with cold beers in your hands, watching the dogs loll and listening to the night sounds of the neighborhood build.

Just think, you'll be able to say, we grew it and brewed it ourselves!

Picture what it could be like, leaving with him. You will acknowledge what you've been saying across the aisle with your eyes. You will walk around the airport together and maybe miss your flights. He will reach out for your hand, and over drinks at the bar he will tell you that the only thing he doesn't want in life is kids. You will get a hotel room and wander out into the neon night.

Behind his head you see the sign for DEPARTURES, and the cars are moving in a steady stop and go. Your eyes are drawn to the lights.

Tomorrow you will eat soup at home with crackers and goat cheese. You will watch your husband make a circle with his spoon around the bowl, like he has something to say. Outside the dark will keep getting closer. The rain will keep falling and falling until the yard is slick with mud. The night will keep pressing and circling until the glass turns from blue to black and all you can see from inside is you and him reflected. Your husband will look up as he sets down his spoon and his eyes will sink into yours. From across the table he'll reach out. His hand will be warm.

Think of ripping paper out of your planner and scribbling quickly. If you hand it to him as you disembark, as you are collecting your bags and tipping the bus driver who has lifted your luggage off of the metal racks, he will read it as he is doing the same, and maybe he will call your cell phone while you are walking ahead of him towards check-in. If he calls, you will answer.

Think of statistics. Think of how easily you could become one.

The bus is pulling into the terminal and when you look out the window you cannot see anything at all except for lights and people's reflections. You suddenly feel tired. You miss the smell of your house; the way your bed was when you left: the sheets unwashed, his body warm and asleep among the covers.

You look up. For a second your eyes meet and you hold his gaze. The bus lurches to a stop.

"Welcome to the Las Vegas International Airport," the driver says. Then he presses some buttons and the doors fold open like the knees of a grasshopper.

"Watch your step," the driver says as he hands you your bags. He is wearing fingerless gloves and dark sunglasses, and everyone is trying to get off of the bus at the exact same time.

Keep your planner in your bag. Leave after him. Stay at the back of the bus until he has collected his bags and is already making his way through the revolving doors. Stay, even if he looks back, and he will.

MICHAEL SCHMELTZER

While You Were Sleeping

From our data we suspect the songbird dreams of singing
—Daniel Margoliash, University of Chicago biologist

The scientists monitored
individual neurons firing
while the zebra finch sang

and those notes echoed
in the minute chasms of the brain
while the delicate bird slept.

A songbird dreams of singing
and what do you suspect
I dream of, the one you left

without a voice? When the sky
strips off her blue sari
to reveal every twinkling freckle

on her dark skin,
I dream of the airport motel
we made love in

while our spouses dreamt
us home. I dream of hijacked planes
crashing into the twin towers

of our marriages.
And what about you?
What melodies reverberate

in the terminal of your sleep?
Does the song shape the body
beside you, or does it mirror

the body that no longer sings,
the body of the one
who watched you sleeping

and listened to you breathe?
In & out, a solemn hymn,
then nothing, then a name

that fell from your lips like an egg
pushed from its nest, a name
you swore in the morning was mine.

Michael Schmeltzer

Blizzard, 1996

I. What We Told Our Son

Because the dog was sick with age,
would not survive

another season. Because she stopped
eating the bits and scraps of meat

we gave her. Because the blizzard approached
like a buzzard to a body

and a good flurry makes the most beautiful
animal burial, merciful

as it throws itself down
handful after handful.

II. Through a Window Blurred by Moisture

The dense silence ensuing the gunshot
makes me question

whether I heard the sound at all.
Then, the shriek of my son

like a rabbit maimed, the creaking
front door, the stomping of my husband

clearing snow from his boots.
I watch a cloud curl

out of my howling son's mouth
and wonder about wounds

in the dead
of winter, whether steam rises from them

against the falling snow.

ANDREW ALLPORT

Purgatorio

non per vista, ma per suono é noto (Inferno, XXXIV)

I spent a year there, searching for the right line,
trying to translate that long silence
into sight: neither darkness nor brightness

but snow falling on snow, the radio losing strength
in the tunnel. Even static has its edges, its windows.
Even the truth can be dressed in curtains, trees, a forest,

a fortress. Underneath, my mountain was pathetic:
man-made, catastrophic, it could hardly bear
weight, its summiteers barely cared if I blessed

or damned them. I never imagined my tragedy
would be so full of extras, spinning chairlifts,
ascending without effort into the empyrean,

or that the scene itself would have no season,
clocking a few bitter hours of winter, then a spring
so warm we could have swum. In an unconsolidated space

nothing connects, and you slide. Who first broke
the news? A red paging phone told me
the king will come early to his idyll, and die

with a smile on his face. The archetypes will not
hold, I heard the radio say, I heard the first canto
of avalanche safety say the odds are zero, oh, o, o, o

and our job is recovery, not rescue.
So I spent a January sun, handling shovel and probe,
close-reading layers of snow—rickety, slippery

as a stack of small books, red spines, green. A weakness
for the wild insides of places, people: it took him
down. My beacon calls out, bat-blind, to the body:

you're getting colder, colder, no—now you're hot,
hotter, you're so hot you're on fire, you're burning—
and there it was. A face, encased in a second face,

a mask of ice, his breath. In an unconsolidated space,
death is half the story. We wrapped him in silver,
laid him in the litter. A numb remembrance

of the knots remains at hand. It was all by the book,
I remember: the sled, the rope, the weight, the boots.
The world read into, each object animated

by the same unbelievable sight, indelible
as the range of light: the calm town of stone
where we gather each spring around the marker we made,

we made it resemble (how could we not) a mountain.

NIK DE DOMINIC

Apologia, Louisiana

Here is the sound. It is the sound of water. It is the sound of rushing. It is the sound of being surrounded. It is the sound of innumerable helicopters above, around us. The sky blackens in blades. It is the repetitive whir of a ceiling fan off balance, improperly hung, threatening to loosen itself through its own motions, its own undoing, and behead us both. Until then, we will be cool and forget the wet in our skin, the way it crawls. It laps around us, this sound, this water, our skin. Here our bodies converge and separate. Here it will begin and in beginning it will end again.

This place is evaporating into the sea. The topography of the continent literally disintegrates into the water. It is a place that by all accounts should not be here. They warned us against settling it—its bogs, swamps, and ghostly apparitions of gas in the moonlit humidity of night. Men disappeared into this place, into its wet loam; that or they came back mad and raving—lunatics with bulging eyes and signs tattooed on their bodies, appendages missing. The scars should've been enough to keep us out—but hubris, a belief in conquering both land and man has brought us here and kept us coming back since those prescient warnings, that and we want to die because we know that to die is to live and those unaware of the danger of their curious and tentative position in the world are already dead.

We think ourselves clever. Dangerous and clever. We want to exist in another briefly at the edge of the world until the sea swallows us up. We want to be swallowed.

There was a fear in California that the big one would come, the fires would rage, the mountains would slide into the sea, and the state would split along the San Andreas. As long as we uttered it though we knew it could not happen because we know utterances cannot manifest—like the child who utters each and every possible way to die because death, he knows, is unexpected. Sometimes childish beliefs are all we can grab hold of in the gale. Sometimes they are the strongest because of their whim and their buoyancy. Sometimes they are the only things that will float.

Let us be children. Adults in their concreteness sink to the bottom only to be forgotten or excavated later by uninterested third parties, parties that do not understand the import of the creatures they hold in their hands, these things they removed from their proper resting place. All bodies must come to rest and this is why we left—because we are restless.

There were others before—this coming together and separating, this movement away—us. Before Pangaea, Pannotia. Before Pannotia, Rodinia. Before Rodinia, Nuna. Parts like where we are now, though, were lost or forgotten. Gobbled and swallowed by the seas: the Lapetus, the Panthalassa, the Paleoasian, the others. What does it matter, a name, these names so familiarly foreign on the tongue?

I peel an orange carefully so that I may preserve the rind. I allow it to tear as it wants to tear. Sometimes I rip violently, mimicking what I would think the earth does and other times I rip slowly as I know things drift apart. I do not eat the fruit but leave it intact—pith to flesh to pips. It is the ocean, the body that supports these other bodies. I reassemble and reassemble to resemble. I work parts together that were never connected to see how they fit, see what is lost and forfeited in this semblance.

This process takes ten minutes. In my mind I scale that time to a billion years. Many died and much was lost. A civilization or two collapsed under its own weight. I duct tape a final configuration to the wall. I leave the orb wrapped in a paper towel on my desk to sit.

Today oil laps the shores, its orange glint in the sun and opalescence soak into the sands, the white beaches of the Gulf sullied. I know this is our undoing but I cannot help to marvel at the beauty of it, the beauty of us and what we were. An egret rises out of the horizon into the gloaming. In these blue hours, everything becomes a shadow of what it once was and here is where we shall build.

JOSEPH P. WOOD

Inauguration Night

The Presidential bed is a slush-locked barge. The Presidential bed amplifies our sighs. The Presidential bed vetoes abjuration. The Presidential Bed is the nation's bed, always.

The rivers in America pour straight to the chapel. The chapels in America unhinge the Plains. There are mountains, there are deserts, vast miasmal swamps— we secrete our secrets there and migrate flittingly.

I mean to say we, the citizens, are desolate children. I mean to say we, the citizens, are hard-aged alley cats. We tip over trash barrels and unfurl our tongues shamelessly. We, the citizens, have weak sweet chins.

CHRIS HAVEN

4077th

When Hawkeye Pierce looked at Hot Lips it was hard
    to understand what he really wanted but it taught us
        chase and rebuff and how neatly the world divided
            into doctors and nurses and sweetness withheld.

When Hawkeye Pierce drank with Trapper but not Frank
    in the Swamp, it didn't take much shine to have a party
        but it took bombs and bodies to end it, the world divided
            into friends and enemies, each one a target.

When Hawkeye Pierce yelled into Radar's phone to order
    Adam's Ribs from Chicago, Chicago was as far as home,
        and the meat would have to make it through a world divided
            by unsure borders: tiny, parallel Koreas.

When Hawkeye Pierce got dressed in white and jiggled
    his hands inside another man's wounds, he was always
        angry and blood-spattered, and the world was divided
            into those who could keep it in and those who couldn't.

When Hawkeye Pierce went nuts it was because the chicken
    was really a baby and when any baby dies, it makes a man
        go nuts because the world is divided into men, women,
            babies and other things waiting to be killed.

When Hawkeye Pierce heard about Henry Blake's chopper,
    his nose and mouth—for once silent—were covered by a mask,
        his eyes the only survivors in a world dividing its attention
            between the distance and the body beneath.

When Hawkeye Pierce himself finally heads home,
in a similar chopper, B.J. says his only goodbye in stone.
The dust swirls, and longing in this world is always divided
from its reward. He never gets to eat those ribs.

CHRISTOPHER ANKNEY

When I Was A Boy The Sun Was A Horse

for James Reiss

Clouds were a dreamer's sheep, pure
white or devilishly gray.

Ponds were always the La Brea tar pits
trying to swallow more beasts.

Every forest my father's hidden kingdom.
Every half buried tire, piece of litter, rusted bike frame

a magical clue in the three-year crusade
between his vanishing act and salvage—

found cracked to pieces at the foot of a wall
a kingdom an hour down river.

What was left of the body a litany
of punctuation.

On the drought-riddled beach
at Clear Lake the next summer, hundreds

of choked walleyes littered the beach—
and we two boys imagined them as plagued

soldiers of Normandy. Stuck in crawls,
their lips blue petals in bloom

for the soul's escape—pulled to shore
by boat-waves and a hot round

of adrenaline meant to grease
the body's machinery into action—

so many boys awakened
in June's hot stampede.

HARRY MARTINSON

Sång till zigenerskan

Tältet, seglet, den vita himlen
och ditt brösts bleka druva—
med sådana syner blev jag erövrare,
for med kärrornas bentorra hjul
skramlande ur dammskyn
hän mot ljusa Thebe,
hän mot mörka Trondheim;
där spådde vi i porslinskoppen
och händerna
fräckt och frånvarande
medan våra själar samma kväll reste bland antipoderna.

Song to the Gypsy Woman

The tent, the sail, the white sky
and the pale grape of your breast—
with such sights I became a conqueror,
traveled with the bone dry cart wheels
rattling out of clouds of dust
towards bright Thebes,
towards dark Trondheim;
where we prophesied
boldly and absent-mindedly
in a porcelain cup and in our hands,
while that very night, our souls traveled in the antipodes.

Translated by Lars Nordström

Jessica Reidy

Hyssop in the Forest

Into the nameless he dissolved, the name spoken
everyday, the name the Gypsies called him, the name
his mother knew in secret. He gave his name to wild dogs
and bullets, he smiled at the officers with blue eyes
dusted with hair, yellow-faded. Some Gypsies looked like that.

He gave his name to dogs and iron for the words
of suit and rifle, for miles of bodies recycled,
for a pair of clean boots and and roots that rotted
like the patrin he ignored in his mother's glade.
He reported every caravan but his own.

His mother shook inside her teacups, deeper
into rows of light-starved trees. She wore
white while he lived, boiled his names and tossed
out the water. Ground hyssop in the mornings
sprinkled the saffron-stained wheels and sang.

He pulverized faces, flung lime over
mounds of children in ditches. Dirt barely
blanketed their dissolving forms. She baked
bread with bitter herbs and salt and ate it
every evening in penitence for a nameless man.

He shouldered body after body into great, gaping
ovens, consuming blank familiar eyes. He unwove
gold coins from hair like water, from girls he saw
bathed by mothers at the forest-edged river, pretended
he never whispered their Gypsy names in tall grasses.

His mother waited for officers, but no one came.
War slowly closed its jaws, but she kept the family
in the deepest mosses. No one came for years, the bitter
herbs eaten and sprinkled, the fires drawn for all his clothes,
bitten by flames, children warmed by his crackling shoes.

In the trial days, the unnamed found the door and wheels,
boots taken, execution set. Her bleached sleeve pointed
him back through the grove emptied into choke-full graves.
Pointed to bullets and dogs, woven women chewed
by fire. She gave him bread for his journey to these places.

JUAN FELIPE HERRERA

Mud Drawing #3—The Kalashnikov

Came down the mountain
& I saw them watering cows by the mud wall
I noticed my father Antonov burning off their clothes

Came down the mountain & I stumbled
On the grave stones of Shugakaro where the grandmother's lay
After my father met them out in the open
The women dragged their children into a cave
I do not know why the others were hiding
In a circle around the split tree of the village
Came down the mountain as the sun broke

Some refused to hide
Some refused to crawl
Some held a marriage ceremony later in the night and
Sang the songs of lovers about to taste their flesh
Others formed a circle around them & hummed
& bowed their heads & churned their bodies
As if they were one
My father's open face of fire-flowers
Did not matter to them
Came down the mountain in full gallop
With my sister mortar
And many brothers of the Kalash

After the ashes cleared I fell
By the stumps of flesh
I heard their whispers & furies I
Could not stop listening & peering into them
As my master slept

In my language of Kalash I spoke to them
For the first time I said –

> *Take me with you*
> *wipe my face*
> *I am famished and bloody*
> *I suffer from tempests*
> *from implacable winds between my temples*
> *I want to taste what you taste*
> *cruel breads*
> *stews of the desert*
> *putrid waters*
> *I only know the young hands and*
> *The uncertain fingers of my masters*

So I was born
So was my destiny
It is the mountains that I love

I call to them & I call to them
As I fall by your side

My name is Kala.

STEFANIE FREELE

Wild Child: An Interview with T.C. Boyle

T.C. Boyle is the author of twenty-two books of fiction, including his most recent titles, Wild Child *and* The Women, *as well as the forthcoming* When the Killing's Done. *He is a longtime member of the English Department at The University of Southern California, and was elected to the American Academy of Arts and Letters in 2009.*

SF: After 12 novels and eight short story collections, does writing come easily to you?

TCB: How I wish. Like everyone else who sets pen to paper (or rather, fingers to keyboard), I have to drive myself to produce. But what keeps me going is the great joy that creating and molding something brings. This is the central joy of my life.

SF: Is your writing mostly intuitive or how much is conscious?

TCB: Let's say that roughly 99 percent is intuitive. The other 1 percent derives, I suppose, from the fact that I am sitting upright and alive in the world while writing, though I may not always be aware of it. Of course, I do conduct research and make discoveries about themes and plot, but this happens in a mysterious, subconscious way, for the most part.

SF: In "Admiral" we learn about cloning, and in "Sin Dolor" the narrator is a physician who discovers a boy who can't feel pain. These stories must take some significant research. How do you tackle research?

TCB: I do enough research to stimulate the process of story-making. I cannot be an expert on everything, but I can be expert enough to put my seduction over on you.

SF: What is your own editing process look like?

TCB: It looks like a computer screen. I edit endlessly as I go along. I do not shift scenes around or write beyond where I am at the moment. Thus, when the final lines come to me, the story is done and ready to deliver, after perhaps a very light run-through. What you see in print is almost exactly what the finished manuscript has become through the days, weeks, months and sometime years of allowing it to find its way.

SF: Fresh metaphors are not easy for some, but yours are marvelous and lively: "… while her own mother was as feeble as a dandelion gone to seed, she was supremely capable of worry." When are your metaphors born and how?

TCB: Metaphors are the very soul of fiction—they help give prose its beauty and artistry. All metaphors are spontaneous. You can't make them up beforehand and save them for insertion in a likely place—the work and all its elements must be organic.

SF: I read in a February interview with Jenny Shank with New West Books and Writers, that you "would never consider" working on more than one thing at once. Since you focus on one project, do you mean you have no stories in your backlog?

TCB: No, there are no stories in my backlog. I finished a novel, *When the Killing's Done*, last July, and have since turned to short stories. There are six new ones, the last of which, "In the Zone," set in Chernobyl three years after the reactor exploded, I premiered at the L.A. Times Book Festival the day before sitting down to your interview. The other five have either recently appeared in print or are accepted for publication. (For those interested, "My Pain Is Worse Than Your Pain" appeared in the January *Harper's*, "A Death in Kitchawank" in the January 18 issue of *The New Yorker*, and "The Silence" in the current fiction number of *The Atlantic*, while "What Separates Us From the Animals" will appear in a future issue of *Harper's* and "Good Home" in *Playboy*. "In the Zone" is just now going out; when I learn where it will be published, I will announce the information on my website, tcboyle.com.) As for now, I will turn to the research for the next novel.

SF: You mentioned in that interview that you write until you get unstuck. How do you get unstuck? How long does a story take you to write from idea to the finish line?

TCB: I don't know. Perseverance, I guess. Perseverance driven by the very strong desire to become unstuck.

SF: Do you ever have down-time between projects, or do you leap gleefully toward the next one?

TCB: Not much. After a novel I turn to stories. On finishing and delivering the 370 page manuscript of *When the Killing's Done* (to be published in March of next year by my longtime publisher, Viking Penguin), I took a brief vacation in Costa Rica (a vacation geared toward collecting material for a future story, by the way), spent some time in the Sequoia National Forest, where I often go to write and brood, took a five-week hiatus for the book tour in support of *Wild Child*, and have arrived here, at this moment, answering your questions.

SF: "Did he somehow come to understand that people were his tribe in the way that a bear instinctually consorts with other bears rather than foxes or wolves or goats? Did he know he was human?" What sort of research went into *Wild Child*? Did you forage for food in the forest, naked and filthy?

TCB: Of course. Don't we all? For Victor's story, I relied on historical accounts and my own experience as a wild child. (See my 2000 *A Friend of the Earth* in this connection.)

SF: Before he even earns a name, Victor the Wild Child is described as having no shame. He would run naked, defecate on the floor, grab potatoes from a fire with bare hands. What was it like writing about such an unusual character—one who doesn't possess the basics of communication and knows nothing of "civilization"?

TCB: It was a pure joy, because we all want to revert to the primitive. Who doesn't want to snatch potatoes out of the fire or defecate on the gleaming marble floors of some potentate?

SF: "Bulletproof" grapples with the current saga of Evolution vs. Intelligent Design: "and because I was weak . . . and didn't care whether Jesus and all the saints in heaven were involved in the equation or not, I got out of my car . . . " Do you think the two groups will ever find a common ground? What are your beliefs about our humble or not-so-humble beginnings?

TCB: The most difficult thing for me in "Bulletproof" was in trying to see the other (non-Darwinian) side of the coin. This, I think, is my favorite story in the collection, because it was so surprising to me when the opposing elements came together in those last few pages.

SF: Speaking of evolution, how has your writing evolved since your first published work?

TCB: There's a whole lot more of it, for one thing. For another, I do think I've moved on from being satisfied with design only, so that I think the newer stories are a bit fuller and more character-oriented, though, of course, I continue to work in all modes and hope that I always will.

SF: You write using wide and varied voices. La Conchita: "So hip. So Honda." The Unlucky Mother of Aquiles Maldonado: "but this was no ordinary smell, no generic scent you might encounter in the alley out back of a restaurant or drifting from a barrio window—this was his mother's cooking! His mother's!" How do you do write with such a range of tone and voice?

TCB: I have no idea, except that it is my job to be able to inhabit my characters and to present their points of view credibly, amusingly, dramatically. That is half the fun, no? By the way, I love the quotes you've chosen, as I never see the stories in this sort of relation, but am instead deeply invested in each of them only in the time of its creation.

SF: Is there a pure T.C. Boyle voice?

TCB: That is for you and other readers to say. I would hope that my prose is recognizable and distinct from that of others. I wouldn't want to say—or pinpoint—how. Again, that is for the reader to determine.

SF: Of all the short stories you have published, including this new book, is there a favorite?

TCB: To my mind, these are finished stories, good stories, provocative and entertaining stories. As to favorites, that is always difficult, because I stand behind each of them. Still, if you take a peek at my response to your question about "Bulletproof," I think I may have tipped my hand here.

SF: The book jacket reads: "There is perhaps no one better than T.C. Boyle at engaging, shocking, and ultimately gratifying his readers while at the same time testing his characters' emotional and physical endurance." What happens to your emotional endurance as you are immersed in writing these stories?

TCB: Emotional endurance? An odd phrase, no? It's enough for any of us to have enough emotional endurance to make it through a single day without shooting ourselves. Let's just say that I am moved by my characters and their predicaments because these characters are just like all of us, floundering around in search of meaning.

SF: What is next—or not next—for T.C. Boyle?

TCB: Ah, there must always be a next—the new and the surprise of the new—else we experience personal entropy. As I've said above, I hope to begin a new novel shortly, the writing of which, if I am very lucky and still in possession of a willing body and active brain, should begin sometime this summer.

An Interview with Tara Masih

Tara L. Masih is editor of The Rose Metal Press Field Guide to Writing Flash Fiction *(a ForeWord Book of the Year) and author of* Where the Dog Star Never Glows, *which* Publishers Weekly *calls "striking and resonant."*

JP: *Publishers Weekly* describes *Where the Dog Star Never Glows* as "memorable for any fan of *New Yorker*-style literary short fiction." One of the Amazon reviews labeled the collection as "Multi-cultural Adventure Stories." Are there dangers in being labeled? How does being labeled sit with you? Do you agree with these comparisons and how would you describe your style of fiction?

TM: Once you make your work public, you have to be prepared for all sorts of reactions: bad reviews, angry reviews, and yes, being labeled and misunderstood. I've written before about people's need to label, and I'm used to it, so it doesn't surprise me. People like to compartmentalize; that way they have some sort of handle on the object or person. I think there's even a subtle labeling that takes place with the issue of gender. Many people automatically place writing into a certain category when they see the author is male or female.

The important thing is that both reviews were 100 percent positive, and I'm grateful to them for their insightful feedback—they each got a good handle on different parts of my writing style, which I don't like to describe myself. It's not one thing or another. It's neither traditional nor experimental. It's a blend. It's been called poetic, and it's been called sparse. It's been likened to *New Yorker* fiction, and it's been recommended to "a wide variety of readers." Labels aside, reviews are very important to small press authors to get the word out, and every positive review, subjective or not, is a chance to reach a new audience. So, best to let the reader make her or his own decisions, I think, and not get caught up in the exact language of the review.

JP: The *Field Guide to Writing Flash Fiction* seems to be doing very well (A ForeWord Book of the Year Bronze Award, #6 on Small Press Distributions' nonfiction bestseller list, a NewPages.com New & Noteworthy Book, a recommended nonfiction book on *Poets & Writers*'s Summer 2009 reading list, an Amazon.com Top-100 literary reference book). What were the challenges in putting together that terrific guide? The surprises along the way? Did you expect that sort of success?

TM: I hope this sounds prescient rather than arrogant, but yes, I knew it would be successful. Did I know it would win an award? No, I could only hope; but I knew it was being published by a good press that would reach the right audience, I knew I had a banner list of contributors who were all passionate about the subject—the real key to any kind of success—and I knew I had the training to pull it all together in a way that would make the book accessible to a general audience as well as an academic one. The main challenges came with acquiring permissions in some cases, and in getting hold of many of the rare texts needed to complete the historical introduction. Surprises? I had no idea the short-short story had such an extensive history, or that people like the late comedian Steve Allen and Bozo the Clown were writing them.

JP: The intro to the *Field Guide* is amazingly in-depth. Tell me about your research.

TM: I would not have been able to do the research without the Internet. The vast amount of information now available online allowed me to track down historical information, magazines on microfiche, and family members related to important contributors to the genre. I had to travel to various libraries, but my own hometown reference librarians were helpful in getting me information when I reached an impasse. The Internet even allowed me to track down some very rare books on the subject, original cover and all. Covers are so important when doing this kind of research. Sometimes, the jacket copy told me more than did the book itself. I kept finding more and more information I had to follow up on, and the intro that was expected to be around 12 pages became 30.

JP: As you write about race, culture, and place, your stories are set all over the world. Are you a traveler who writes, or a writer who travels? What is your next destination? Where would you love to write about? Is there a place that you are itching to investigate?

TM: I just started reading John Gardner's *The Art of Fiction*. I highly recommend it. In it, he discusses how writing and books existed before movies and TV and other modern forms of entertainment, and before we had the technology to travel more quickly and with less fear of harm. Books were a way for the reader to travel to different places and worlds, and to teach people about different cultures and people. I think I still fall into this old-fashioned, if you will, desire to take the reader to a different place, both physically and emotionally (*Heart of Darkness* by Joseph Conrad is a favorite). If I could travel and write about one place right now?—Malaysia. But I don't pick the place and then write about it. I travel, and let the stories surface on their own. Sometimes they do, sometimes they don't. It took me three trips to Puerto Rico to write the story "Delight," set in the beach town of Rincon.

JP: Despite the varied locations in which your stories take place, it seems there are themes of longing and love that are common throughout your work. Was there a conscious decision to build your stories around these ideas? Is there an overarching goal—perhaps to lessen the distance among people and cultures—in considering your writing as a whole?

TM: I think you've stated it really well, "lessening the distance between people and cultures." Being bicultural, it is virtually impossible to see only one side of any problem or issue. The world view is always kaleidoscopic. Sometimes, I think it would be easier to have the stone-hard conviction some people have that things should be a certain way. But mostly, I'm grateful to have the background I have, which allows me to float between many different worlds, and to (hopefully) bring those worlds together in some way in the imaginative worlds I get to create as a writer.

Do I think about this when I'm writing? No. I haven't planned certain themes, they just keep working themselves onto the pages. I'm obviously drawn to characters on the fringes, loners who are struggling with many of the same issues the rest of us struggle with. It's just that their predicaments are more enhanced and become more mythic when they are removed from society in some way. It's my belief that these characters make for more interesting storytelling.

JP: Of all the writing/editing-related gigs you've done, which is the one that jazzed you the most? Exhausted you the most? Strengthened you the most?

TM: Well, when I published my first two books, I waited for this huge exhilaration or epiphany to happen when I held them in my hand for the first time. I didn't get that feeling. Of course, there was excitement and joy and fulfillment, but not on the level I had expected. So I find what strengthens me the most and "jazzes" me up is that first tingle of inspiration, then following through and finishing a piece of writing I like—whether it be an essay, poem, or story—and then having it accepted. Those moments, for me, are what it's all about. The joy of the creative process, the magic that happens when you imagine something into being, and then that moment when someone says it's worth putting out there. You gain strength with each acceptance, and with the connections you make with people who get something positive from your work—whether it be a tiny piece of flash or a whole collection.

Re-Creation: an Interview with Esther Cross

Esther Cross was born in Buenos Aires in 1961. She is the author of four novels, The
Chronic Winged Apprentices *(Emecé, 1992),* The Flood *(Emecé 1993),* Banquet of the
Spider *(Tusquets, 1999), and* Radiana *(Emecé 2007); and the author of two collections
of short stories,* Divine Proportion *(Emecé, 1994) and* Kavanagh *(Tusquets, 2005). She
co-authored, along with Felix della Paolera, two books of interviews:* Bioy Casares at the
time of Writing *(Tusquets, 1987) and* Conversations with Borges *(Editorial Fuentetaja,
2007). In 2002, she released The* Insulted and the Injured, *a documentary film that she
co-wrote, co-directed, and co-produced with Alicia Martínez Pardíes. She has translated
Richard Yates's* Eleven Kinds of Loneliness *(Emecé, 2001) and William Goyen's T*he
Faces of Blood Kindred and Other Stories *(Editorial La Compañía, 2008). She has
been awarded both Fulbright and Civitella Ranieri scholarships. She teaches writing in
Casa de Letras, Buenos Aires, and for Fuentetaja, of Spain. She is published regularly in
several culture magazines and supplements.*

SP: What started you translating?

EC: I read Richard Yates's *Eleven Kinds of Loneliness*, and was overwhelmed by
it. I fell in love with the way he wrote, which is directly, sparingly—yet richly at
the same time. Also, something Yates said in one of his stories, "Builders," about
using words honestly. That's how Yates writes, he uses words honestly. I did some
research and found that *Eleven Kinds of Loneliness* had not been translated into
Spanish. I immediately decided I wanted to bring the book to the Spanish-read-
ing world.

SP: Who are some of your favorite Argentine translators?

EC: Enrique Pezzoni, who brought us *Moby Dick*. Borges, who made some great
translations despite that quite often, his style is prominent. Félix della Paolera,
who translated Dylan Thomas's *Under Milkwood*. Rodolfo Walsh, Cortázar—
among others.

SP: Tell me about your translation processes. How do you go from concept to
completed product?

EC: When I decide which book I want to translate, I read it from beginning to end to capture a general sense of it. Then I read it again to capture the rhythm of the words, the voice of the narrator, the writer's style. Then I sit down and do a first draft of the translation, not worrying about getting it right word for word, but trying to capture the rhythm, the voice, the style. Then I go through my first draft, polish the details, make sure word choice is correct, that phrases make sense, that I am getting all that is needed to make an honest translation.

SP: About the "voice" of the narrator or writer. Is that difficult to translate some-times, even if you hear it clearly in the original language?

EC: Yes. But it is also what I enjoy about being a translator. I think that is the key between a good translation and a great translation—capturing the voice.

SP: Is it difficult to get the rhythm of the words?

EC: Of course, because Spanish and English are very different languages. English is more plastic than Spanish, more pliable. Spanish is more rigid. Often, in Spanish, you need two or three words for one word in English, so sometimes you will write a very long sentence, whereas the original writer wrote the sentence economically.

SP: And what do you do when you come to sentence or phrase where you just cannot capture the proper rhythm?

EC: I never give up. With Goyen it was not easy, because he has a talking quality, derived from the oral tradition. In interviews he speaks about the breath of the sentence. His fiction reads like someone is sitting down and telling you the story. Once I was able to "hear" his voice, it was a lot easier.

SP: Now that we are talking about Goyen, what attracted you to him and his writing?

EC: His uniqueness. His powerful story telling. He has a quality that is similar to Faulkner, but of course he is not Faulkner at all. Many people call Faulkner's style Southern Gothic. I like to call Goyen's style Texan Gothic. It may be related to Faulkner, Flannery O'Connor, and Carson McCullers—but his landscape is Texas. What makes Goyen's stories impressionable is their orality, their musicality, and their subject matter. He said that he was inspired by his mother's voice, the way she talked, how she almost sang when she spoke. Goyen also loved music—which his father did not like because he thought it was effeminate, and he forbade Goyen from playing the piano—so Goyen's mother bought him one of those mail-order music courses, and he made a cardboard keyboard and sat under his covers at night and played music silently. His music playing, and as was later, his writing, had to be done in secret from his father. He was literally an undercover musician and writer. Sometimes, at night, he would pretend he was asleep and play his cardboard piano while he listened to his family talk in the living room—stories about sawmill workers, woodsmen, farmers, ranchers, out-of-work small-town people, the Ku Klux Klan. When he was older and started to write, he wrote those voices he heard while he was playing music.

SP: Which of the two was most challenging to translate—Goyen or Yates?

EC: Yates. Because he is grammatically precise. Goyen is poetic, freer, looser.

SP: The stories you selected for *La Misma Sangre* are not solely from *Faces of Blood Kindred*, but are from a number of Goyen's books. What were the factors in your selection process?

EC: I found that most of his stories fell into two groups—urban and rural. I chose the rural stories.

SP: When you translate, in general, do you feel you translate into Argentine Spanish, Latin-American Spanish, or Spaniard Spanish?

EC: If it comes down to a choice, I choose Argentine Spanish, especially if I am being published here in Argentina. If I am translating for a publisher is Spain, of course, I use Spaniard Spanish. Overall, though, I try to think I translate into the language of translation.

SP: So, when you are translating, do you feel you are copying something, or re-creating something?

EC: Re-creating. I try to be loyal to the original work. I know I can never copy something exactly, especially with language. I try to capture the *spirit* of the book. You have to re-create and not copy in order to respect another person's work. If I may draw a parallel, it is like restoring a painting. In restoration, when the restorer fills in an absent part of the painting, or re-creates a part that was damaged, he performs what is known as tratation. If you look at the painting from a normal viewing distance, you see it complete. If you move closer, put your face right up to the painting, you will notice the restoration because the restorer worked with very thin lines. The restorer did that on purpose. She is telling you, "I am restoring the original painting, but I am not the original painter." As a translator, I know I will never be able to reproduce the writer's writing. I will try to get as near to it as I can, but I will not copy the writing. That would be too difficult.

SP: Does that mean you feel a translator's presence should be somewhere in a translation?

EC: No. Those lines I spoke about are not the translator's presence, but the translator's respect. The lines are there, but not the translator.

SP: You chose to translate two North American authors. Is there any particular reason for that?

EC: I guess that it has to do with my admiration for North American writing. I believe that the 20th Century narrative was what it was because of North American writers—not only, but mostly. I also feel there is a wonderful lack of solemnity in North American English that makes it playful. North Americans use the English language with a freedom and familiarity that is wonderful.

SP: Do you find translating language of one culture into language of another culture difficult?

EC: Yes. Without a doubt. Because language is derived from culture and culture from language.

SP: What do you do when you come to a word or phrase or a scene that does not make sense in your culture?

EC: I always try to stay true to the original. There are some exceptions, especially in word-choice, but the scenes must remain in the same order for the reader to understand the situation.

SP: What about metaphors, similes, and double meanings. How do you deal with them?

EC: You have to give up something sometimes when dealing with figurative language. It's inevitable. You strive to make it best as possible. Changing a word is hard, but not impossible. Sometimes you can find a similar figure of speech—just as long as you don't change meaning. Sometimes when you are meticulously reading a text you will find figurative language that the author did not intend. Usually that happens with the genius writers. Their unconscious minds at work. If you try to reproduce any of that, it is kind of like trying to show the submerged part of an iceberg. You can attempt to show as much of it as you are able, but you will never be able to show it all. That would be too ambitious. There is just too much mass there. Lifting the iceberg out of the water would change the aesthetics of the tip.

SP: What about story titles? Do you often have to change them to make meaning?

EC: Quite often, but not always. This is because titles are an introduction to the story, or an overall interpretation of the text. If that introduction or interpretation does not make sense in the culture of the translated language, a change must be made—something representative.

SP: Do you take a long time getting to know the author you are translating?

EC: Yes. (She holds up a two-inch thick book that she has held in her lap during our conversation, a biography about John Fante). I would like to translate his letters and that is why I am reading his biography. I always research the author.

SP: Why do you feel it is important to get to know the author?

EC: If I know the author, I know how his mind works. If I know how his mind works, I know how he uses language.

SP: When you are working on a translation, how do you work—do you focus solely on the translation, or are you able to juggle other things, like your own writing?

EC: I would prefer to work solely on the translation. Keep my mind focused only on that. Sometimes though, I have to work on two projects and it works out. It's difficult, but it can be done if it is necessary. You have to have a lot of faith in yourself if you want to work on your own writing while you are translating a genius.

SP: Then, do you feel that your own writings and your translations complement one other, or contradict one other?

EC: I think they complement one another, like all your lifetime writings do. They are linked. They are united. From each translation I make, I learn something. When I go back to my own writing I feel I have changed, I feel I am a better writer.

SP: What kind of advice would you give to writers about to embark on their first translation project?

EC: A translation will never be perfect; you just have to get it as close as possible. The closer you get it, the better the translation is. Have tenacity. Never give up, even if it feels like it is not working. Have a very good dual-language dictionary, and read all you can about the author.

SP: As a final word, then, what is the major role of a translator?

EC: To introduce the reader to the writer, then step back, and disappear.

Tiny Excerpts From Small Presses

Jane Bradley
Are We Lucky Yet?
Press 53

You smell his man-smell the way a recovered alcoholic makes the mistake of suck-ing in the scent of a whiskey floating by on a waiter's try.

from "Lost Souls Go Wandering"
originally published in *Confrontation*

John Brandon
Citrus County
McSweeney's

At the age of twenty-nine, he'd already experienced three things that mostly only happened in books. (1) As an infant, he'd been stolen from the hospital by a nurse. The duration of the abduction had been six hours and he'd been unharmed, but still. (2) He had unexpectedly inherited money. It was only $190 grand and he'd blown it in two years traveling around Erope, but still. (3) He had chosen his permanent residence by throwing a dart at a map. There hadn't been a town where the dart had stuck, but there weren't many towns in Citrus County, Florida. Citrus County was a couple hours north of St. Petersburg, on what people called the Nature Coast, which Mr. Hibma had gathered was a title of default; there was nature because there were no beaches and no amusement parks and no hotels and no money. There were rednecks and manatees and sink-holes. There were insects, not gentle crickets but creatutres with stingers and pincers and scorn in their hearts.

Miracle Boy and Other Stories
Pinckney Benedict
Press 53

My father flung himself into the manure pit, to save his oldest son. They tell me that he was overcome by the methane in an instant. Maybe he managed a brief laugh before he succumbed, as Albertus had. My uncle, who was stacking hay in the loft with my younger brothers, and who arrived at the mouth of the pit only seconds after my father did, followed him without hesitation. Then, selflessly, Ptolmey, the older of the twins by a matter of minutes. The Cunobelinus. Did any of them, did they all manage a final chuckle at the absurdity of their situation? They inhaled the methane, as unbreathable as the atmosphere of some distant alien planet, and they died, while I stood in front of the dairy barn and watched the car with the beautiful woman in it dissapear down the road to the west.

from "The Angel's Heritage"
originally published in *Appalachian Heritage Magazine*

Hot Springs
Geoffrey Becker
Tin House

Her mother was walking out to the sidewalk, nude except for her running shoes, the reflective strips of which flickered in the thin light from the street lamps. Her boyish body was right there on public display for the neighborhood: her flat bottom; her small, white breasts; all her most secret places. She paused for a moment and looked at the house, and their eyes met. Her mother smiled and waved, then gave a thumbs-up, fluffed her hair, and proceeded to walk down the street.

Test Ride on the Sunnyland Bus: A Daughter's Civil Rights Journey
Ana Maria Spagna
Bison Books/University of Nebraska Press

For my dad, I thought, maybe running was transcendental like prayer, liberating like a beatnik road trip, only minus the drinks and the chicks and, well, everything, but the wind in your hair, and maybe when you're over forty and the father of three, the wind in your hair is enough. That, and the fat slabbing off like arctic ice, feet slapping like a metronome, and sometimes, every so often, sunlight slicing through the smog and clarity at last!

Agaat
Marlene Van Nierkerk, Translated by Michiel Heyns
Tin House

how does sickness begin? botulism from eating skeletons but where do the skeletons come from? Ioco-disease nenta preacher-tick-affliction smut-ball bunk black-rust glume-blotch grubs beetles snails moths army caterpillars all inisible onsets soil is more long-suffering than wheat more long-suffering than sheep soil sickens slowly in hidden depths from tilling from flattening with the back of the spade from heavy grubbing in summer wind i am neither sheep nor wheat did i think then i was god that i had to lie and take it did i think then i w as a mountain or a hill or a ridge . . .

The Physics of Imaginary Objects
Tina May Hall
University of Pittsburgh Press

The townspeople who side with my mother would like to fill the hole with tons of dirt and gravel. I've spent innumerable town meetings explaining that a hole is not something to be filled; there is no way to do it. The only thing to do with a hole is to take measurements and photograph it and tell it over and over. And to stand next to it, regularly, as close as possible.

The Butterfly Collector
Black Lawrence Press
Fred McGavran

If the staff here and television shows are any indication, fat people have taken over the country. Sometimes the people on television start hitting each other, but they are so fat that no one is ever hurt. People watching from an amphitheater yell, "Jerry, Jerry!" that must mean, "Hit them harder," because the people on stage keep right on pounding. Then come the commercials, where everybody is normal size again. So maybe the fat people haven't taken over the country after all. Maybe it's just here.

from "Lillian"
originally published in *Storyglossia*

The Illustrated Version of Things
FC2
Affinity Konar

So of course, she hits me first. She has all the grace of soap in a sock but her hands don't clean me, she just lays me down, she lays me all to splattery and my eyes, they're outbleared by some sting she's put there, thick as signature. And I choose only to lie there, becuase when you're the one who gets hit first you can lie about anything.

The Taste of Penny
Dzanc Books
Jeff Parker

When Russians, in the course of normal conversation, describe a lecture as "exciting and inspirational" the Russian word for which is "pathetichiske", I hear only "pathetic." At the kiosks late at night, young men ask for "preservativi" and I'm imagining cured pears when it's the Russian word for "condoms"; when I hear "narciss" on the lips of a young woman strolling through the garden with her lover my immediate mind thinks "self-involved prick" when it somehow means "daffodil.

from "False Cognate"
originally published in *Best American Nonrequired Reading 2006*

CYAN JAMES

I Go to the Ruined Place:
Contemporary Poems in Defense of Global Human Rights
edited by Melissa Kwasny & M.L. Smoker

Lost Horse Press
ISBN-13: 978-0-9800289-7-3
2009. 168pp. $18.00

Hard stories are not hard to find. Just hard to listen to. Hard to analyze, too, when you hear the catch in the teller's voice, and see water beginning to crowd the corners of her eyes, and you smell old blood.

It's like that when you read the poetry collection *I Go to the Ruined Place*. It begins in Sandra Alcosser's "Blue Vein":

> To be human is of the earth, crumbling
> Is humus. Is humility. Bleeding
> We fall down. A dog licks our blood. Sometimes
> We eat songbirds because we are hungry
> A poet might refuse to speak after
> Shelling. Another sings until they starve
> Him, not because he plots against the state
> Because he makes his own song.

There is, immediately, the conflation of earth and human flesh, the evocation of the creation story, a slight echo of nursery rhyme, and the thematic introduction of the poet as simultaneously fragile and enduring. Of course, it's not really the poet who lasts. It's the song.

The poems in *I Go to the Ruined Place* are songs that want to last. These poets want to embed their words like thrown stones that will not easily be forgotten.

The collection spans a wide range of work detailing particular abuses; the thematic backbone that holds the poems together is the act of witnessing the violations humans enact on one another. It's a dizzying and sometimes heart-cracking read, at times uneven, often compelling, full of vivid details.

A collection of this scope and deliberate ambition cannot escape certain questions. First of all, is it even poetry's role to address human rights abuses?

It proves to be a tricky endeavor. Trauma is by no means taboo in poetry. But readers so commonly encounter trauma, it is challenging to find words that prick hard enough without seeming contrived. Words, particularly when one struggles to express the strongest of feelings, often wear thin; sometimes the threads fail, the fabric of communication tears, and the poets are left naked, somewhat ugly, not quite sure where to put their hands (or where they want us to put our beliefs).

Words cannot always do proper shrift to carnage. The attempt is intrinsically dicey, because poetry imposes an order and structure, a logic of cohesion, where, in the midst of trauma, no such order may be detectable. Yet the poets gathered here try hard. Ellen Bass, in "Bearing Witness," writes:

> But we draw a line at the sadistic,
> as if our yellow plastic tape would keep harm
> confined. We don't want to know
> what generations of terror do to the young
> who are fed like cloth
> under the machine's relentless needle.

Her poem attributes injustice to the machine-like nature of civilization's march, and even helps us question our own complicity in the construction of mechanized injustice. Here she succeeds where many of the other poets in the collection seem balked by the enormity of what they attempt to describe.

By dealing exclusively in trauma and oppressive violence, many of the poems in this collection rub the humanity away from the very people they are trying to tell us about—the litany of rough images carves these people into mere, abused shells, which could be counterproductive to the collection's whole endeavor.

It helps to preserve and restore humanity when the poet is artistically skilled, has practical experiences in injustice, and is, above all, willing to take a few risks. Tamiko Beyer runs such a risk in "Report":

> —burn cigarettes burn palm ear
> shatter collarbone kick slash face
> burn matches burn stomach crack
> ribs kick puncture face burn
> cigarettes burn forearm thigh
> crack skull kick puncture stomach
> burn cigarettes burn palm ear
> shatter collarbone kick slash face
> burn matches burn stomach crack

ribs kick puncture face burn
cigarettes burn forearm thigh
crack skull kick puncture stomach
burn cigarettes burn palm slash
ear face skull burn palm

The poem is a simple conglomeration of hard, plain words repeated without narrative. The violence connoted is brutal. But it's the repetition that really starts to compel the reader—the relentless patterns concretely set up the rhythm of trauma and dramatically demonstrate the mindless banality of torture.

Is this use of accrued violence effective? What *is* the most effective way, after all, to depict the terror of trauma without sensationalizing, glamorizing or soft-pedaling it? There is the danger that details told in an especially lurid fashion allow the reader to suspend the belief these poems demand. A sense of hopelessness may be instilled as well—the reader may not know how to respond, especially if the poet strikes a sour note. For example, let's consider Ellen Bass's "Bearing Witness" again:

God is
the kicked child, the child
who rocks alone in the basement,
the one fucked so many times
she does not know her name, her mind
burning like a star.

The details beg the reader to be shocked. Yet the final image is somewhat clichéd. Are we meant to read this as an echo of the child's limitations, or simply as a weak metaphor? Christi Kramer demonstrates a better command of detail in "The Recaller, the Reckoner. The Effacer of Sins. The Witness." Two priests rigged with bombs who are about to detonate themselves during a church service. But a man serving tea gets in the way:

Glass, gold flecked glass, coal, fractured sugar cube, sliver of
     gold spoon, bird from
the pattern on the rug set loose, prayer beads unstrung, heart, morsel
     of date, no sound,
a window, a window, steam of cascading tea—bent bowing, light,
Silver serving tray rolled away.

The details themselves tell the story. Kramer stays stark and focused. Her understatement accentuates the subject, and the delicacy of the diction creates an even starker contrast to explosiveness of the violence.

Her poem reminds us that it is not enough, in some senses, to have a traumatic story; one must also practice traumatic storytelling. Sadly, the task is complicated by translation. The translator must "get it right," for one thing. And then the poet is at a remove of one language's distance, and cannot be sure if the poem conveys the exact linguistic meanings intended, much less unpacks its cultural baggage accurately and in a way a Western reader can understand and appreciate. So not only is artistry involved—cultural communication must occur as well, and this depends on the skill, intention, and integrity of both poet and reader.

At times, it also seems like a struggle when some of the Western writers strain to express the depth of the human rights injustices happening across an ocean, in a different language. There are, however, outstanding poems that resonate. One of them is Joel Long's "Taking Down the House," about a woman searching through rubble for her son:

> *Go inside when the wind blows*, she told him.
> *Go inside.* Her son is a stone. His teeth
> spill in her hands like rice. Her son is God.
> She does not recognize him. She lifts stones,
> his hand like cold tar when frost comes,
> lifts, bringing the floor light, bringing dust
> radio, dead of voices, the speaker cone torn.
> *Go inside when the wind blows. Go inside.*
> The wind is blowing now.
> The wind is blowing now.

The images are appropriate to the place and time. The language is concise and measured; it has propulsion, shows mastery of tone and rhythm, and sets up an engaging narrative arch clinched with evocative use of repetition and viewpoint.

Poems like these delight the reader and provide motivation for sifting through the rest of the anthology. And even in the weaker poems, there are flashes of brilliance and chunks of clear insight that will stick with readers.

There remains a final question: What sort of response do these poems desire? Are we supposed to simply bear witness along with the poets? Or does a poetry collection like this demand us to somehow take action? It's difficult to say. Many of the poems indicate no concrete action; many of them talk of injustice that happened long ago. The poems that simply portray anecdotes or stir readers' emotions risk ignoring the greater opportunity of urging redress and lasting change. Perhaps it's the poems' accumulative weight that eventually demands a response, and a determination to prevent these injustices from happening again. Perhaps there are even fragments of hope:

> But one day you wake up and the sun is shining on the snow.
> Suddenly the iron weight is off your chest. Nothing is changed.
> The boy's head is still torn apart by a bomb. The husband is still forced
> under and drowned. The months of beatings and shocks don't go away.
> But for a moment it feels fresh, like being born again.

—Ann Hunkins, "One Day You Wake Up"

CHARLES HOOD

Nox
Anne Carson

New Directions
ISBN-13: 978-0811218702
2010. n.p. $29.95

Nox is a book centered on absence—it negates even its own book-ness, since it is an unpaginated, accordion-folded scroll with the heft of a Bible, delivered in a box that is coffin/decompression chamber/treasure chest (circle one), a box whose cover just says *Nox* in almost imperceptible ink and has a torn photo of a lad in goggles and swing trunks sepia toned onto the front lid. Elegant, minimal, enigmatic.

The photo, we learn, is of the author's late brother, a Kerouac bad boy who lived abroad, mostly out of contact, and died similarly, and whose absence has left a considerable wound. And the title? Latin for Greece's Nyx, the goddess of night, it calls to mind the term to put the kibosh on something—my boss nixed my request for a raise—as well as the recently discovered third moon of Pluto, that once-planet which now hangs around the faculty water cooler, demoted to adjunct status. *Nox* could be coroner's shorthand for finding a residue of noxious chemicals in the suicide victim's lungs. If you are unkind you note that it rhymes with bagels and lox. Way to go Red Sox. Nox nox, who's there.

So an anti-book with night for a title. There is, quickly let us read into the record, much amazing work here. Anne Carson is one of those poetry gods whose work, on average, is so far beyond mine it makes me want to kill things, myself included. This book is flat out brilliant. It is also (as of this review's writing) sold out. The initial print run sold out, other than a $150 collector's edition. We all should praise this, and maybe envy it.

Brilliant then. That it also is, oh, I don't know—self-indulgent?—may or may not change its value for you. In the end, so were *The Cantos*, and Pound remains brighter for me than the Pleiades. Perhaps all of poetry is one long act of self-indulgence.

Taxonomy before judgment. Here more specifically is what the book is: it is a replica of a section-numbered notebook on grief in the form of a Japanese scroll that also is a meditation on/renewal of vows with a poem about a deceased brother by the Latin poet Catullus. Oh, we all remember him—Pound wrote about him.

Some pages are single words; other pages are photographs; others replica scotch tape and graph paper. If one just takes the English language text, we end up with a sad and moving exploration of what it means to grieve and remember. But this is also something more: book as artifact, book as memory log.

Okay, right on—except with George Oppen's *Daybooks* or Claudia Rankine's *Don't Let Me Be Lonely* or even the postmodern fortune cookie scraps of Sappho, their fragments and excised spaces draw power from the implied social contract of things being left out. There is a sense of negative space being used as a compositional device, and also that the page's collaged-in blank un-said-ness ties back into what is known but cannot be said, because it implies the horrors of racism or the speaker's ambivalence about being a war veteran or even just the nibbling insect mandibles of time. Their negotiations via silence and blank space (however voluntary or involuntary the creation of that blank space is) reveal a larger historical or socio-political commentary. In contrast, with this book Carson's silences are the silences of grief or horror or incomprehension, as she tries to find a *private* way to understand a human life no longer directly being lived on this planet.

If a book like *Kaddish* is grief as lunch-hour at Home Town Buffet, *Nox* is grief as a breadcrumb trail through the forest. The breadcrumbs happen to be diamonds (lucky us) and the forest can represent the process any of us goes through as we process our own losses and absences. Yet publishing a book (as opposed to writing one or keeping a journal or seeing Herr Doktor Professor Shrink on Tuesdays at 2)—to *publish* a book is to imply an audience, and an audience implies readers, and readers imply language that connects on some level, any level, even if it is the level of hopscotching hybrid language poetry metacognition.

And that is where I say that some of the diamond-bright croutons ain't enough. I can't connect enough to care. *Of course*, you may now say, *of course you don't, you're a man*. We all know how bad men are at having feelings and shit, especially feelings of loss and regret. But I don't know. Frank Bidart is a man, and his tours of sadness and loss in "Ellen West" or "The War of Vaslav Nijinsky" do it to me every time. And it's not like I haven't done my homework—dead parents, runaway children, failed marriages, lost jobs and lost friends and lost cars and lost manuscripts: it's not like I haven't paid my own personal dues in the country western bar of sadness and longing. It seems to me that to create a shrine to a person living or dead via a very singular (some might say pretentiously singular) book implies that at book's end, the reader will care, or at least see why the author cares, about that person. We will be invited to participate in the understanding of the mystery of a life, a family, a death, a meaning.

I want with all my language poetry-fed heart to enjoy an otherwise blank page that replicates a scrap of paper that says "*multa*/see above *multus multa mul-*

tum." But I don't, I don't enjoy it. And that is it—that is the whole page, what I just quoted—the referent-less directive to "see above." See God? See the rest of the book? See the ceiling light's glass bowl filled little dead bugs? Right, I have tried to learn languages, have done translation, understand the infinite pleasures of found text. But to me the "multa multa" page isn't wise or insightful, it just conjugates pabulum.

That I am put off surprises me since the next items on my personal reading list are recent books by Ron Silliman and Carol Snow, technical articles from the *Journal of Mammalogy*, abstruse but well-illustrated art history. Stray words and random associations light my candle more times than not. Maybe I need a sense of playfulness if we're doing minimalism, and not the Rothko funeral chapel of black on black under 20 watt bulbs. Much of the book does work. Here's is an example of a great line: "I wanted to fill my elegy with light of all kinds. But death makes us stingy." To consider what we hoard in death makes for provocative reading.

And yet here is an example of a not-great line pair (from a facing page to section 10.3): "**atque**/see above *atque*." Now previously in the book we did already handle this charming potsherd of a word, so this is not without context. And it follows a series of pages playing with and off of the word *ave*, with all the Christian tradition that implies (including Frank O'Hara's sex-in-the-movies poem, "Ave Maria"). I "get" why she herself might put it in a journal or day book. I just don't get what I am supposed to get, reading it now. I need more candles, or else to have the breadcrumbs closer together.

Non quo, sed quomodo: not by whom, but in what manner. If she wasn't already famous and if I didn't approach her breadcrumbs with the reverence we pay holy relics, what would we make of this? I am not sure we would enjoy it, be sustained by it. But maybe so: some friends love this project, and the fact is, we *do* know she is good and serious and famous, and as such, we *do* read it open-heartedly. There is never language without context, just as there is never loss without regret, or it wouldn't be loss. And it may be too that even if I claim that 20 percent (or twice that or half that) doesn't work, that hardly negates the other percentage that does work, and in fact works wisely and well.

All that said, I still want bigger candles. In a parallel universe or out past the undiscovered fourth moon of Pluto, I long for a remix version of *Nox* that is less nocturnal and more crepuscular, perhaps even (in Carson's bravest act of all) fully and eye-blindingly diurnal.

MARGARET ROZGA

High Notes
Lois Roma-Deeley

Benu Press
ISBN-13: 978-0-9815163-9-4
2010. 67pp. $16.95

"You cannot sing a song and not change your condition," declared Bernice John-son Reagon in a 1991 interview with Bill Moyers. Poet Lois Roma-Deeley affirms such a belief in the power of music in *High Notes*, her third collection of poems (Benu Press, April 2010). Roma-Deeley's work also makes clear that while the song may be free, the life that produces it often is not. A song is a hard-won ac-complishment; its power to provide moments of reprieve and to forge an endur-ing vision of earthly salvation moves first through pain.

Roma-Deeley's background testifies as well to a belief in the integration of the arts. She has collaborated with visual artist Beth Shadur to produce works that weave words into paintings with themes of identity and social concern. She and Shadur were co-curators of the widely exhibited, three-phase, five-year Poetic Dialogue project. In its third phase, "Collaborative Vision," this project paired 30 poets with 30 visual artists to create together works that combined words with images. *High Notes* itself began as a collaborative project, a jazz opera, with music by composer Christopher Scinto.

The poems in *High Notes* deliver with lyrical intensity specific dramatic plot points in a story of the struggle for beauty and music in a racially segregated world. In subtle ways, the book contextualizes the incipient civil rights and women's movements. An Italian American and professor of Women's Studies as well as Creative Writing, Roma-Deeley presents a group of characters who "represent Italian-American, African-American/White, African-American and British origins." She reports that audiences have been receptive to her portrayal of these characters. Her enthusiastic publishers, LeRoy Chappell and Lesly Chappell, who are African American and Native American, respectively, focus on literature with social justice content.

The 1950s world of these poems is a far cry from popular images of 1950s in-nocence. It is a world where addiction seems like the only possible alternative to a thwarted pursuit of happiness. On tour through cities like Detroit and Kansas City, these characters find a grim reality of cheap hotel rooms where "yellow walls grow thin." Each of the five characters suffers an addiction, whether to drugs (sax-ophonist Jake), power (drug-dealer Harry), grief (Sugar Baby), anger (Jasmine), or hope (the angel). In the opening poems, each character can only sing the recur-ring line of an addiction, each voicing a variation on the insistent, "Give-it-to-me; give-it-to-me; give-it-to-me . . . "

Basic facts of these intertwining stories are outlined in the list of dramatis personae. The poems themselves, then, like redemptive songs, plumb the depths beyond that outline. The language, with frequent internal and end rhyme, pulls the reader from the sidelines into the experience. Jasmine June, like a band leader counting the tempo, sounds out a series of words that echo the long o sound: "I already know/about Jim Crow." Thus when "the music finally flows/into the trumpet, piano, bass and saxophone," that music is a source of power to sustain her beyond the immediate moment: "I can see the future." Given her sensitivity to the song even before it is played, she can move beyond the cash counting task that begins this poem into a vision of a possible future:

> I have this feeling
> a thousand wings are beating
> against "Colored Only" signs . . .
> this, our some day, some time,
> this seventh heaven dreaming . . .

Still this vision of a heaven on earth seems only remotely possible, and there is the question of all the life between songs until that "some day." Even moments of success have undercurrents. Sugar Baby notes that "Now the light inside my eyes is raw, / and every time the audience applauds/ it hurts."

Into this volume of mostly free verse poems, Roma-Deeley weaves the firm logic of English sonnets, sometimes where they might at first seem most surpris-ing. In "Arguing with Angels," for example, three subtly rhymed quatrains build toward the concluding couplet and the key question of this book, "How will you live?" The sonnet's last line provides the answer as gesture. "I make my hands a cup: with only this." Likewise in "Improvisational Memory" Jasmine raises from her point of view a similar, though more forward looking, question: "Now what will you do?

Bernice Johnson Reagon in that 1991 interview explained to Bill Moyers that "the purpose of a song is to get singing going." Her explanation does more than belabor the obvious. It tells a truth about music: its effects endure beyond the sounding of the last note. It also tells a truth about freedom and redemption:

the arts have power to transform experience, to sustain us, to point the way to freedom even as they provide a freeing experience.

For the characters in *High Notes*, the art that carries such an effect is most particularly music. For Roma-Deeley, poetry shares in this power. The surprising and inevitable open ending of Lois Roma-Deeley's *High Notes* concurs with Johnson Reagon's assertion. "The Biography of Now" concludes with another seeming truism: "In the stepping—/the lifting of the foot, the foot set down into the dust—/we are moved." The hidden difficulties of lifting the foot and setting it down in dust are made clear in the music of these poems even as their music also lifts the foot.

RAMOLA D

Live from Fresno y Los
Stephen Gutierrez

Bear Star Press
ISBN-13: 978-0979374531
2009. 120pp. $16.00

"Don't they say those on the outside try hardest to get inside? And the farther away you are, the greater your effort?" That's the voice of the young maintenance man dreamer and playwright in the innovative "Lucky Guys"—oddly obsessed with his nose, despairing over his sick father, fantasizing he is JFK as he raises a flag. He then drafts a play tracing the rise of his favorite burger joint in the greater Eastside—a play, intriguingly enough, that features mirror images from his world: a son "abominably ugly, full of self-castigation," a father "afflicted with a terrible disease," and a storyline that rocks and flails and weaves itself sinuously into his own life. So a character created merges into a character he creates, and a picture emerges of a life among the "vatos of Los," characters vibrant and alive, taking refuge with each other, through the modishly self-conscious lens of his voice, often deprecating, comic, almost absurdist, and, ultimately, in the freshness of its simplicity and youth, raw and engaging.

Voice in fact strikes a reigning power in these eight stories that make up *Live from Fresno y Los*, a Before Columbus Foundation 2010 American Book Award winner. From the sadly dissipated La Helen, whom La Gloria meets in La Marqueta many years after "the old days," to the recording star Freddy Fenders, who drinks his loneliness down, to the striving, thriving Harold, who is unafraid to embrace his inner "cholo," yet is made to pay for it by his seemingly threatened and less radical Mexican-American "vatos." Voice leads us into these stories, with their small, intimate cameos of lives in streets and barrios in East Los Angeles, lived often on the edge or the middle of a pervading violence, punctuated with uncertainty and a sense of displacement. What we hear is the rough simplicity of energy and youth, distilled through a chorus of voices compelling in their honesty, insistent in their intimacy. Even Chato in "Chato's Day," whose essay of violence with his girlfriend stops one cold as he becomes, if not entirely sympathetic, credibly human through the close reveal we have of his life via an intimate narrative voice. Whether told in first or third-person, it's an insider's voice: direct, candid, clear; it doesn't take long for each story to hook a reader, the sharp clarity of the voice sounding like a friend on the telephone—persuasive and intent.

Mood, too, is drawn with delicate deliberation. In prose with echoes of Hemingway and Diaz—almost minimalist yet adroit with description, just imagistic enough to compel attention—Gutierrez excels in evoking the mood of a time and place. In "Just Everything," seemingly a simple story of Walter and Nadia's love, of a moon "the size of a grapefruit," and nights of rendezvous, all sorts of things combine to give a sense of edgy nostalgia to the piece: the shift midway in perspective from the narrator to Walter, the retrospective narration, the side stories (of Walter's friend Fernando, busted for theft and smuggling, of Nadia and her friends), the evocation, not just of a moment, but a whole period of time. There is also a shift in perspective from the narrator to Walter, the retrospective narration, the side stories—of Walter's friend Fernando, busted for theft and smuggling, of Nadia and her friends, the evocation, not just of a moment, but a whole period of time. "The Barbershop," focused as it is on a father's last trip for a haircut, swerves nevertheless into bittersweet nostalgia through the sons' childhood memories of their father driving through their neighborhood, and becomes as much about a father's love for his sons as the sons' love for their father.

While the turns and flashbacks feel unstructured and confusing on occasion, some stories stand out for their brilliant, improvisational feel—the sense of a new form, a new language informing them: the magical, jazz-infused "Feeding the People" is one, in which Walter Ramirez, ardent musician, singing "Helen's Song" on stage (with Santana) detours into singing of another Helen, who, amazingly, shows up in the audience. "Harold, All-American" is another—a compendious sweep of a story, an almost-novella, which takes us through both Harold's journey from Catholic school to public school to embracing his Mexican identity, and Frank, the narrator's, own journey from public school to Catholic school to becoming a writer, and all their struggles to know and be known—"barrio-tainted maybe, suburban-influenced to some degree . . . We were all ethnic, different, separate. We were stamped alien against everybody else in America. And that's a lie too, a big lie."

Women in these stories are girlfriends or wives, central in some essential way to the heroes of these modern-day quests yet apparently never center themselves. The exception is La Gloria, who speaks of her once-friend La Helen—a story that, as the title warns, leaves you wanting more. Yet these are gritty, clear-eyed stories of lives and relationships pursued through adversity, of special East Los neighborhoods remembered, and people loved—the emotional heart of these stories anchors this collection, never sentimentalizing their subject, often very lightly touched on, just calmly glinting through.

ADAM GALLARI

Drenched: Stories of Love and Other Deliriums
Marisa Matarazzo

Soft Skull Press
ISBN-13: 978-1-59376-271-1
2010, 248 Pages; $14.95

Marisa Matarazzo's *Drenched: Stories of Love and Other Deliriums*, consists of ten loosely interconnected stories divided into two parts, and though this division is an unnecessary break in an otherwise free-flowing book, readers should be prepared to be immersed in a restless world where the line between reality and the landscape of the mind is ineffably blurred. Matarazzo's universe is opaque, one of, as her subtitle suggests, almost feverish delusion in which characters remain clouded by a veritable fog that seems to obscure all but the hint of their outline. In *Drenched*, Matarazzo begets fewer full beings and more human mirages, visible at a distance but who, up close, vanish like vapor whisked away by a strong ocean breeze.

From the opening bravura of a story entitled "Deliquesce": "Our liaison. One summer long. It ends when I break the building. I meant to impress her. And cool her, in the heat. Grievously I'll never know if it does. Because she disappears, washes away, gone. Vapor." Matarazzo announces herself as a writer first and foremost wedded to the beauty and mystique of language. It comes as no surprise, then, for the reader to discover that she is the daughter of a linguist, and not surprisingly, Matarazzo seems to know where her strengths lie. Initially, her work appears much less interested in offering the reader a clearly defined narrative than in regaling them with the musicality of her lyrical prose styling.

"Deliquesce" takes as its theme the volatile and dynamic love affair of a nameless female narrator and her woman-acrobat lover, whom she presents as:

> the strongest and most delicate looking woman I have ever seen. Her torso: compact, muscles like cables wrapped in skin. Her hands: smooth and pale and straight fingered. Glimpsing them, I wish I had a fever. She would press her hands to my forehead and my temple. Her face: soft cheeks over strong bones. Blue eyes—deeply blue, like paint-tube colors. They are cerulean. But they sometimes change—azure, cobalt, ultramarine. Long back eyelashes she flaps open and closed, a little slowly.

Here Matarazzo offers readers their first encounter with the main narrative voice, known later as His Love, and who will dip in and out of many subsequent stories, which run the gamut from the comically absurd to the remarkably poignant. In "Freshet" a town of adults overcome with frustration at all of their baby-sitters having become sex-crazed and pregnant, devises a plan to regain autonomy over their own lives—give their children over to the ocean: "The kids gather close. The tides rise. Rolls over the sand. Waves stretch and stand high, then break and crumble and foam over the kids. A few are knocked over. They splash into the spume, and flop and turn. Some stand, slip, fall again. Upon withdrawal, wave water cradles the spilled kids, rocks them clear from the beach and into the sea. Some kids notice. Point, grunt, perplexed until they capsize and are slipstreamed away." And in "Hangdangling" two young lovers are spirited away by flood waters while performing sexual acrobatics on a trapeze-like apparatus attached to the mast of the ship they've constructed together.

In *Drenched*, Matarazzo conjures a haven where even the most insane and vile seem acceptable, understood as harmonious with the rules of this world. Matarazzo is not one who lacks for imagination or talent, and her mind, which so effortlessly jumps from the illogical to the whimsical, offers readers moments that, at their best, leave one squirming and uncomfortable yet transfixed and unable to look away. Such is the case with Danguy Weck, the child protagonist of "Cataplasms" who, after a possibly lurid encounter with his neighbor (Matarazzo keeps most hard detail off the page) takes a knife to his voice box and then attempts amateur surgery on his attacker, Budweiser Dad:

> (Danguy) swabs his knife and Budweiser Dad's abdomen with rubbing alcohol. Makes a clean entrance into the liver area of his stomach. The diamond knife parts skin like it is melting it. Carefully poking, he locates the liver . . . grabs hold of it. Lifts and pulls it out. With his other hand he grabs the fish from the bucket. It is barely moving. The fish in his left hand, the liver in his right, he notices they weigh about the same.

After which, Danguy Weck and his sister, Little Sis, are spirited away by their father to live in a Russian hideout pod located somewhere within the Arctic Circle. And even where absurdity seems to reign, Matarazzo's writing succeeds when she allows the reader to access the humanity of her characters, no matter how muffled that humanity might be.

However, despite all of its merits, *Drenched* too often relies on an unnecessary cuteness and the gimmick of the idea rather than the power of its rendering. Unlike Marilynne Robinson, John Banville, or even Jeanette Winterson, all of whose brilliantly baroque sentences and paragraphs build upon each other, making the next just as necessary as the last, Matarazzo seems, perhaps, an author in love with her own ability to put words on the page, however meaningless they might be to the scene at hand. Matarazzo's book would be strengthened by being condensed. Her greatest strength is also her greatest weakness, as too often the reader is led through a world of empty details that masquerade as lyricism, where after too many diamonds one becomes blinded by their shine and numb to their effect.

"Fisty Pinions" serves as an example Matarazzo's over-writing. It follows the obsession of one Ronnie Scartoon—many of Matarazzo's characters possess such sexually ambiguous names yet, with one notable exception, are always female—with Ashlyn Aschenbecker, a tragically beautiful young woman who, after the death of her parents, has attached ashtrays to her breasts and chain-smokes into them. Such overt irony (Aschenbecker is German for ashtray) shifts the focus away from her skill, and the long paragraphs to nowhere, and let what otherwise would be engaging and powerful moments fizzle into tedious listing:

> Then the big sound of her heart. Not beating, just one long, loud boom: This is what it is like to see Ashlyn Aschenbecker at the sushi counter in the supermarket. Ronnie Scartoon turns and examines the shrimp through the case. Lays her hand against the cool curve of the glass. A thin fog outlines her palm and fingers. She removes her hand, leaves a sweaty print. She looks at her shoes. Steps one in front of the other. They click softly on the linoleum. She crosses thirty-two tiles. Stops. Breathes. Looks. Ashlyn Aschenbecker is wearing brown boots with worn and pointed toes. The cuffs of her jeans break just past the ankle of her boots and drag lower behind her heel . . .

Moreover, when she attempts to temper the magic of her world with reality she stumbles. "Henchmen," the longest and most linear of *Drenched*'s ten stories, returns once more to "His Love" who is stalking a mysterious Kelly Green, the male CEO of Target, in order to assassinate him. When she encounters the first of Green's henchman, Tom—the other two being Dick and Harry, another unnecessary coyness—the reader experiences the thrill of the unknown, yet both subsequent interactions with Harry and Dick follow a similar progression to that of Tom. Soon it becomes apparent to the reader that nothing will happen, and by the time the fourth and final henchman, an unnamed German characterized only through the occasional asides about his accent, arrives, whatever tension might have been built has evaporated from the page, leaving the reader more curious than satisfied with "Henchmen's" sudden and less than grand dénouement. Frustrating, as it has come from a writer who has repeatedly shown she is capable of much better.

In all, Matarazzo's debut is an imaginative and evocative piece of sensual prose fiction, one that will surely arouse emotion in its readers, and garner as many adamant defenders as it will harsh critics. And though Matarazzo is not a writer to be taken lightly, hopefully as she grows, she will rely more on her prose than her ideas to carry the bulk of the weight. *Drenched* is an ambitious first effort, and one which should be applauded for the risks it takes. Fear of not reaching the other side of the canyon is no reason for one not to try and jump it, and in *Drenched* we have Matarazzo's raw skill on display, a skill that hopefully, with time and maturity will deliver the book such an author is capable of writing.

The Bad Life
Frédéric Mitterrand

Soft Skull Press
ISBN-13: 978-1593762605
2010. 320pp. $16.95

"You can never be too careful; nothing ever unfolds the way you expect it to," writes Frédéric Mitterrand in his memoir cum autobiographical novel, *The Bad Life*. If it's true that Mitterrand has lived "the bad life," then he has found very good words with which to express it. As provocative as it sounds, the book's title does not fairly represent its content, which paints in Technicolor prose the life of a privileged child born into Paris's *haute bourgeois* sixteenth arrondissement, his struggle to conceal his homosexuality, and the personal relationships that have affected him—deeply and in surprising ways. Published in France in 2005 as *La Mauvaise Vie*, the title translates as easily to "loose living," but it could also be taken to mean "the wrong life," as in not quite right—the fifth button in the fourth buttonhole. This square peg translation supports the book's overarching themes of otherness, rifts, disappointed expectations, and dreams built like houses of cards twitched to collapse.

At times so intimate it feels as if we are overhearing the author's confessions to himself, Mitterrand's memoir highlights the circumstances that have formed his character. A television personality, filmmaker, gay rights activist, and writer, he is the nephew of former French president François Mitterrand. In 2009 Nicolas Sarkozy appointed the author to serve as France's Minister of Culture and Communication.

Not surprisingly, the book reflects a love of cinema. Its chapters do not follow a chronological sequence. Instead, Mitterrand elegantly stage-directs a timeline in which past and present sometimes meet, but always with fluid effect. Each chapter is itself a motion picture; the book, a collection of little movies, each a different genre. Throughout, Jesse Browner's English translation captures the very French "ah, well . . . such is life" tone.

In the opening chapter, "Childhood," we learn not only of his upbringing, but also of the manner in which he is bringing up his adopted Moroccan son. The second chapter, "Litany," pays homage to "people met and never forgotten":

They all left me with an undying ember, a violent feeling of loss and nostalgia, a dream-like desire that continues to blaze...like a breeze over the inner sea of regret and loss; every desirable stranger reminds me of someone else, of several others. The first few times it happened, I was very young. These experiences were very confusing, filling me with fervor, enthusiasm, and anxiety, but I didn't understand the cause of my emotion or where its extraordinary strength might lead.

In dreamlike sequence, the author offers a procession of characters and his brief encounters with them, including the film stars he meets as a 12-year-old after sneaking into a movie audition and getting a key part. Yet the revelations assigned to his parents provide the most telling details:

I've been able to pull off this whole scheme without their knowing; their obedient little boy is a dissembler leading a double life. My mother feels guilty for not being sensitive enough to my feelings; my father is concerned for the future of a child who creates his own hidden realities. Neither of them reproaches me, but it's a painful shock to them. They have no better idea than I do of the true reasons behind my ability to conceal myself, my capacity to lie by omission, this nascent tendency to live apart.

The "Quentin" chapter invokes an *In Cold Blood*-like scene, perpetrated by someone once close to Mitterrand's older brothers. Pondering the if-onlys of existence, the author grasps at understanding based on his own relationship with the perpetrator of the murder/suicide:

He had high expectations of his death, he was hoping precisely that it would tear him from his isolation. That is surely why he . . . required the assistance of Christine, Sacha and Bronia, who would accompany him and remain forever at his side. . . . As for the rest of us who remained behind, our love for Quentin had long since become insufficient."

With "Howard Brookner," the author speaks of his too brief encounters with—and the disappearance into thin air of—an American director whose William Burroughs film showed in one of Mitterrand's art-house theaters. Evoking scenes from a budding but doomed romance, the author feeds us breadcrumbs that lead us to understand what he himself did not: "At that moment, in the film, there will be nothing but an exterior night shot of the deserted street spread out before the black Mini." Only later does the author learn, via callous messengers, that his deep but fragile connection to Brookner has been severed by AIDS.

"Tenderness/Tenderezza" proffers a love letter to Catherine Deneuve, who is never named. Mitterrand simply refers to "you." This second-person epistolary chapter unfolds as a confessional, and by dint of confessing to "you," he is really confessing to us, the readers. The author manages to stay just this side of stalker by exposing so much of his own fragility: "I'm the kind of boy who opens his heart to strangers on the train."

By far the most controversial section, "Bird" takes us into the author's fraught world as he pays for sex with young male prostitutes in Bangkok. "I spend lavishly to ease my conscience, I turn it all into a novel in my head." Couldn't put it down. Bad life, capital B.

The final chapter brings us back full circle to "Childhood." Both he and his Moroccan son reappear, but this time, the scene plays out at the funeral of a former lover. But there's no time to "get caught up in the mythology of our wonderful former lives, the adventure of the movie business and all those fabulous people we'd known" because as ever-present cell phones remind us, life rings forward. Ah, well, such is life.

Mitterrand claims the book is neither autobiography nor fictional novel, but rather an "autobiography which is half real and half dreamed." Even if the book defies classification, it has not defied scrutiny by the world's media. In October 2009, a Member of the European Parliament and of France's right-wing National Front party, targeted Mitterrand, quoting sections out of context on French television, accusing him of sex tourism, and demanding his resignation. President Sarkozy was called upon to defend his minister of culture, which further fed the furor. As the book bubbles in a ragout of international political scandal, one delectable question surfaces like a lovely, sweet bite of root vegetable: Is *The Bad Life* a good read? Tuck a serviette at your collar and get out your big spoon. The answer is yes.

JACOB M. APPEL

We Are Never As Beautiful As We Are Now
Adam Gallari

Ampersand Books
ISBN-13: 978-09841025
2009. 155pp. $15.95

A majority of Americans now grow up in suburbs. That is certainly true of the majority of students attending MFA programs in fiction. In contrast, a disproportionate share of short stories by today's ambitious young writers are set inside Appalachian cabins, inner city tenements, prairie farmsteads and—with all too much frequency—on fishing excursions and drinking binges in the Deep South. Anywhere, it seems, except the manicured subdivisions that these would-be authors know best. The suburbia that once inspired the twisted comedy of John Cheever and the pitch-perfect tragedy of Richard Yates is now regarded by many aspiring talents as a cultural desert to be mocked or ignored, rather than mined for literary gems.

Into that void steps Adam Gallari, a Long Island native whose refreshing and perceptive debut collection, *We Are Never As Beautiful As We Are Now*, embraces the suburban landscape that so many of his peers have rejected. His characters may make occasional forays across New York City or even sojourn in Los Angeles, but they are most at home (and most convincing) when cruising the streets of Levittown or the college bars of Poughkeepsie. The deep authenticity which pervades all nine of Gallari's stories, including several written from a daring second-person point-of-view, and particularly his ability to capture the voice of contemporary masculinity, makes the author a natural literary heir to such psychologically-precise stylists as Tobias Wolff and Stuart Dybek.

Gallari's stories are explorations of manhood and maleness. Nearly all of his protagonists have a direct connection to athletics—Gallari himself played first base for the Vassar College Brewers from 2005 to 2007—and the specialized language of the diamond and dugout adds texture to his prose. At the same time, his stories are almost defiantly lacking in machismo. Frank, the romance-addled pitcher who narrates "Throwing Stones," speaks for a whole clubhouse of Gallari protagonists when he says of baseball that "very few guys actually get to tell the game it's over. The game usually tells them." In one way or another, Gallari's young men have been told by the masculine world that their game is over. That means an end to bar-hopping for Danny in "No Cause for Concern" after his drunk driving conviction costs him his license and confines him to the only watering hole within walking distance. For Matt in "Good Friend," the end of the game means the loss of male intimacy that comes from betraying his ex-teammate. However, the most searing defeats in Gallari's stories are failures at love. What cements these pieces together, more than setting or voice, is theme: *We Are Never As Beautiful As We Are Now* is, at its core, a poignant disquisition on heartbreak.

The boyfriends and ex-boyfriends and would-be partners in Gallari's stories—in contrast to the emotionally-stunted and wisdom-bereft men who populate so much contemporary fiction—share considerable insight into the nature of human relationships. For example, Dave in "Good Friend" observes of his jilted buddy, Matt, that "whenever he set his mind on a girl, he jumped into it like a man who jumps into wet concrete and then starts blowing on his feet to speed up the process. . . . " The self-awareness of Gallari's men renders them highly sympathetic, all the more so because recognizing their own shortcomings does not enable them to overcome the limitations. These young men know why their relationships will fail—but also recognize that they do not possess the gifts, often creative or intellectual, to change their romantic destinies. The second-person voice of "Reading Rilke" captures this paradox of "understanding without power" when describing pillow talk between the story's hero, a baseball-star-turned-bartender, and his Shakespeare-loving ex:

> It was during those moments that you knew it couldn't last—though you were never certain, then, that you wanted it to. You saw the eventuality of her leaving as something obvious and concrete because you knew who you were. She knew what she wanted to be. Because, secretly, you knew that your way of thinking was smaller than hers. You wondered if, secretly, she knew it too.

That is not to say that Gallari's male characters lack erudition. In fact, that is one of their greatest charms. Gallari can conjure up college athletes who reference the classics—sometimes with whetted irony, as when one narrator compares his own father hewing logs in order to work off his frustrations with Achilles battling the Trojans. But, as Frank recognizes in "Throwing Stones," helping his girlfriend study for her college history classes will not turn him into her scholarly match.

If Gallari's stories are touching, they are also quite funny. In "No Cause for Concern," he taps into the hilarious "logic" of the drunken mind as the narrator reflects on his DUI arrest: "He rolled through a stop sign, and the officer was waiting for him. Behind some hedges. Wasn't there a law that hedges on corners had to be a certain height so drivers could see over them? If the hedges had been lower he would have seen the cop waiting." His wit can also be unforgiving, as when the protagonist of "Go Piss On Jane" realizes that the only difference between "Catholic discipline and military discipline" is that "the military gives you a gun." His humor can also display original wisdom, such as the observation that another character "always felt hubris to be a necessary evil." By giving his men minds as supple as their bodies are sore and spent, Gallari transforms us from spectators into invested fans.

The most mature and complex story in Gallari's collection, "A Beautiful Lie," manifests all of the author's strengths. The principal character, Reid, is a college ballplayer who has his pitching arm injured in a brawl that he instigated. When his ex-paramour, Maeve, invites him into New York City one night he kindles a hope for renewing their romance. He recognizes the complexity of her allure and the futility of resisting it:

> She was beautiful and fickle, yet smarter than she let on, or so he liked to believe. There was something siren-like about the way she reentered his life after long absences and beguiled him into situations that she must have known could only have caused him pain. And each time he let her.

But as the pair bicker—over Reid's jealousy and his unwillingness to apply to medical school—the damaged athlete realizes that Maeve "possessed a level of artistry and sophistication that he couldn't attain." He abhors himself for holding her talents against her, but he cannot resist doing so. The story's concluding scene, in which Reid exposes himself at his most vulnerable, proves truly enchanting.

One might easily fall into the trap of concluding that Adam Gallari's pensive, idealistic protagonists reflect a new kind of man: sensitive yet virile, capable of both athletic endurance and intense friendship, not extraordinary in any way but actualized enough to articulate his own deficiencies. Those are indeed Gallari's men. But such men have always existed. What has been lacking is a literature that gives these men their due. Since the heyday of Raymond Carver and Larry Brown in the early 1980s, middle- and working-class masculinity has come to be associated with hapless and befuddled blockheads incapable of interpreting their own failures. Gallari's inspiring first collection provides a bracing antidote to that rather constricted approach to manhood. At a time when short fiction's leading stars from Robert Olen Butler and George Saunders to Kevin Brockmeier and Elizabeth Graver have embraced a naturalism of the paranormal, Gallari's hard-fought stories offer a dose of unadulterated realism at its finest.

Contributors' Notes

TORY ADKISSON is originally from Los Angeles, and is currently an MFA candidate at the Ohio State University. Tory's poem "Scarecrows" won the Potomac Review poetry prize and will appear in Issue 48 of the *Potomac Review*.

ANNA AKHMATOVA (1889-1966) was a leading Russian poet during the first half of the 20th century. Her volumes were immensely popular during the 1910s and 1920s. *Requiem* (1938) is a powerful indictment of the Stalinist Terror, and *Poem Without a Hero* (on which she worked from 1942 until the 1960s) is a complex, multi-facetted modernist masterpiece.

AARON ALFORD is pursuing a Ph.D. in Creative Writing at Texas Tech University, where he teaches and serves as an associate editor for *Iron Horse Literary Review*. His nonfiction has also appeared in *River Teeth*. If you hit on his grandma, he will fight you.

ANDREW ALLPORT holds a Ph.D. in Literature and Creative Writing from the University of Southern California. His chapbook, *The Ice Ship & Other Vessels*, is available from Proem Press. The epigraph of his poem "Purgatorio" is translated as "found not by sight but sound." He lives in the mountains.

R. A. ALLEN's fiction has appeared or is forthcoming in *The Literary Review*, *The Barcelona Review #64*, *Calliope*, *PANK*, *Leaf Garden*, and elsewhere. His work was selected for *Houghton Mifflin's Best American Mystery Stories 2010* and nominated for *Best of the Web 2010*. He lives in Memphis. www.nyqpoets.net/poet/raallen

CHRISTOPHER ANKNEY loves to explore issues of masculinity, race, and poverty in small-town Ohio through his poetry. His first manuscript, *silent defiance*, seeks a permanent home and has traveled to two countries, while he has traveled to seven countries and dreams of getting to Latin America or Italy next.

JACOB M. APPEL has short stories in more than 120 literary journals including *Gettysburg Review*, *Southwest Review*, *Missouri Review*, and *Virginia Quarterly*

Review. His reviews are forthcoming in *The Georgia Review*, *Ploughshares* and *Rain Taxi*. Jacob is a graduate of the MFA program in fiction at New York University and teaches at the Gotham Writers' Workshop. www.jacobmappel.com.

RUSTY BARNES grew up in rural northern Appalachia and now lives in Revere, MA. He maintains webspace at www.rustybarnes.com, and he can split a playing card in two at up to twenty feet of distance with a tomahawk, then throw a knife and stick it in what's left of the split card. Aren't you jealous?

SHAINDEL BEERS's first poetry collection, *A Brief History of Time*, was released by Salt Publishing in 2009. She loves wide open rural spaces more than you've ever loved anything in your life. Find her online at http://shaindelbeers.com.

LAR's nonfiction editor, **ANN BEMAN** earned her MFA in creative nonfiction from the Northwest Institute of Literary Arts: Whidbey Writers Workshop. Beman lives with her husband and two whatchamaterriers in California's Kern River Valley. Only recently has she become a small dog convert. It's still a little weird.

SARAH BLAKE is from New Jersey, where she once placed third in a fencing tournament. Her poems have appeared or are forthcoming in *Michigan Quarterly Review* and *Sentence: a Journal of Prose Poetics*.

MARK JAY BREWIN JR. was born on one of the last bits of farmed property in New Jersey and learned to appreciate poetry lying on a picnic blanket in the middle of a spring-stubble field in the back country of North Carolina. He has never been the same since.

STACE BUDZKO has been published in *Night Train*, *Hobart*, *The Collagist*, *Rose Metal Field Guide to Flash Fiction*, *Flash Fiction Forward*, *Brevity & Echo*, *Quick Fiction* and elsewhere. He is currently promoting *Authors Anonymous*, a short-short anthology from the members of his writing group, who fully admit they're flash addicts.

JOHN CALDERAZZO teaches creative writing at Colorado State University. His essays, stories, and poems have appeared in *Audubon*, *Bellevue Literary Review*, *Coastal Living*, *Georgia Review*, *Orion*, *North American Review*, and dozens of other journals and anthologies. His work has been cited in *Best American Essays* and *Best American Stories*, and he has won a Best CSU Teacher award. His books include *Writing from Scratch: Freelancing*, *101 Questions about Volcanoes* (for children), and *Rising Fire: Volcanoes & Our Inner Lives*. He recently finished a book of poems, *At the Night Window*.

GIUSEPPE CARBONE is a pediatrician at the University of Southern California and has worked in several countries. He has had reasonable success writing and editing all sorts of scientific material. He has just begun to write fiction, and is pleased that he may have found an audience.

TANYA CHERNOV holds an MFA from the Northwest Institute of Literary Arts (Whidbey Writer's Workshop). She has been published in *Rattle, Isotope, Vulcan*, and *Stringtown*, among others. She is Translations Editor of The Los Angeles Review and cooks the meanest brisket you've ever had.

DANIEL COSHNEAR lives with his wife, Susan, and children, Circe and Daedalus, in Guerneville, California. He is training for a marathon, contemplating smoking and completing a second collection of stories, tentatively titled: *The Hero of My Unfinished Novel*.

BRANDON COURTNEY spent four years in the United States Navy. His poetry is forthcoming or appears in *Best New Poets 2009, Linebreak*, and *Fogged Clarity*. When not writing, he obsessively collects records from the early nineties. He will be attending the M.F.A. program at Hollins University in the fall.

JENNINE CAPÓ CRUCET is a Miami-born Cuban living in LA. Her story collection, *How to Leave Hialeah*, won the Iowa Short Fiction Award, the John Gardner Fiction Award, and was named a Best Book of the Year by the *Miami Herald* and the Latinidad List. She is actively trying to pick a fight with Pitbull the "rapper."

AVITAL GAD-CYKMAN, a former lawyer, designer, and puppet manufacturer, was born and raised in Israel and is now living on an island in Brazil. In her novel *Desert Symphony*, she expresses her awe and her love of the country that has embraced her. In her spare time, she runs.

RAMOLA D is the author of the fiction collection *Temporary Lives*, winner of the 2008 AWP Grace Paley Prize in Short Fiction, and the poetry collection *Invisible Season*, winner of the Washington Writers' Publishing House award. Her work has appeared in *Blackbird, Agni, Prairie Schooner, Green Mountains Review, Indiana Review, Writer's Chronicle, Full Moon on K Street*, and *Best American Poetry 1994*. Her fiction appears in *Best American Fantasy 2007*, and *Enhanced Gravity:*

More Fiction by Washington DC Women Writers. She teaches creative writing at The George Washington University and at The Writer's Center, Bethesda. She blogs at http://afterviews.blogspot.com/

Along with other teenaged boys from the handball choir at his Glendale church, **ORMAN DAY** spent a vacation parading through Disneyland as a Christmas tree, swinging handbells, and fending off bulb thieves. Later, wearing a home-made "Super-Frog" outfit, he won a boat on "Let's Make a Deal" and marched in the first Doo-Dah parade.

NIK DE DOMINIC lives in New Orleans and drives a 97 Saturn given to him by someone in the English Department where he went to school. He'd never seen nor heard of this person before. He appreciates the kindness of this mysterious person. Nik is an editor of *The Offending Adam* and the *New Orleans Review*.

JAQUIRA DÍAZ is pursuing an MFA in Creative Writing at the University of South Florida, where she also teaches. Her work has appeared or is forthcoming in *The Southern Review*, *Harpur Palate*, *The Southeast Review*, and elsewhere. She's obsessed with sushi, coffee, road trips, and her two troublemaking dogs, Taína and Chapo.

ALEX DIMITROV is the founder of Wilde Boys, a queer poetry salon in New York City. His poems have appeared in the *Boston Review*, *Yale Review*, *Best New Poets 2009*, and *New York Quarterly*. He works at the Academy of American Poets, writes for *Poets & Writers* magazine, and has received a Hopwood Award from the University of Michigan.

STEFANIE FREELE's short story collection *Feeding Strays* was a finalist for the Book of the Year Award and the 2010 Binghamton University John Gardner Fiction Book Award. Recent fiction can be found in *Glimmer Train*, *Vestal*, and *Night Train*. Stefanie is the reclusive Fiction Editor of *The Los Angeles Review*.

ADAM GALLARI is an American ex-pat working pursuing a PhD at the University of Exeter. Originally from New York, he holds an MFA from the University of California, Riverside. His work appears in *The Quarterly Conversation*, *Fifth Wednesday Journal*, *TheMillions*, *anderbo.com*, and *The MacGuffin*. His debut collection, *We Are Never As Beautiful As We Are Now*, was published by Ampersand in April 2010.

COREY GINSBERG collects masters degrees, shoes, and obscure facts about The Beatles. She lives in Miami with her toothless daschund, Joey, and is looking for a home for both her collection of poems and her collection of essays. Her favorite writer is Kurt Vonnegut.

ELEANOR GOODMAN has a Masters in Creative Writing from Boston University, and writes fiction, poetry, and literary criticism. She has lived in Shanghai and Beijing, and is currently translating a book of contemporary Chinese poetry. Her website is www.eleanorgoodman.com.

MEGAN GREEN is the assistant editor of the poetry journal *Rattle*. Her poems have appeared in such publications as *32 Poems*, *Ninth Letter*, and *Paterson Literary Review*. Her chapbook, *The Beaded Curtain*, was released by Spire in 2009. She lives in Los Angeles with her husband, the poet Timothy Green.

KATHLEEN GUNTON owes her education and imagination to nuns. Audrey Hepburn and Deborah Kerr (in movies) added romance to the mix. No surprise that Kathleen entered a convent at the age of 17. Prose, poetry, and photography help in living her life as art.

JEREMY HALINEN is a coeditor and cofounder of *Knockout Literary Magazine*. Some of his recent poems appear in *Best Gay Poetry 2008*, *Crab Creek Review*, *Poet Lore*, and *Sentence*. He is a citizen of both the United States and Finland and resides in Seattle, where he was born.

MELISSA HART is the author of the memoir *Gringa: A Contradictory Girlhood* (Seal, 2009). She teaches journalism at the University of Oregon. Lately, she's been writing travel essays and posing for her husband's photos in hiking attire, accompanied by their three-year old daughter. Website: www.melissahart.com

CHRIS HAVEN is from Oklahoma where as a child he watched so much TV that he should list ABC, CBS, and NBC as degrees on his CV. Adam's Ribs are fictional, but the best he's had are from Artz in Austin, Texas. He teaches at Grand Valley State in Michigan.

MICHAEL HEMERY's obsession with family, environment, and class incongruities are voiced in *No Permanent Scars*, his essay collection available for publication. These essays appear in nearly a dozen journals, including *Drunken Boat*, *Passages*

North, *Redivider*, and the book *Fearless Confessions*. He also serves as the nonfiction editor for *Hunger Mountain*.

GRAHAM HILLARD lives and teaches one hundred and thirty miles from Huntingdon, in Nashville, Tennessee. His poetry and fiction is forthcoming in *Clarion*, *Tar River Poetry*, and *Prairie Fire* and has been published widely.

AUBREY HIRSCH is a native of Cleveland, Ohio. Her work has appeared in *Third Coast*, *Vestal Review* and the *Minnetonka Review*. When not teaching or writing, she enjoys reading up on theoretical particle physics, playing Scrabble, and quilting.

About to deploy to Antarctica via a National Science Foundation grant, **CHARLES HOOD** is the author of the recent books *Under the African Air* and *Bombing Ploesti*. He is currently working on six different book projects and two long-term photography portfolios.

A poet, critic, translator and TV host, **XUDONG HU** was born in 1974 in Hubei. He has taught at Universidade de Brasília, and was a fellow in the International Writers Program at University of Iowa. He is now an associate professor in the World Literature Center at Beijing University.

AMORAK HUEY recently left the newspaper business after 15 years as a reporter and editor, including being assistant sports editor at The Grand Rapids Press. In addition to writing poetry, he is working on a mystery novel set in Grand Rapids, where he lives with his wife and two children.

JM HUSCHER lives in Davis, California, where he works in the non-profit industry. He has an unhealthy love affair with his bicycle. In between those long rides, he found time to recently complete an autobiography about immigrating to post-Soviet Eastern Europe with his family in the early '90s.

CYAN JAMES earned an MFA from the University of Michigan, and is currently working on a PhD in public health genetics at the University of Washington. Her work has appeared in *Harvard Review*, *Blackbird Review*, *Michigan Quarterly Review*, *Fiction Writers Review*, and *Beloit Journal of Poetry*. She rock-climbs, dances the blues, does aerial arts, volunteers, and writes bits of her novel.

LAURIE JUNKINS holds an MFA in poetry from Northwest Institute of Literary Arts (Whidbey Writer's Workshop). She has been published in *Rattle*, *Poet Lore*, *Nimrod*, and *Literary Mama*, among others, and has been nominated for a Pushcart Prize. She is Poetry Editor of *The Los Angeles Review* and was once walked in on in the bathroom by Joan Baez.

MATTHEW LABO is a new writer of short fiction and the occasional memoir. He's an accomplished golfer and a voracious reader who lives in Mays Landing, New Jersey. He tries to capture the day-to-day struggles of his characters and expose their flaws.

DAVID LABOUNTY's recent prose and poetry has appeared in *Pank*, the *New Plains Review*, *Pemmican*, *Night Train*, *Unlikely 2.0*, *Word Riot*, and other journals. His third novel, *Affluenza*, was published in 2009. *Affluenza* is a story about debt, consumerism, vanity and patricide told through the financial rise and fall of an insurance executive who lives beyond his means. LaBounty lives in Michigan.

ARIONÓ-JOVAN LABU' is an artist and writer who conducts writing workshops for underprivileged youth at a local community center once a month. He is currently working on a documentary, which traces his family roots from Africa to Cuba and the United States. His first collection of poetry, *Fragments of Struggle* is due to release late summer of 2010.

LAN LAN, born Hu Lanlan in 1967, is one of the leading woman poets of contemporary China. After college, she worked as afactory worker and editor. Now residing in Beijing, she has published several books of poetry, essays, and fairy tales. Her latest book, *Poems*, was published in 2007.

TOM LARSEN was a journeyman printer for twenty years before scrapping it all for the writer's life. His work has appeared in *Newsday*, *Philadelphia Stories Magazine*, *Puerto del Sol* and *Antietam Review*. Tom's short story "Lids" was included in *Best American Mystery Stories 2004*. His novel *Flawed* was released in October.

AMY LEACH lives in Chicago. She is writing a book about animals, plants and stars.

TIMOTHY LIU is the author of eight books of poems, most recently *Polytheogamy* and *Bending the Mind Around the Dream's Blown Fuse*. He lives in Manhattan.

COLIN LOCKARD lives in Beijing, China, and teaches at Peking University. His closest brush with literary greatness occurred in college when he held a job cleaning the toilet in a room that once belonged to T.S. Eliot. "Ordering Drinks en Español" is his first published poem.

DEBORAH A. LOTT writes about child trauma for the UCLA/Duke National Center for Child Traumatic Stress and relives it in her creative nonfiction. Her work has been published in *Alaska Quarterly Review, Bellingham Review, Black Warrior Review, Cimarron Review, Salon*, and elsewhere, and has been thrice named for notable essays in *Best American Essays*. "Mrs. Finch" is part of a book-length memoir.

DON MAGER has published over 200 poems and translations from German, Czech and Russian. His volumes are *Glosses, That Which is Owed to Death, Borderings, Good Turns* and *The Elegance of the Ungraspable, Birth Daybook* and *Drive Time. Us Four Plus Four* (UNO Press 2009) is an anthology of translations from eight major Russian poets including Akhmatova, Pasternak, Tsvetaeva and Mandelstam. www.donmager.org

JILL MAIO's fiction has appeared in *Ploughshares, Meridian*, and *Virginia Quarterly Review*. She holds degrees in Creative Writing from the University of Virginia and Boston University, and teaches at BU's Metropolitan College. A circus aerialist, she has performed in venues from L.A. to Barcelona, and is founder/director of an aerial acrobatics school in Somerville, MA.

OSIP MANDELSTAM (1891-1938) was a Russian poet during the first half of the 20th century. A satiric poem about Stalin led to his exile during which, in *Voronezh Notebooks* and *Moscow Notebooks*, he produced poems of astonishing affirmation. Arrested again in 1938, he died in transit to a labor camp in eastern Siberia.

TIMOTHY L. MARSH grew up in Palos Verdes, California. He has lived in five different countries in the past five years and now resides in Bali, Indonesia, where the surfing is reliably gnarly and glorious. His awards include a 2010 residency at the Vermont Studio Center, and a 2009 Arts Jury Award from the City Council of St. John's, Newfoundland.

HARRY MARTINSON (1904-1978) was a self-taught, working-class writer, a prolific poet, essayist and novelist who often explored his experiences as an orphan, sailor and vagabond. Flora and fauna interested him greatly. In 1948 Martinson joined the Royal Swedish Academy, and in 1974 shared the Nobel Prize for Literature with fellow Swedish novelist Eyvind Johnson.

JASON MCCALL teaches English at the University of Alabama. His work has been featured in *Cimarron Review, New Letters, Fickle Muses,* and other journals. However, most of his pride stems from his undefeated record in grade school spelling bees and a preternatural knowledge of professional wrestling.

JILL MCCABE JOHNSON is the director of Artsmith, a non-profit to support the arts. She is pursuing a PhD in English at the University of Nebraska, and was recently nominated for a Pushcart. Jill and her husband enjoy cooking at their bed and breakfast on Orcas Island in Washington State.

RACHEL MCKIBBENS was born a few blocks from Disneyland in Anaheim, CA. Her work appears in *World Literature Today, The New York Quarterly, FRiGG Magazine* and *Wicked Alice.* She is a New York Foundation for the Arts fellow and her first collection, *Pink Elephant* (Cypher Books) was released in 2009. She resides in upstate New York with her five children.

CLAIRE MCQUERRY teaches writing classes at University of Missouri, where she is currently a doctoral candidate. She lives with her Amazon parrot, Coco, who likes to swing from a perch above her desk while she writes.

SUSAN L. MILLER teaches Creative and Expository Writing at Rutgers University. Her work was published in *Commonweal, Meridian,* and *Iowa Review,* among others. She lives in Brooklyn with her husband and has traveled to Prague, Mumbai, Fes, Granada, Oaxaca, Montreal, Mexico City, Cusco, Madrid, Berlin, and Guanajuato. Next stop: Rome.

ERIN MURPHY's most recent books are *Dislocation and Other Theories* (Word Press, 2008) and *Making Poems: Forty Poems with Commentary by the Poets* (State University of New York Press, 2010). She is not the Erin Murphy who played Tabitha in *Bewitched.*

DARLIN' NEAL's story collection, *Rattlesnakes & The Moon* was recently released by Press 53. Neal is an assistant professor in the MFA and undergraduate Creative Writing Programs at the University of Central Florida, and lives in Orlando and Jensen Beach with Maggie the cat, Brian the human, and Catfish the dog.

BEN NICKOL is the recipient of several awards and fellowships, including a 2010 Individual Artist Fellowship from the Arkansas Arts Council. Before coming to Arkansas, he was a walk-on basketball player at the University of Notre Dame. He is currently at work on a novel about a college basketball coach.

ANGELO NIKOLOPOULOS is a former high school teacher who recently completed his master's degree in literature and creative writing at New York University. His work has appeared in *Boxcar Poetry Review, Ganymede*, and *Gay & Lesbian Review*. He lives in New York City, where he hosts The White Swallow, a queer reading series in Manhattan.

LARS NORDSTRÖM is a transplanted Swede from Stockholm, who settled in rural Oregon in the late 80s after obtaining a PhD in American Literary History. He farms five acres of organic wine grapes, makes a lot of compost, reads, writes, translates, and gives talks on Swedish-American subjects. He has become increasingly interested in the contemporary immigrant experience. www.larsnordstrom.com

STEPHEN PAGE holds an MFA in literature and writing from Bennington College, and a BA in literature and writing from Columbia University. He is the author of a book of poems, *The Timbre of Sand*, and a chapbook, *Still Dandelions*. He likes traveling and spending time with his wife.

BOB PERKINS is an old man. He grew up in Los Angeles and in the suburb where he now lives. He has been a submariner, a lawyer, and a teacher. Now retired, he likes hanging out with his wife and kids, surfing (small waves only), reading, and sometimes writing. This is his first publication.

JOE PONEPINTO is Book Reviews Editor for the *Los Angeles Review*, and a graduate of the Northwest Institute of Literary Arts in Washington State. His work appears in *Vestal Review, Apalachee Review, Fifth Wednesday Journal, The Summerset Review, Raven Chronicles*, and others. He has a novel represented by Andrea Hurst & Associates Literary Management. He lives in Michigan with his wife, Dona, and Henry the coffee-drinking dog. http://otnipenop.com.

COLIN POPE met Jennifer Wrisley through the MFA program at Texas State University. She was a tall, beautiful poet who loved the spiritual and natural worlds. On February 26th, 2010, Jennifer took her life to escape chronic pain. She was a light that should have never been extinguished.

EMMA RAMEY lives in Grand Rapids, Michigan and is co-poetry editor of *DIA-GRAM*. Sometimes she likes to watch Cagney and Lacey and pretend it is still the 1980s. She recommends you try this if you are feeling low or friendless.

MICHELLE REALE is an academic librarian on faculty at a university in Phila-delphia. Her work has appeared in *Smokelong Quarterly*, *elimae*, *Word Riot*, *Monkeybicycle*, and others. Her chapbook, *Natural Habitat*, will be published by Burning River in 2010. Her fiction comes in various sizes, but tends toward the small. She thinks of herself as a miniaturist.

JESSICA REIDY is a writer from New Hampshire. She holds a BA from Hollins University, Roanoake, Virginia. Her Romany-Gypsy heritage has influenced much of her work. She currently lives in Ireland with her husband where she spends her time writing, volunteering, practicing yoga, and plotting new adventures.

MARGARET ROZGA teachers creative writing and multi-cultural literature at the University of Wisconsin Waukesha. Her book *200 Nights and One Day* won a bronze medal for poetry in the 2009 Independent Publishers Book Awards. She has poems in *Capitola Review* and *Memoir (and)*. Her play, *March On Milwaukee: A Memoir of the Open Housing Protests*, has been produced three times since 2007.

CHRISTINA ROSALIE SBARRO is a writer, mother, and mixed media artist. She has a habit for forgetting things on the roof of her car, a passion for eavesdrop-ping in cafes, and a knack for getting paint on her jeans. Her fiction and essays have appeared in *The Sun*, *Mothering*, and *Blue Print Review*. Christina blogs at mytopography.com.

MICHAEL SCHMELTZER earned an MFA from the Rainier Writing Workshop at Pacific Lutheran University. He is a two-time Pushcart nominee and lives in Seattle, Washington, where he listens to a tremendous amount of hip-hop. Poets can learn a lot from Lil Wayne and Eminem. No, seriously.

TARA MAE SCHULTZ is a first year MFA poetry candidate at the University of Memphis. She has work forthcoming in *Touchstone*. She also teaches and loves to decorate her classroom with pictures of pigs dressed up as Spider Man, the Phantom, Peter Pan, and, of course, Santa Claus.

PATTY SOMLO received a Pushcart nomination for "Bird Women," a story set in a mythical Latin American country. She lived in Nicaragua after Sandinista guerrillas overthrew the dictator, Anastasio Somoza. She currently lives with her husband two blocks from the Sunnyside Environmental School and its free-range chickens in Portland, Oregon.

JEFF STREEBY is a horseman, cowboy poet and performer who is training his big Polish Arab mare for 50-mile races. His recent work has appeared in or been accepted by *Flashquake, Rattle, Naugatuck River Review, Oak Bend Review, Verdad*, and others. He currently teaches English in Perris, California.

While **DONNA VITUCCI**'s mail address is Cincinnati, OH, her home's located closer to the Indiana border than to any city—the perfect place to watch each year's four distinct seasons creep in, dress up, disrobe, fall down. She gets kind of jazzed just tracking the life span of her trees' leaves.

DAVID WAGONER has published 18 books of poems, most recently *A Map of the Night* (U. of Illinois Press, 2008) and ten novels, one of which, *The Escape Artist*, was made into a movie by Francis Ford Coppola. He won the Lilly Prize in 1991 and has won six yearly prizes from Poetry (Chicago). He was a chancellor of the Academy of American Poets for 23 years. He has been nominated for the Pulitzer Prize and twice for the National Book Award. He edited Poetry Northwest from 1966 to its end in 2002. He is professor emeritus of English at the U. of Washington and teaches in the low-residency MFA Program of the Whidbey Writers Workshop.

AO WANG received his Ph.D. in Chinese Literature from Yale, and teaches at Wesleyan University in Connecticut. He is the author of several books, including *Quatrains and Legends* (2007), winner of the prestigious Anne Kao Poetry Prize. He is also an accomplished singer and electric guitarist.

When he is not painting sad men wearing funny hats or enjoying beer and Pop Rock slushies, **STEVE WESTBROOK** teaches creative writing and cultural studies at Cal State Fullerton. He also writes poems, some of which have been published in journals like *RATTLE, Good Foot, Literal Latte*, and *Hibbleton Independent*.

CHARLES HARPER WEBB's latest book is *Shadow Ball: New & Selected Poems*, published by the University of Pittsburgh Press in Fall 2009. Years ago, he gave up baseball to play rock-and-roll. Now he's back on the diamond, happily playing with his All Star son.

Joseph P. Wood is the author of five chapbooks and two forthcoming books, *Fold of the Map* (Salmon Poetry) and *I & We* (CW Books). He is co-director of The Slash Pine Poetry Festival and is creating an exchange program for undergrad writers. His email is slashpinepress@gmail.com.

Barry Yourgrau's books include *Wearing Dad's Head* and *The Sadness of Sex*, the film adaptation of which he starred in. He's also author of *NASTYbook*, misanthropic tales for kids that are perhaps inappropriate for children. They share the spirit of his story "Casserole" here. Worldwide Biggies has optioned them.

Yusa Zhuang lives in Singapore. His poems appear in *Sargasso* (Puerto Rico), *Yuan Yang* (Hong Kong), *ditch* (Canada), *The Toronto Quarterly Review*, *Ganymede*, and elsewhere. His has also been anthologized in *Ganymede Poets Vol. One* and *Smoke* (Poets Wear Prada). He has few interests outside of literature and working out at the gym.

Black
Clock

Aimee Bender · Tom Carson · Samuel R. Delany · Don DeLillo
Brian Evenson · Janet Fitch · Rebecca Newberger Goldstein · Maureen Howard
Shelley Jackson · Heidi Julavits · Miranda July · Jonathan Lethem · Ben Marcus
Greil Marcus · Rick Moody · Geoff Nicholson · Geoffrey O'Brien
Richard Powers · Joanna Scott · Darcey Steinke · Susan Straight
Lynne Tillman · David L. Ulin · Michael Ventura · William T. Vollmann
David Foster Wallace · Carlos Ruiz Zafon

EDITOR Steve Erickson

subscribe online   www.blackclock.org
Published by CalArts in association with the MFA Writing Program

creamcityreview.org

featuring images by:

**Sarah Legow :: John Porcellino ::
Cecilia Johnson**

featuring words by:

**Lori Davis :: Jessica Lakritz :: Anna Leahy ::
Gregory W. Randall :: Nicole Callihan ::
Tim Wirkus :: Rick Kempa ::
Melissa Olson-Petrie**

**featuring our annual literary prize-winners ::
Haines Eason :: Eson Kim :: Roger Sheffer**
now accepting online submissions

cream city review

volume 34 issue 1   spring 2010 $12

"Origins" by Sarah Legow

stone canoe

A Journal of Arts and Ideas from Upstate New York

Tom Huff
Stone Canoe
white alabaster, 2006

Stone Canoe, an award-winning book-length journal published each January by Syracuse University, features poetry, fiction, nonfiction, drama, and visual arts from a variety of emerging and established artists and writers with connections to the New York region.

Stone Canoe derives its name from the oldest story of our region—the journey of the Peacemaker who traveled in a canoe of white granite, brought the message of peace to the warring tribes of the Finger Lakes, and founded the Haudenosaunee Great Council on the shores of Onondaga Lake.

Stone Canoe Number 4, published in January 2010, is available at Barnes & Noble, Borders, Follett's Orange Bookstore, Syracuse University Bookstore, and through our web site, both in print and e-book versions.

Visit our site, **stonecanoejournal.org**, for more information about our scope and mission, the annual **Stone Canoe** prizes, and submission instructions.

ep;phany
a literary journal